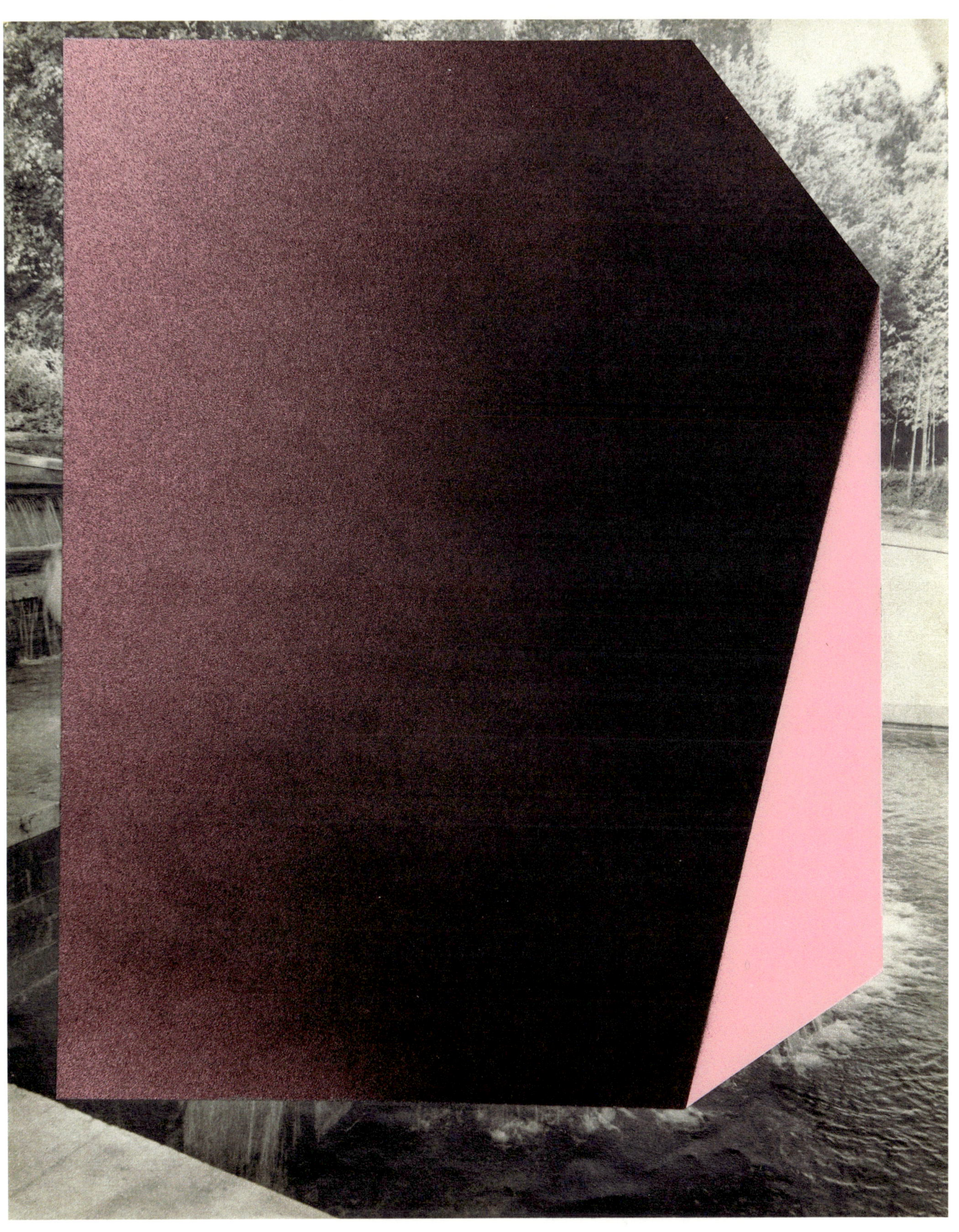

DOWNFALL

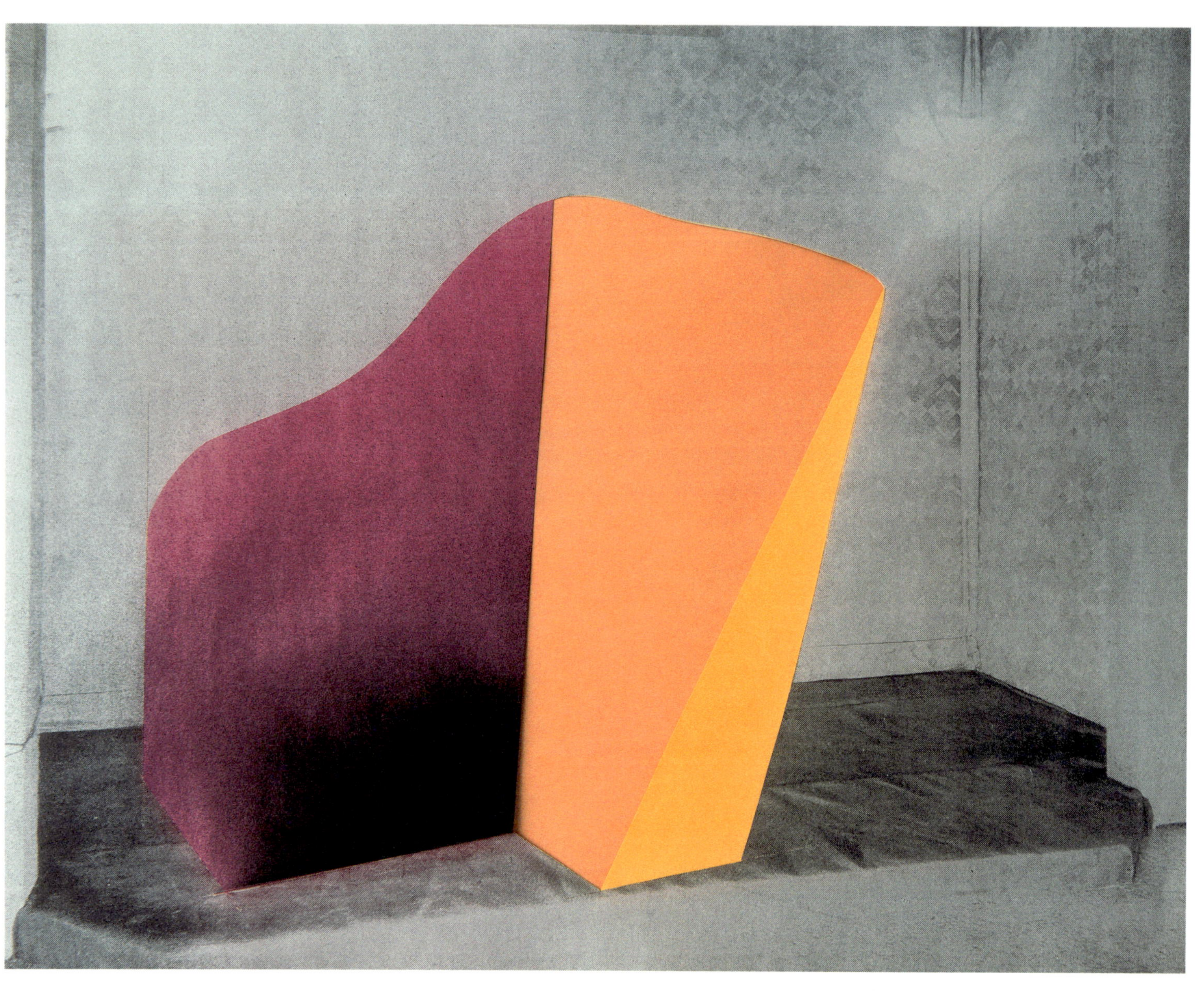

217. Baumblüte

163

BAUMBLÜTE

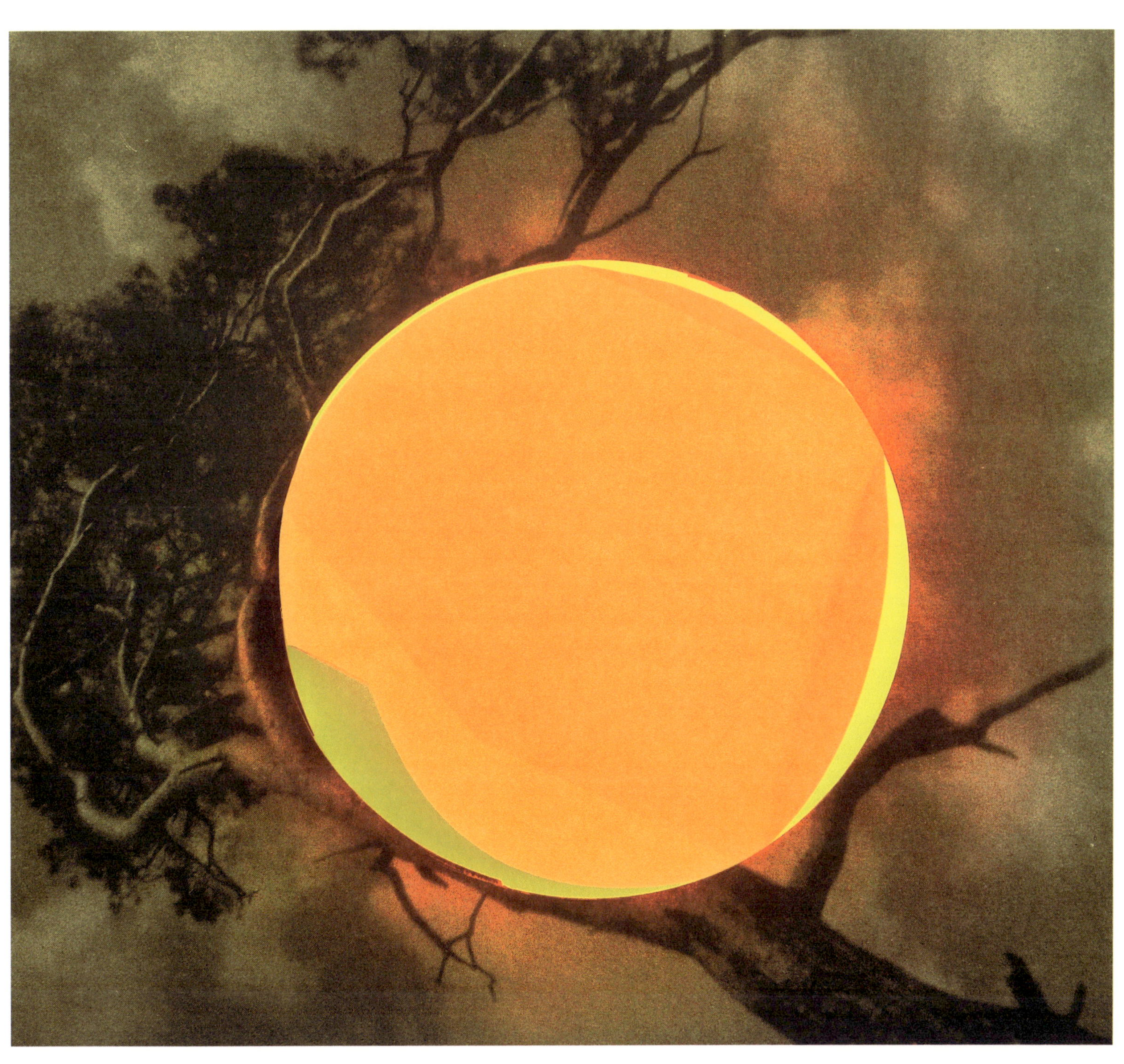

BURNING

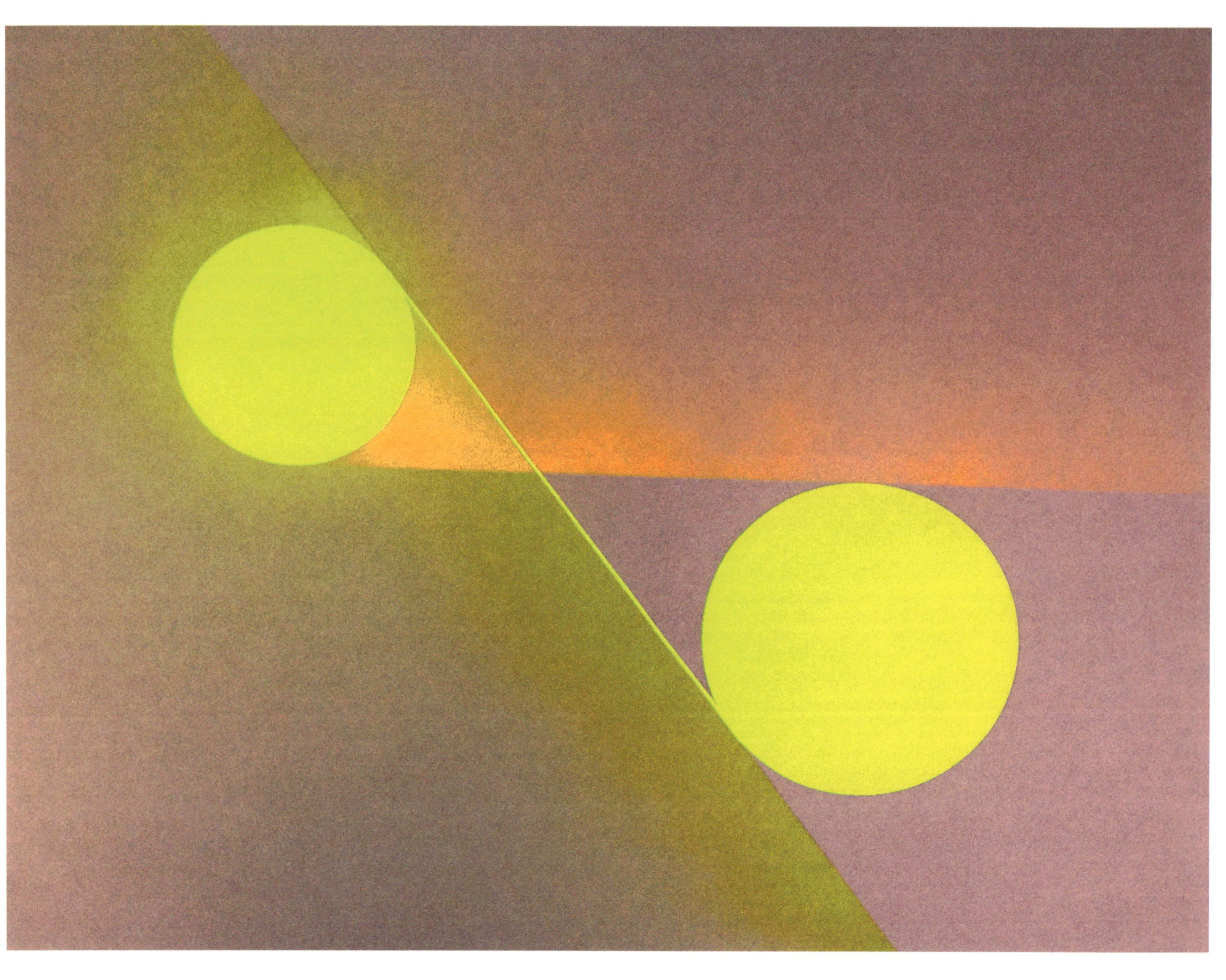

RELATION

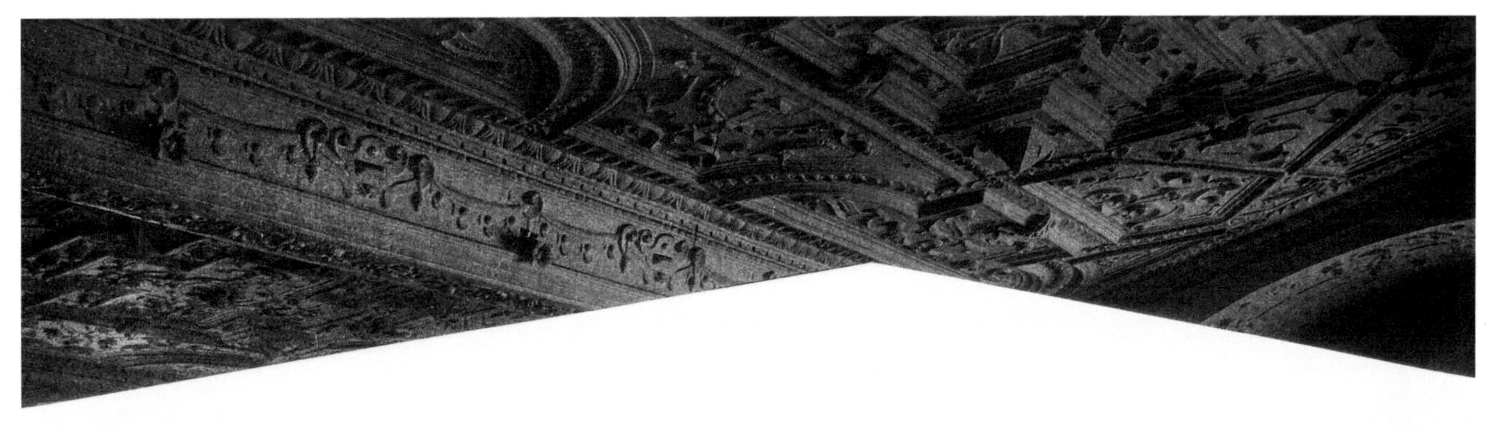

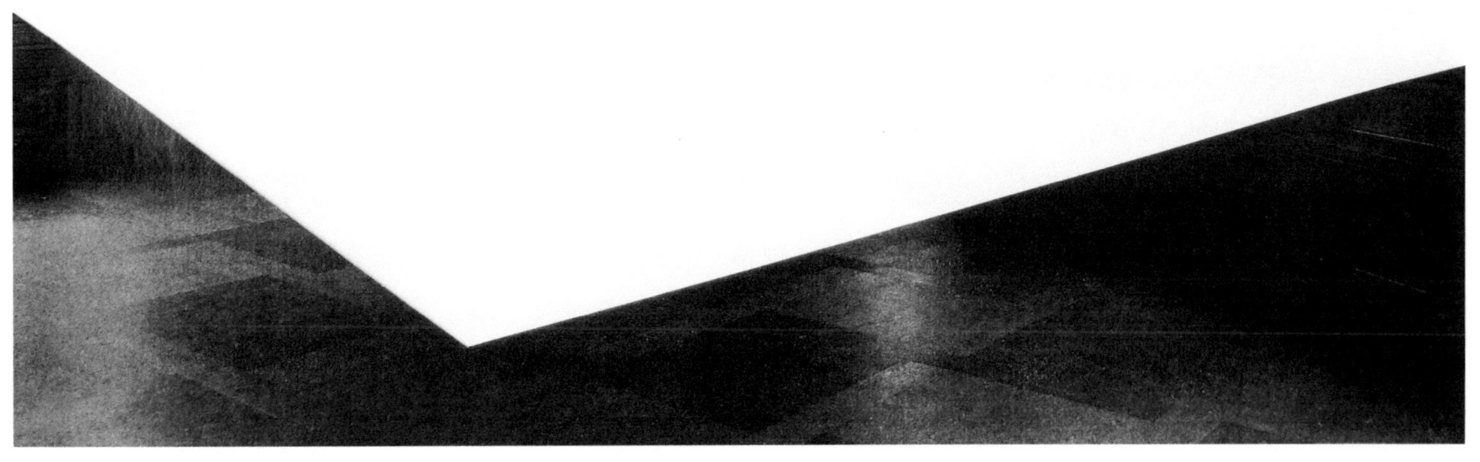

RAUM

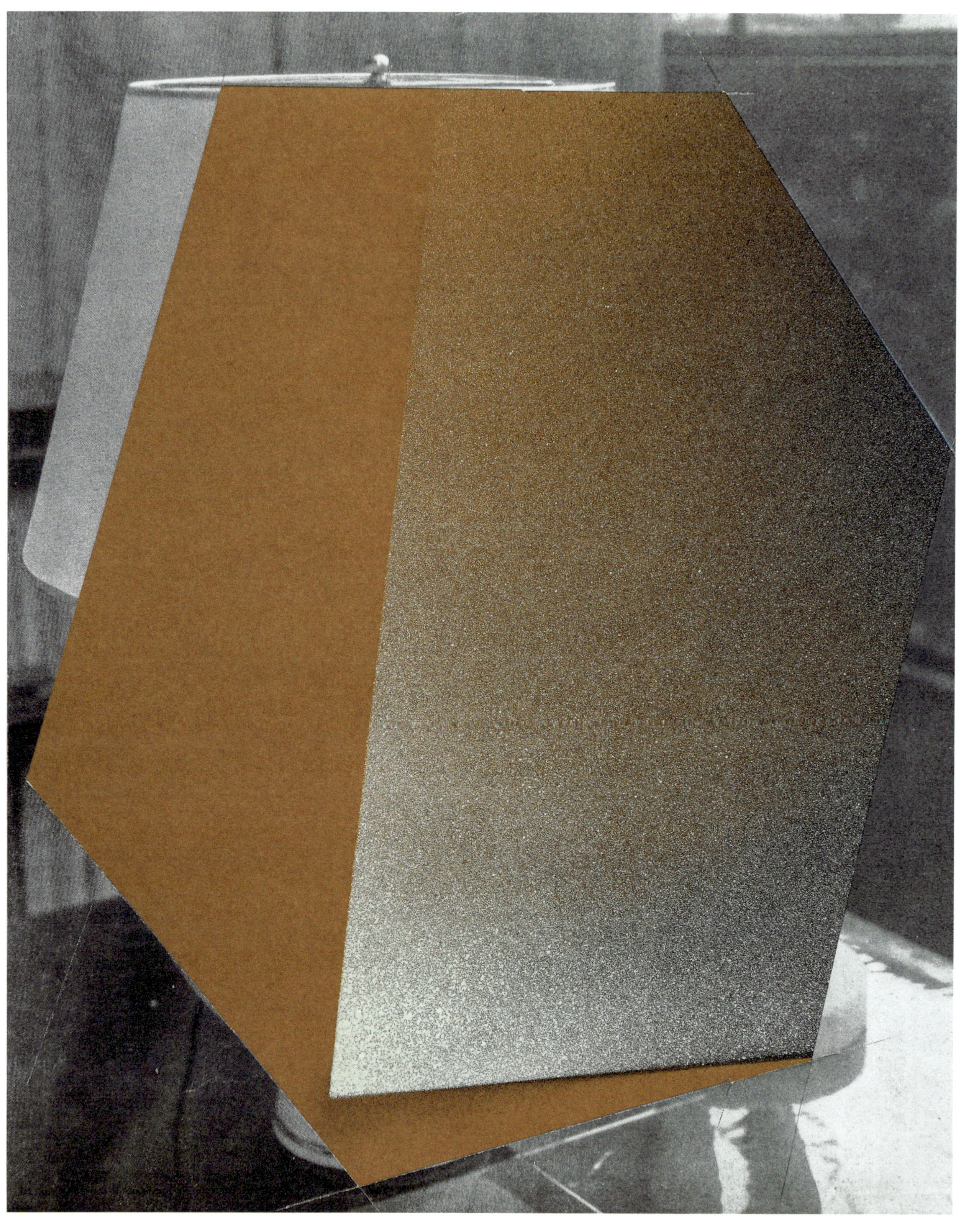

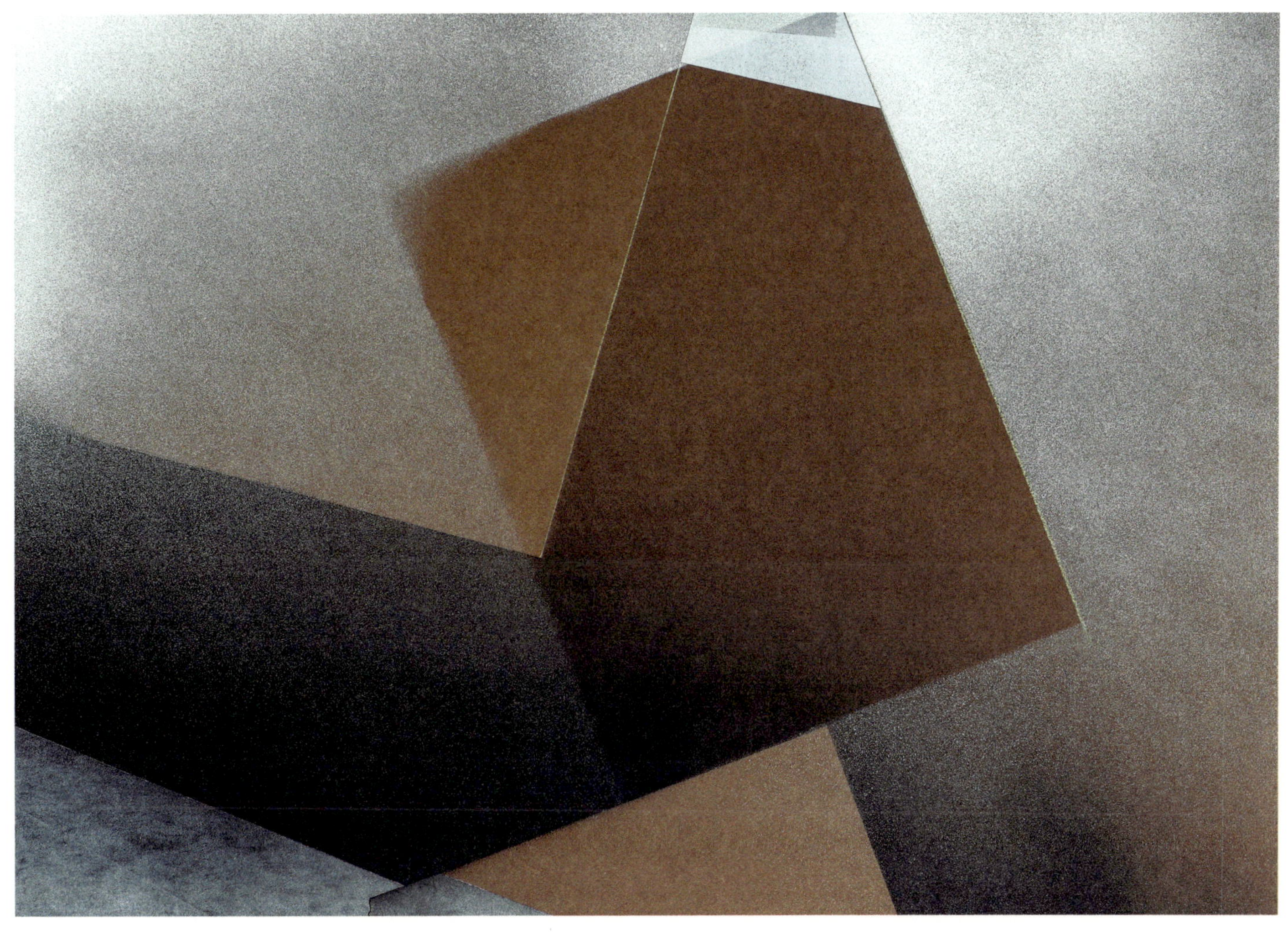

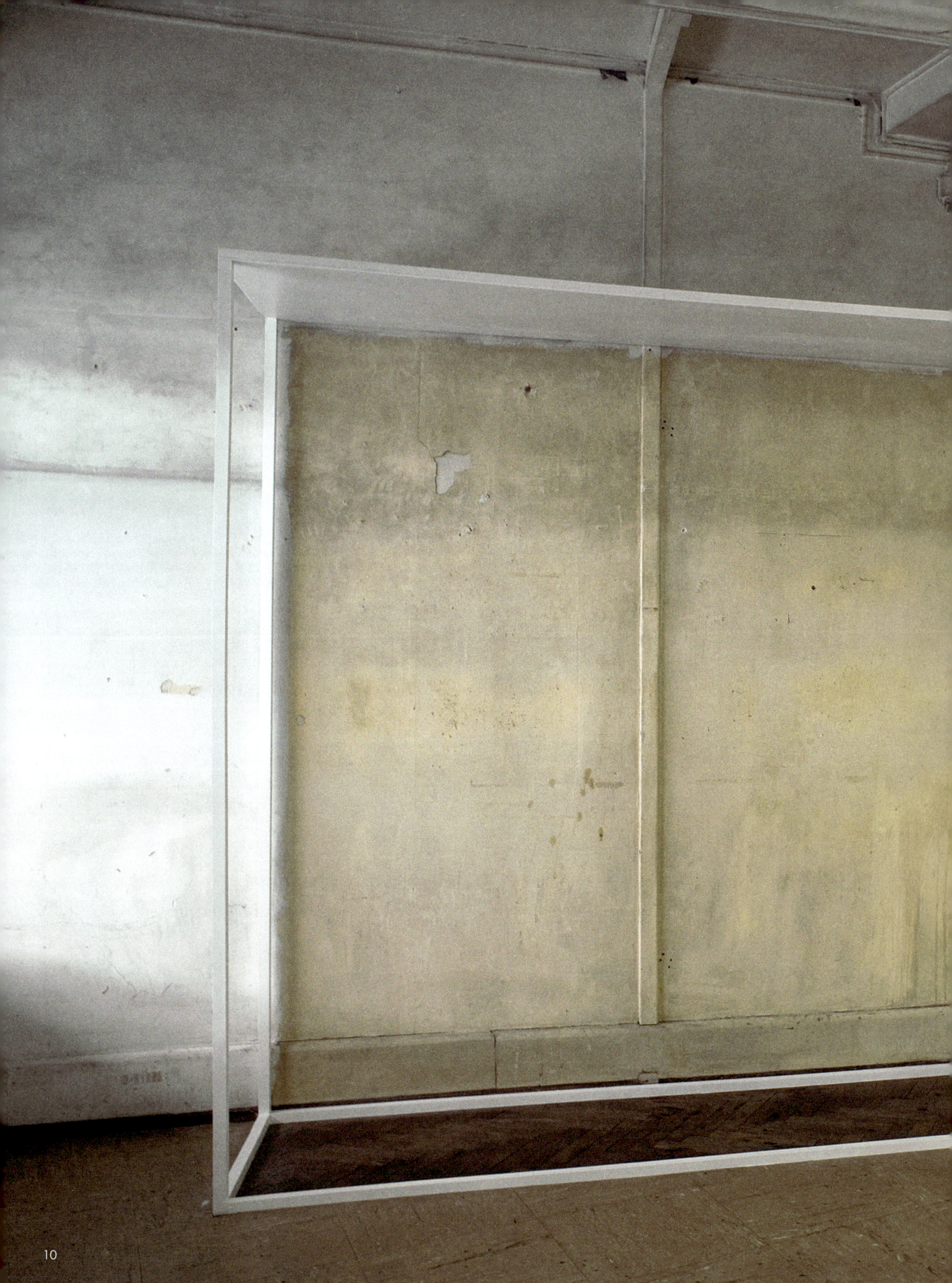

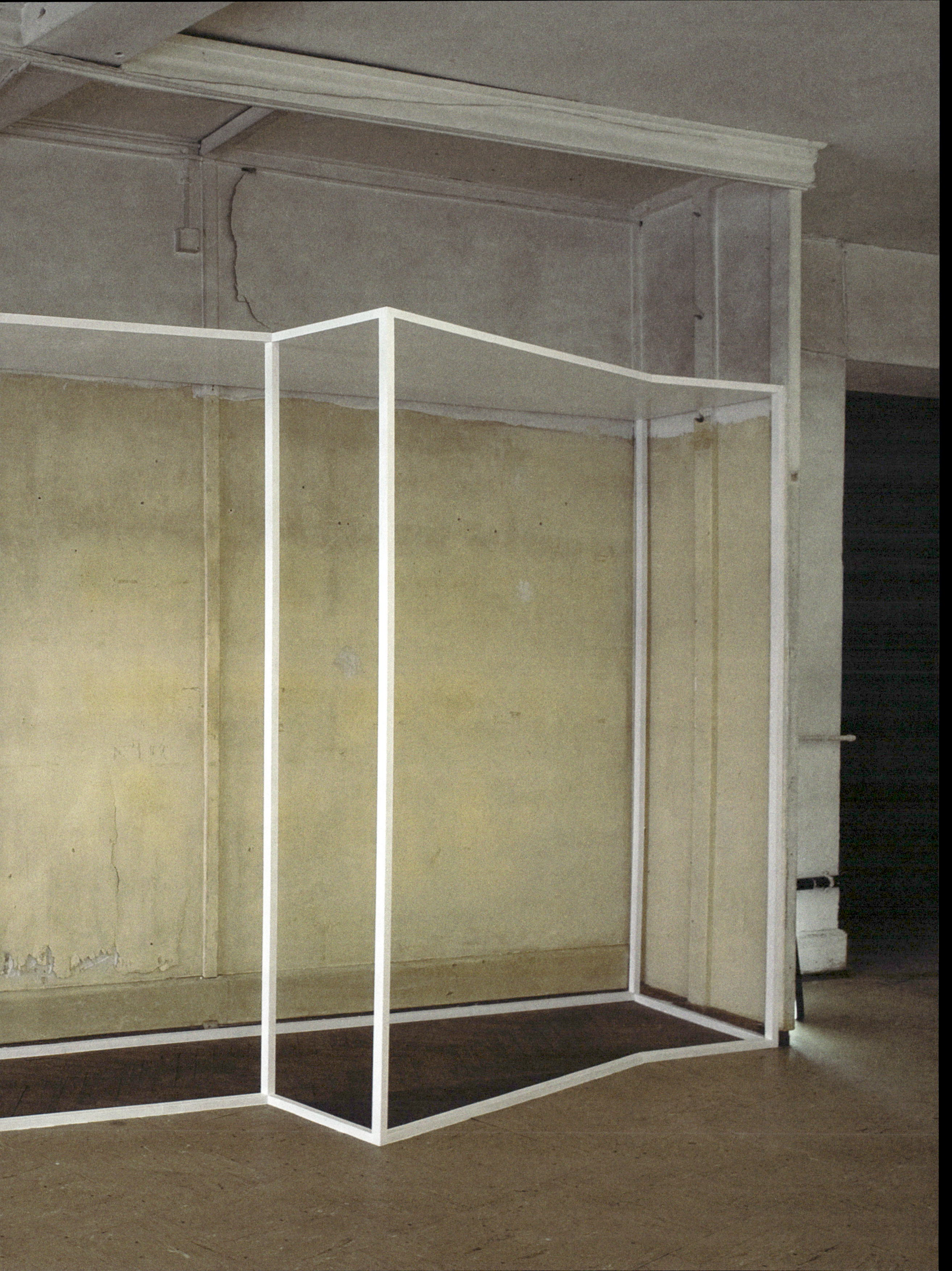

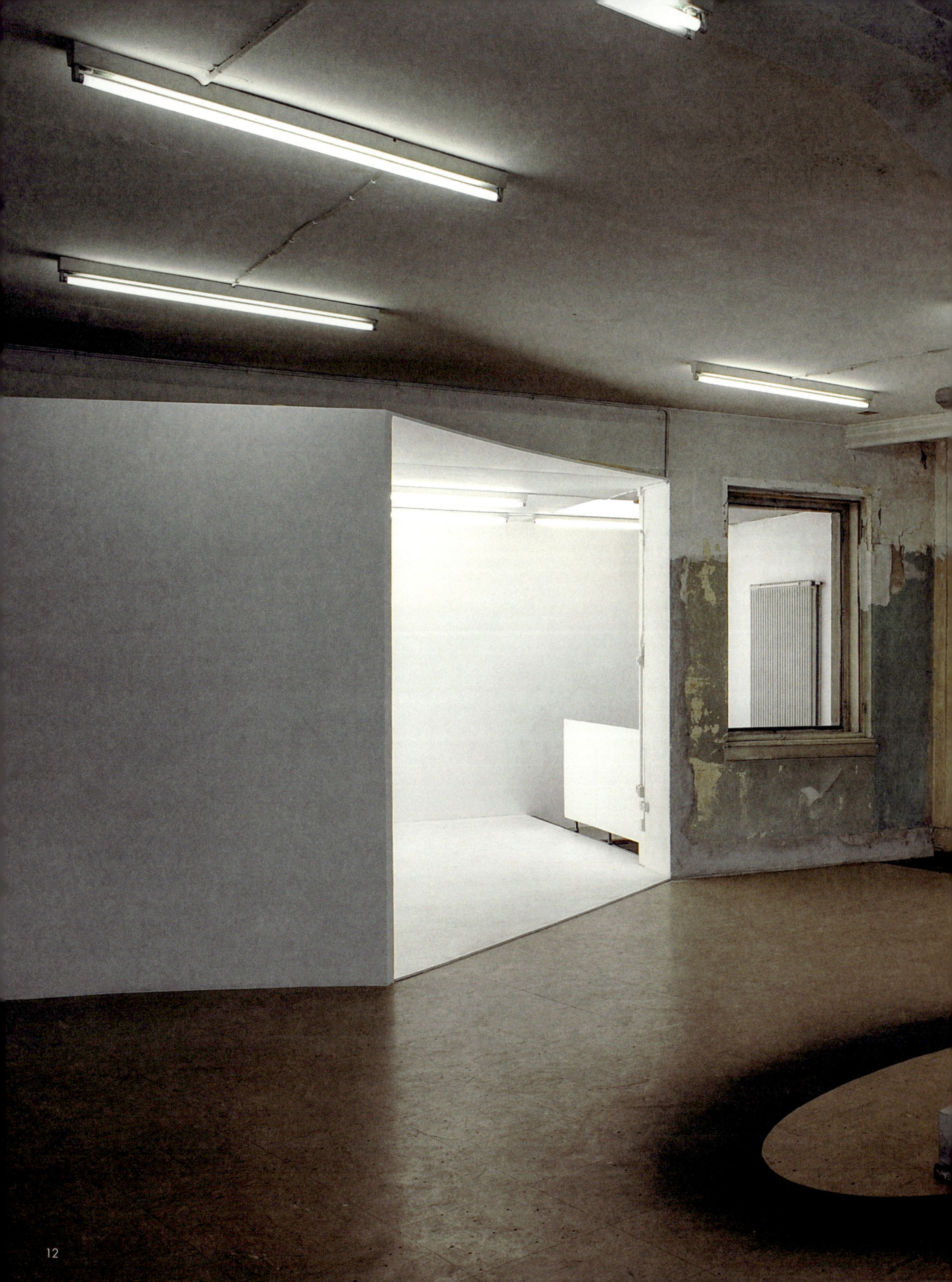

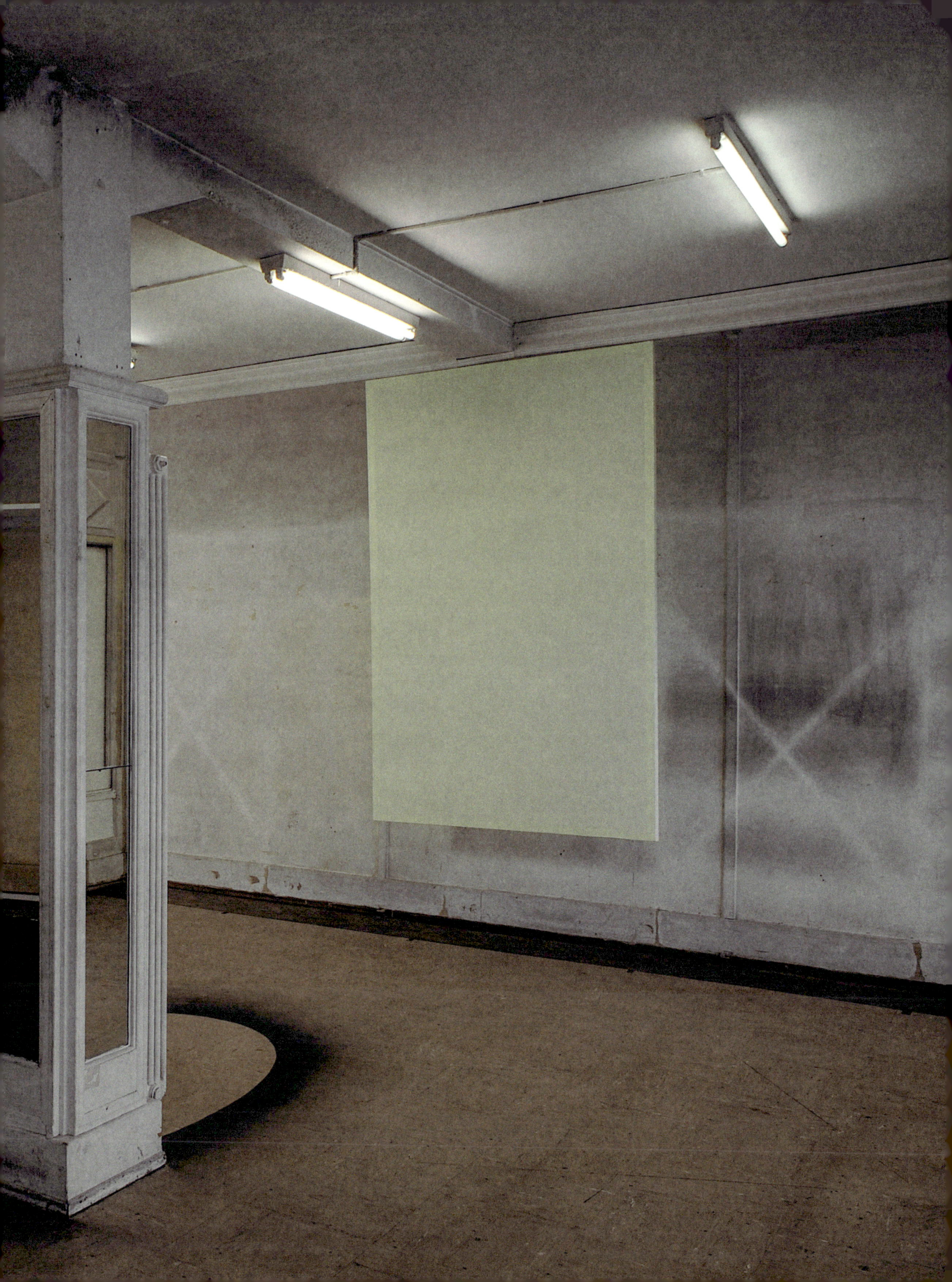

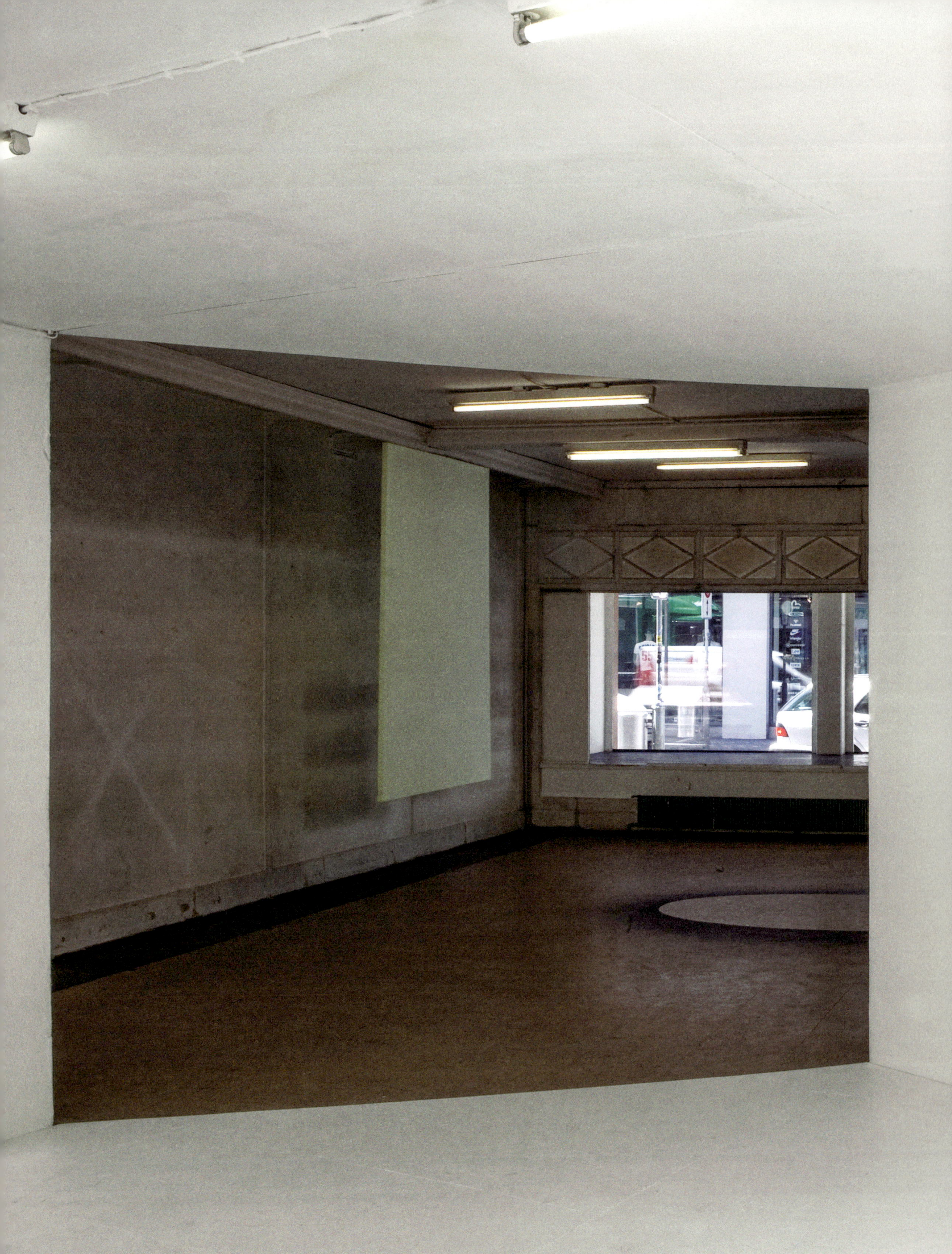

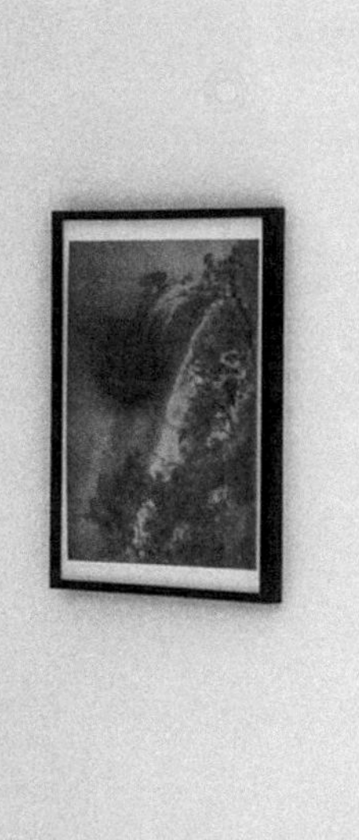
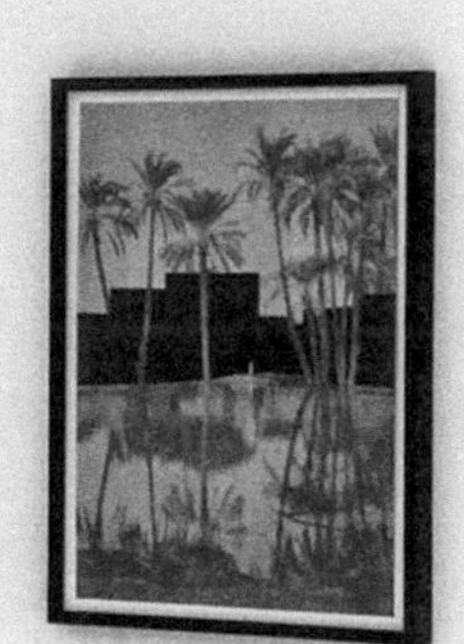
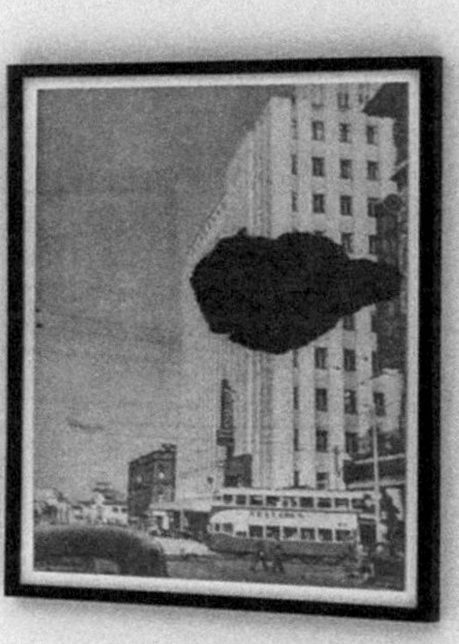

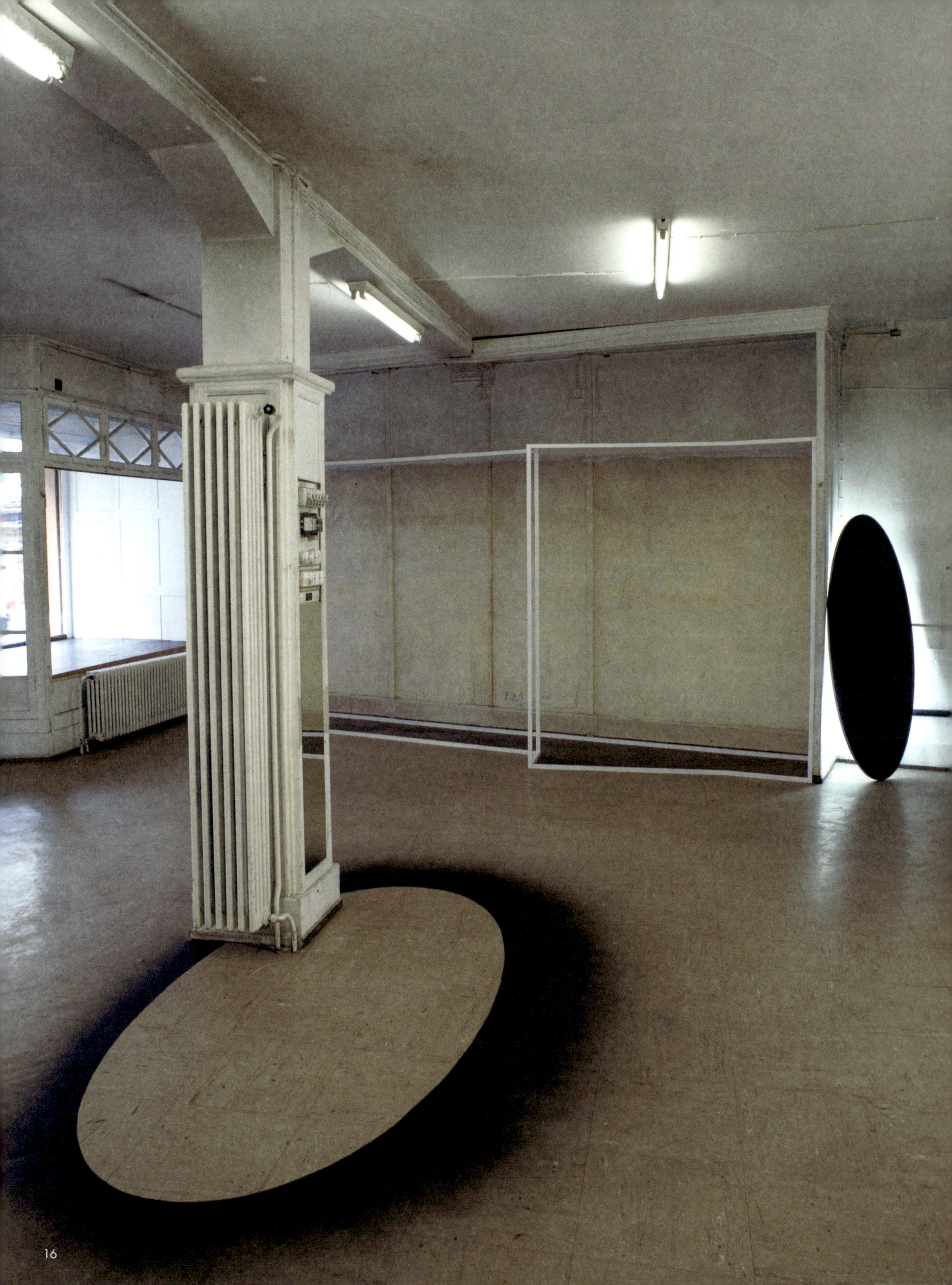

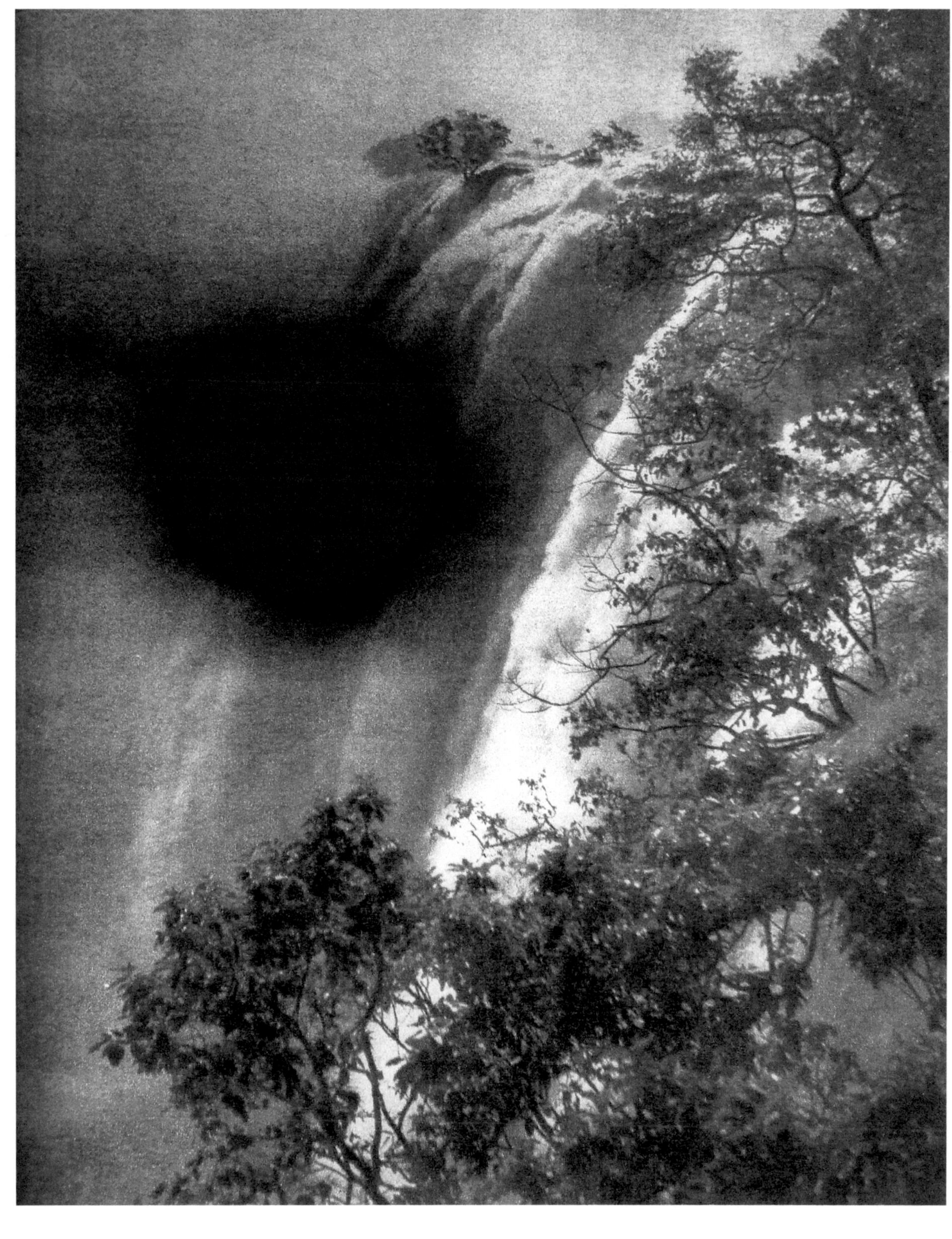

   DIE FLUTEN DES SAMBESI STÜRZEN 107 METER IN DIE TIEFE

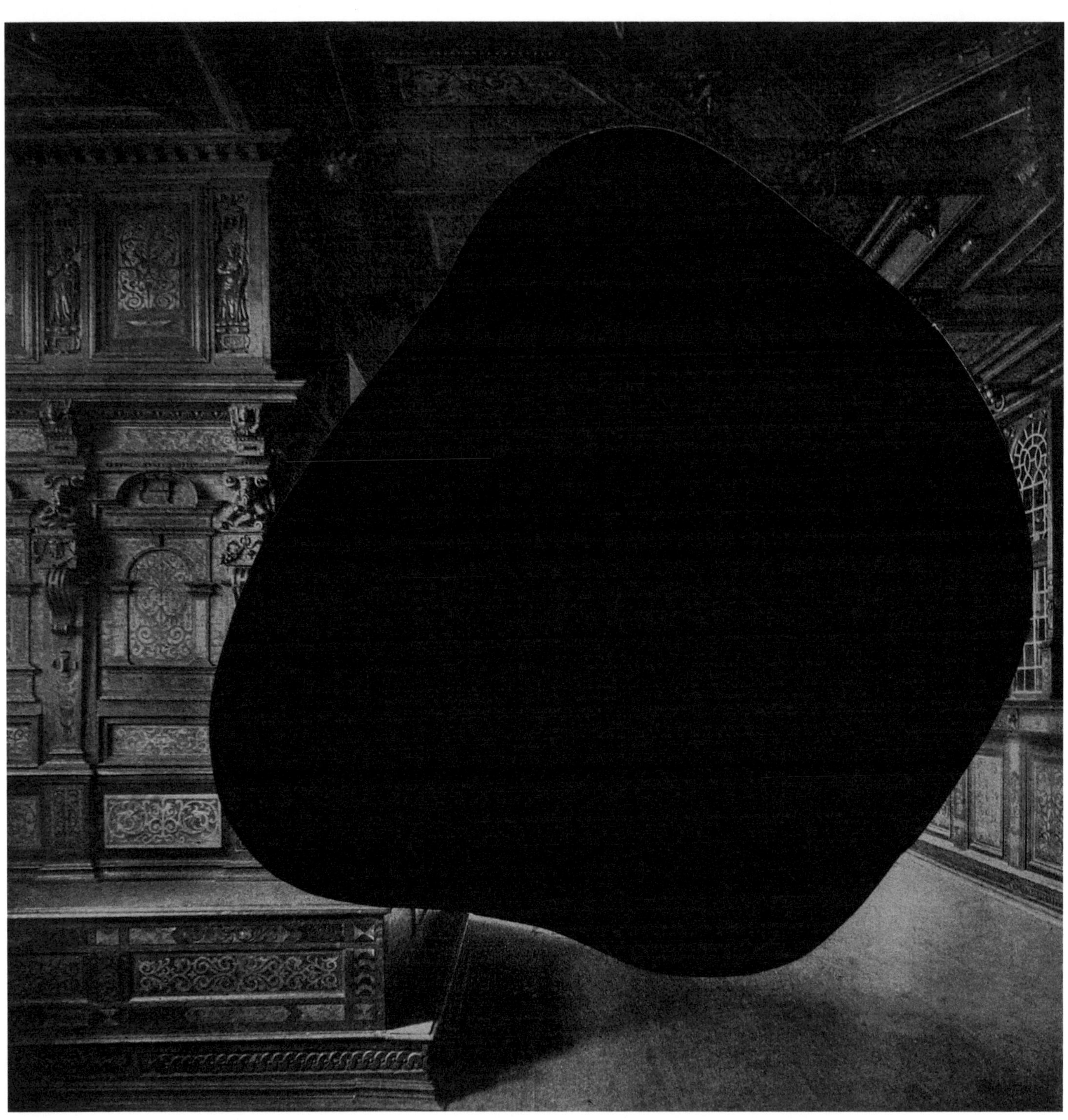

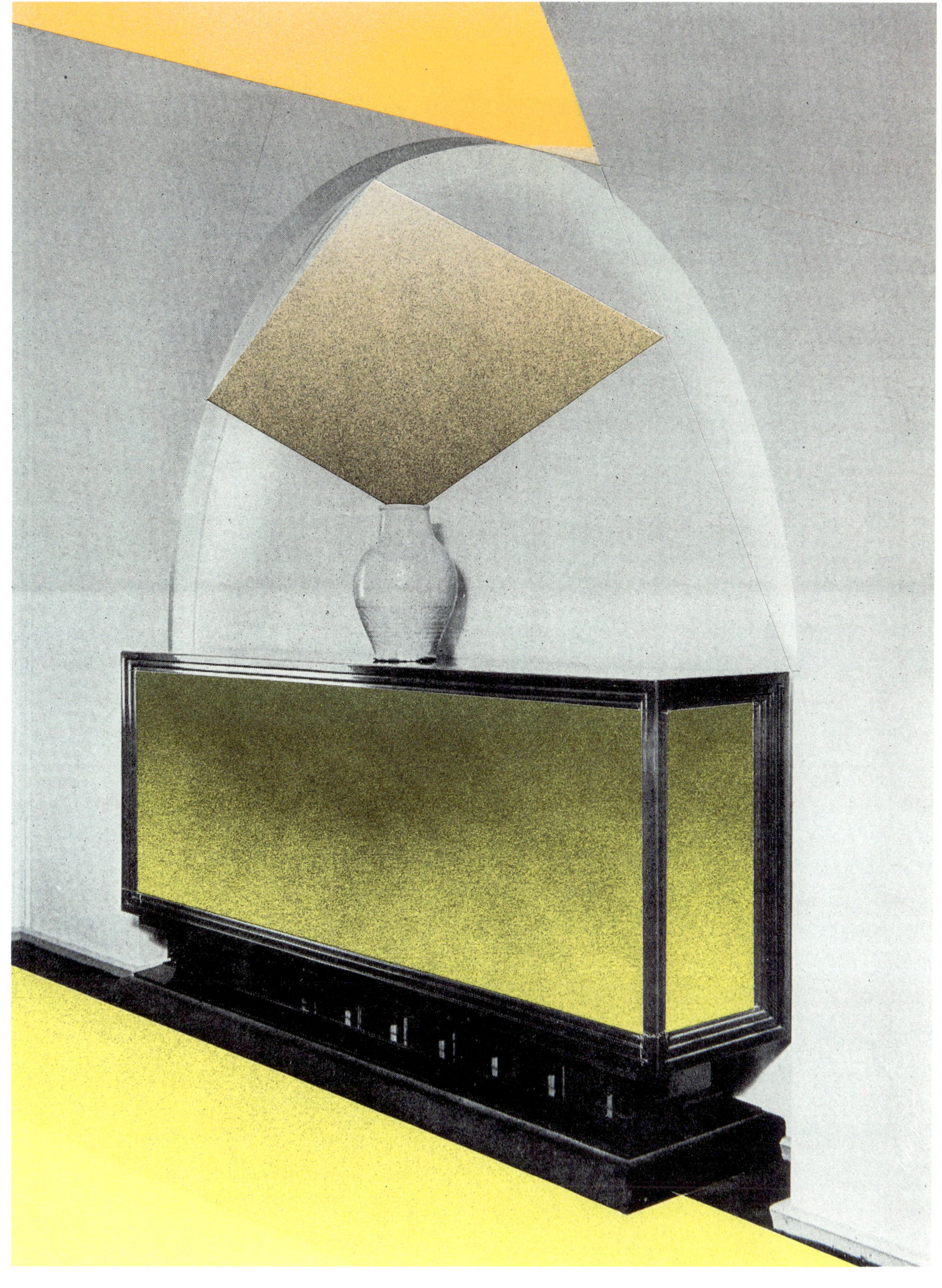

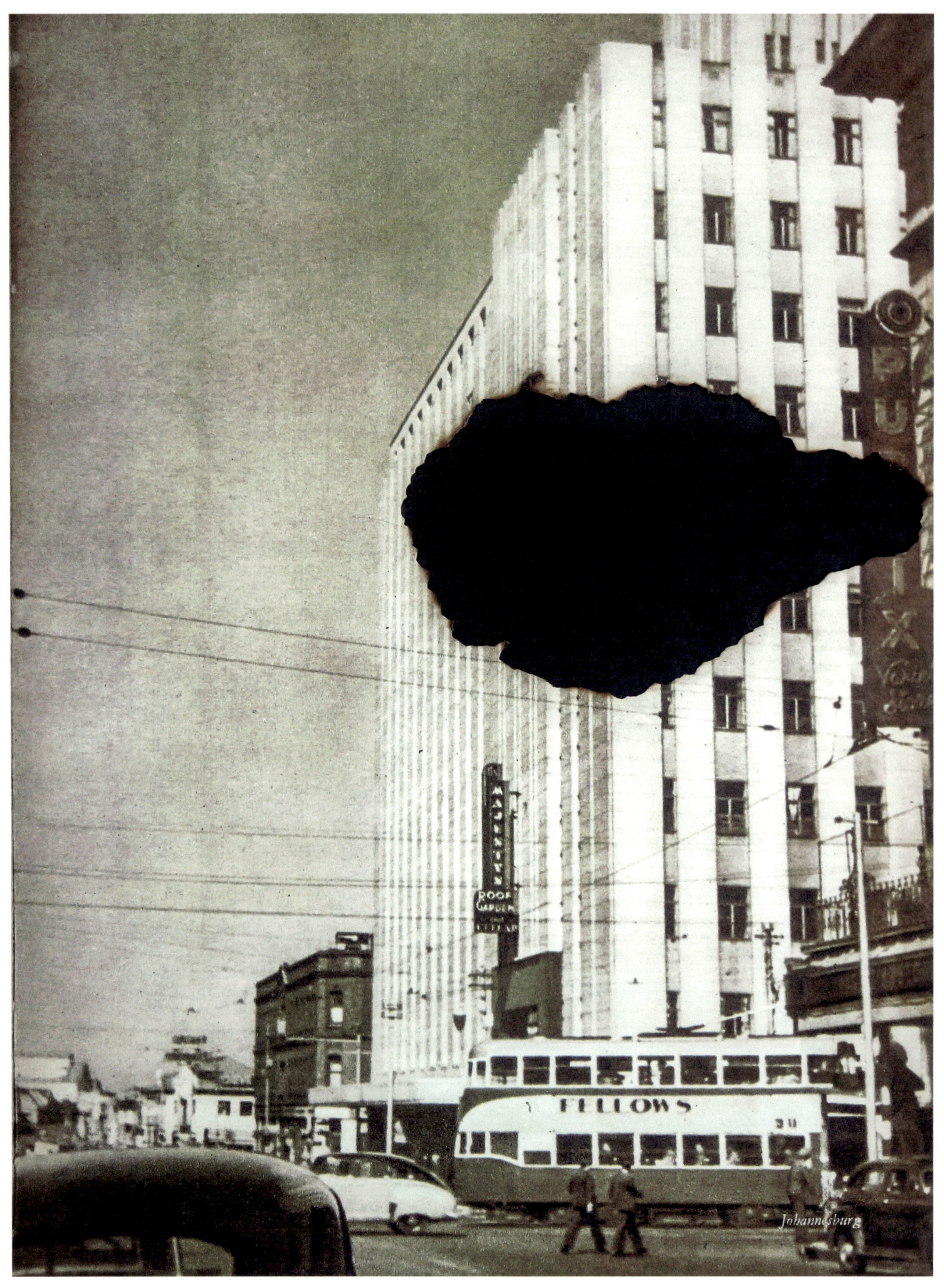
FELLOWS
Johannesburg

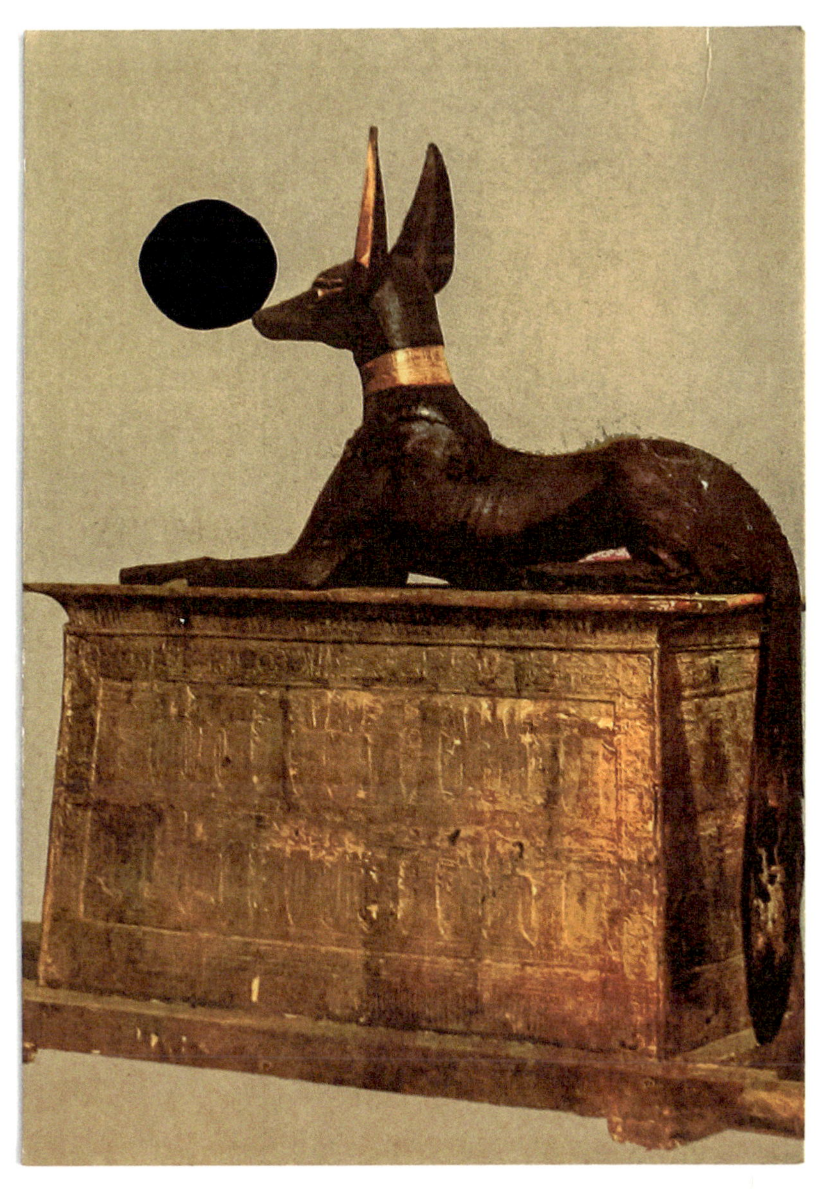

¡SUPERVIVIENTES!

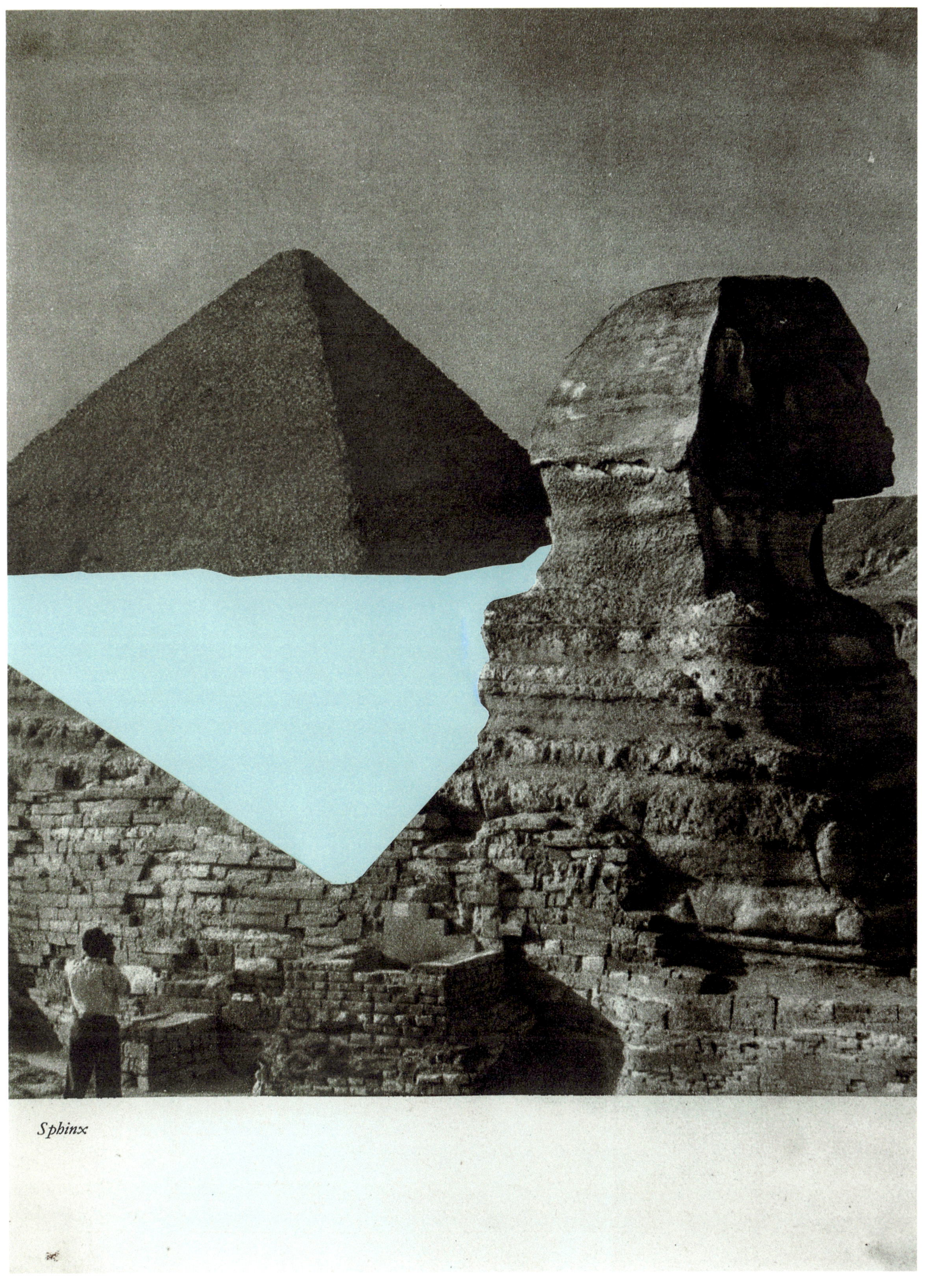

Sphinx

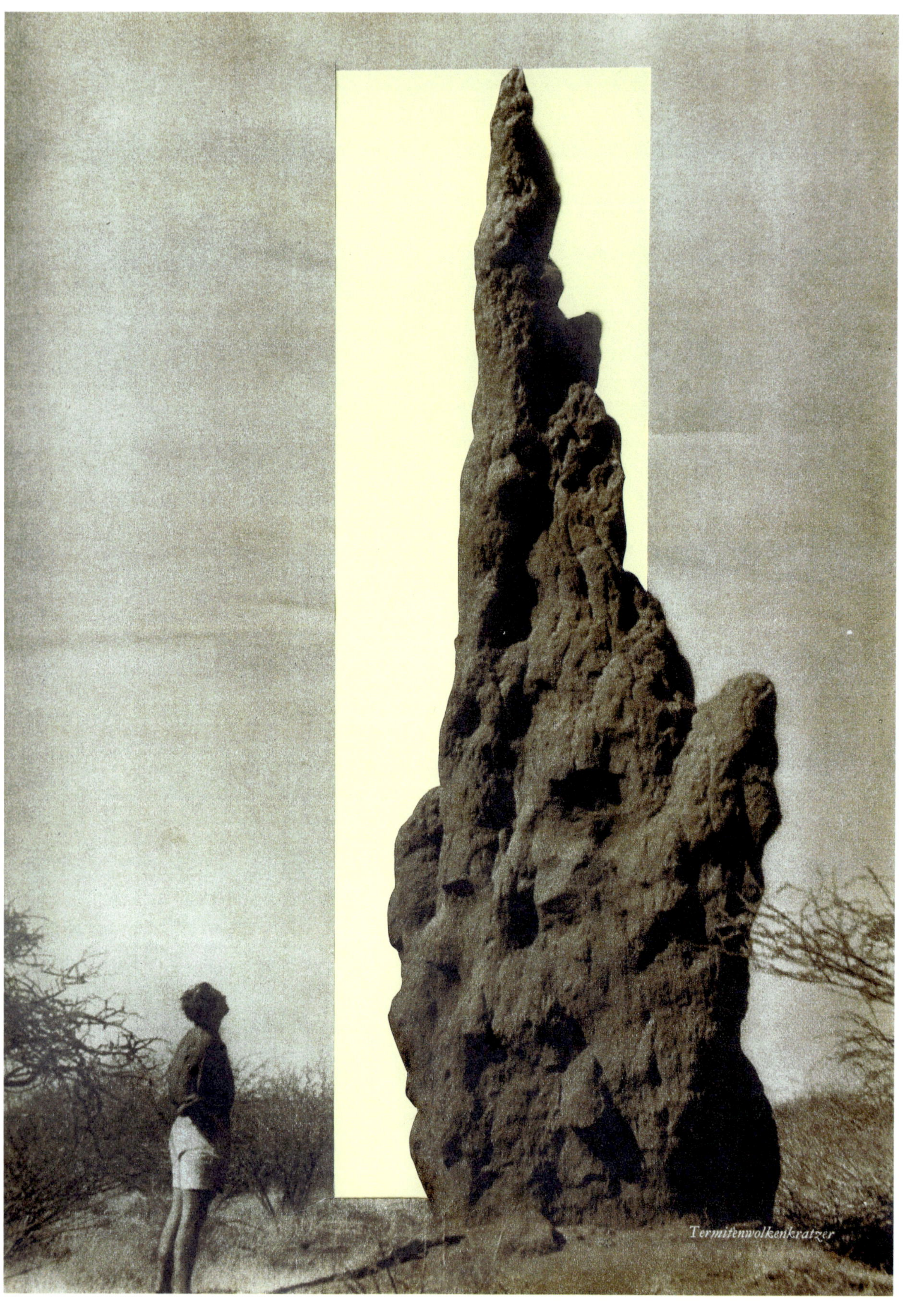

TERMITENWOLKENKRATZER

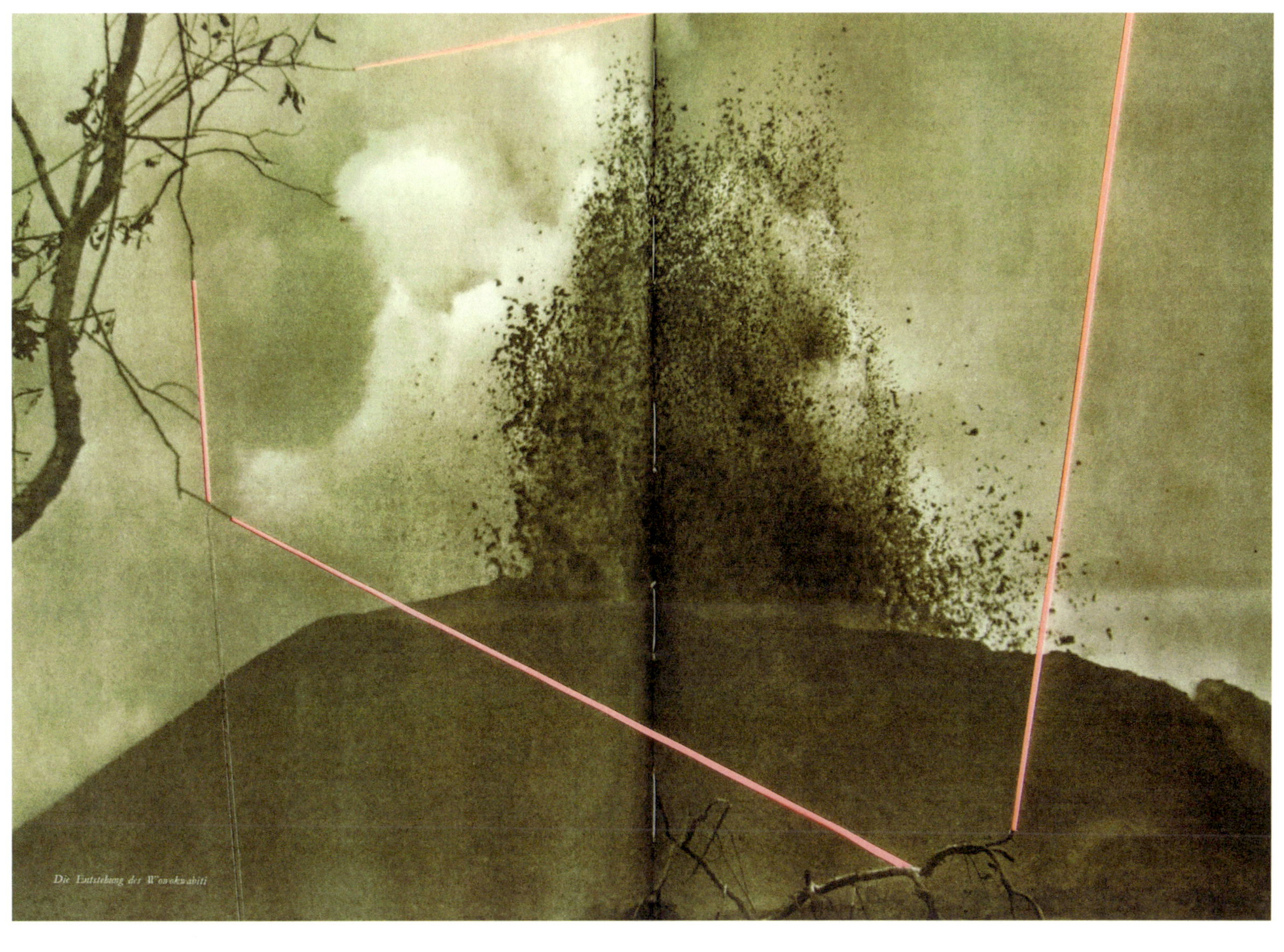

DIE ENTSTEHUNG DES WONOKWABITI

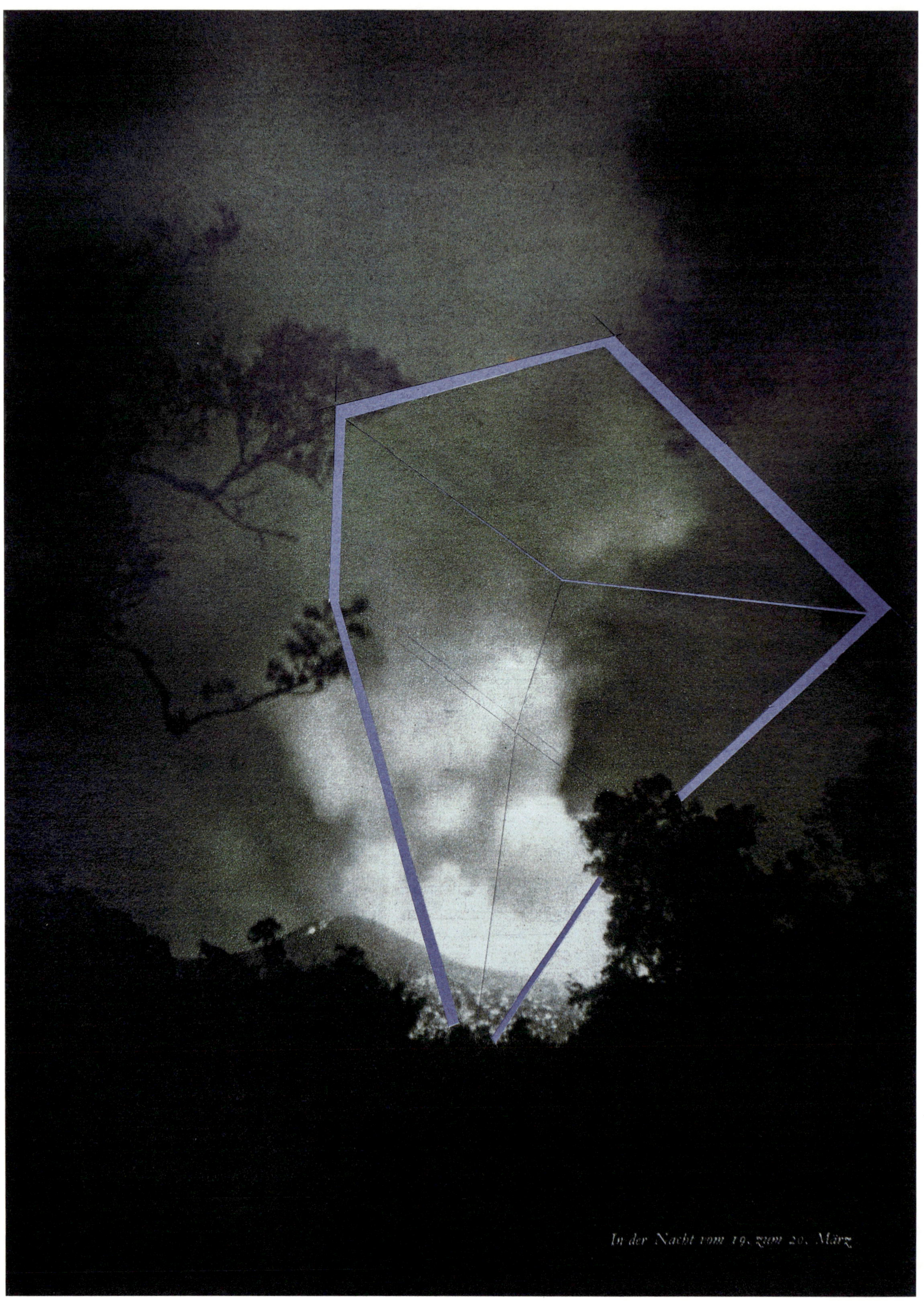

IN DER NACHT VOM 19. ZUM 20. MÄRZ

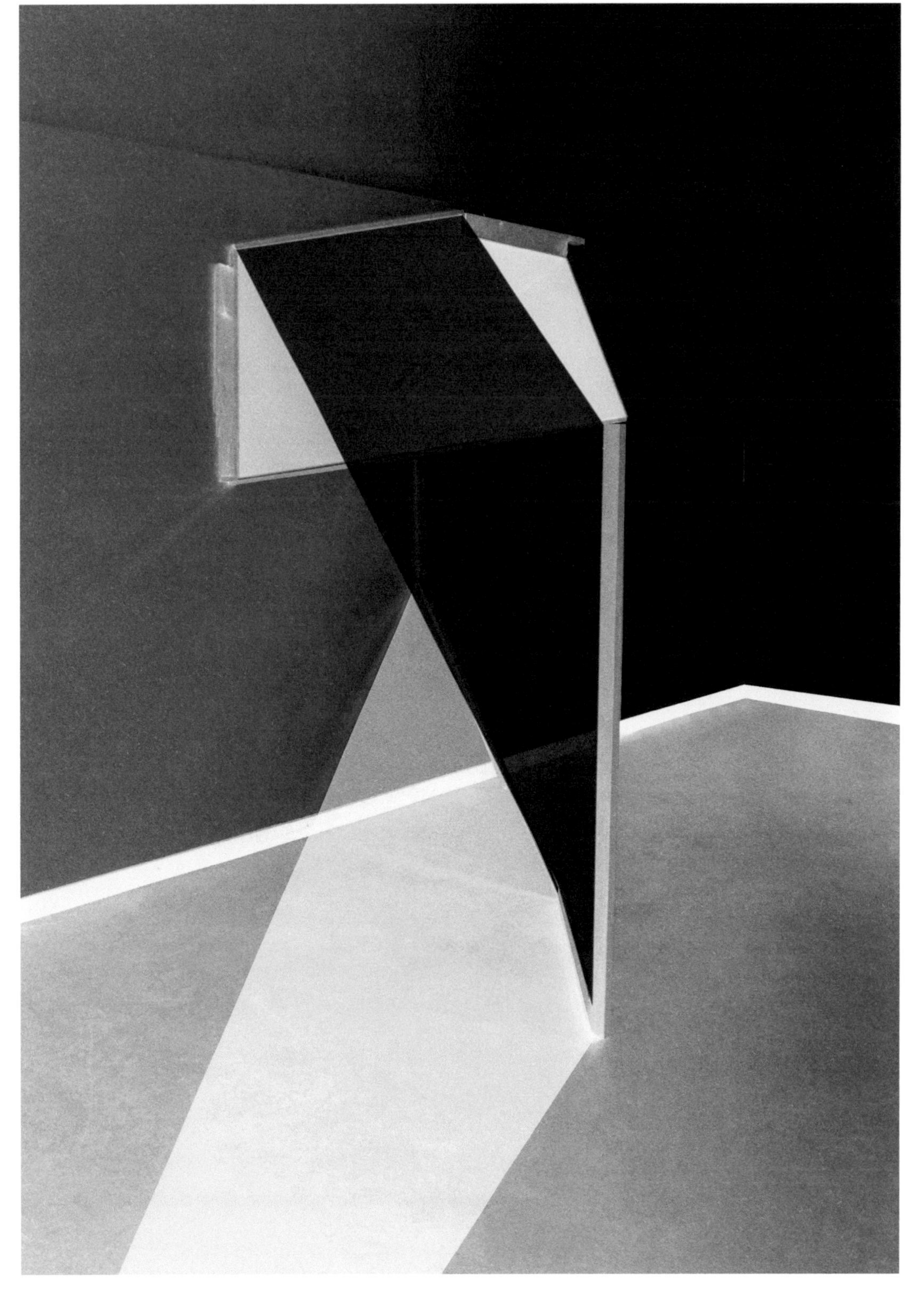

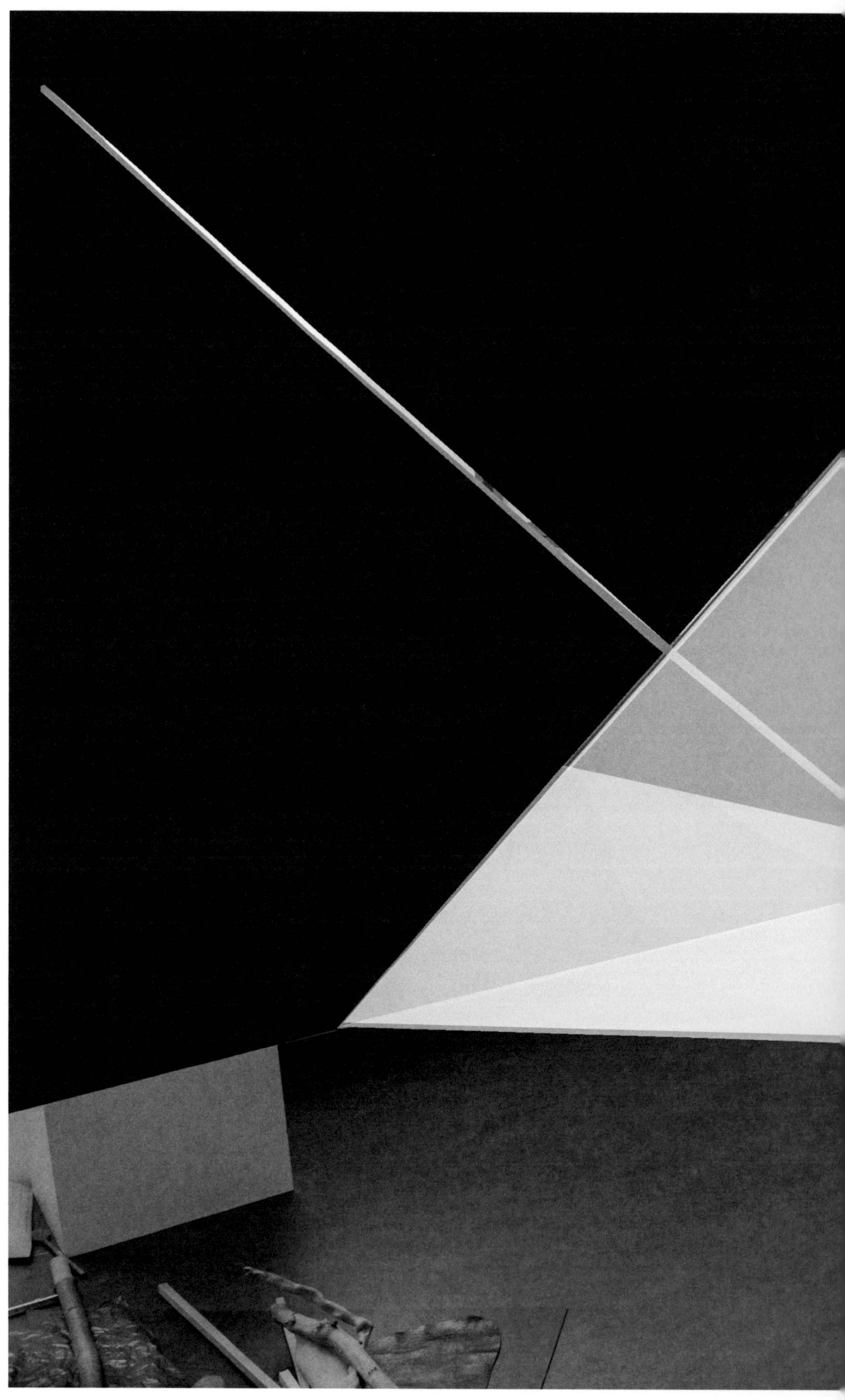

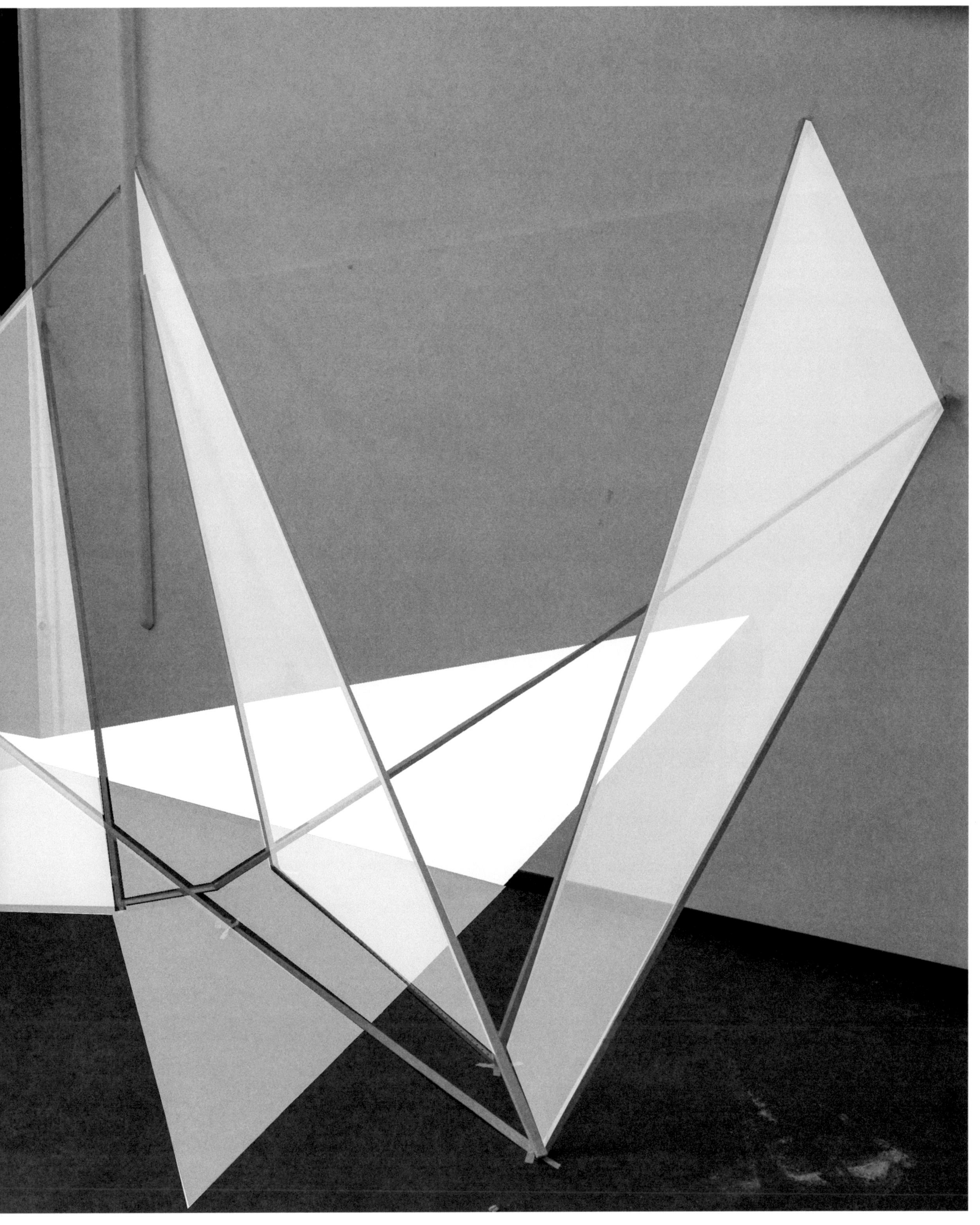

CORNER PIECE

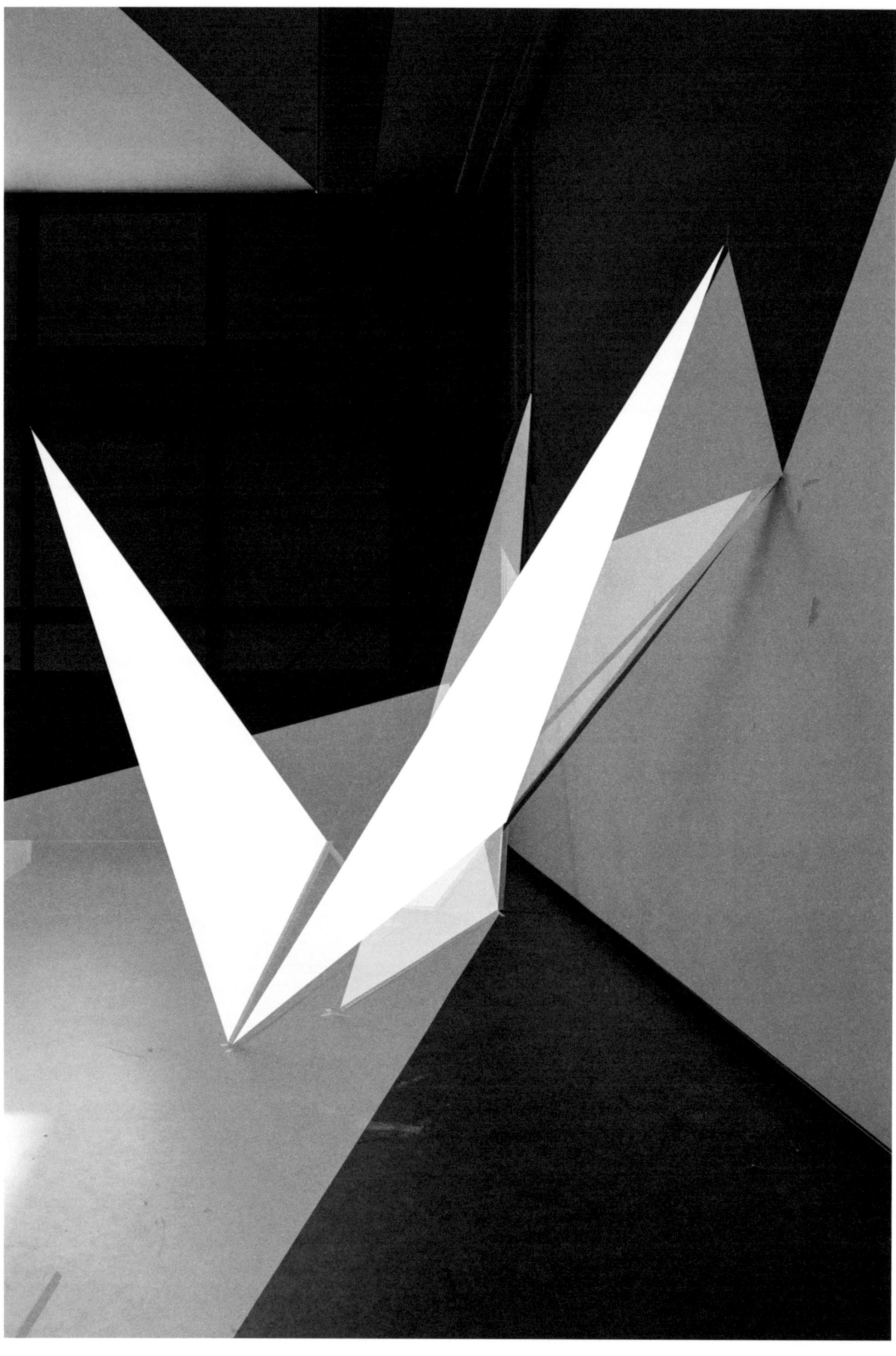

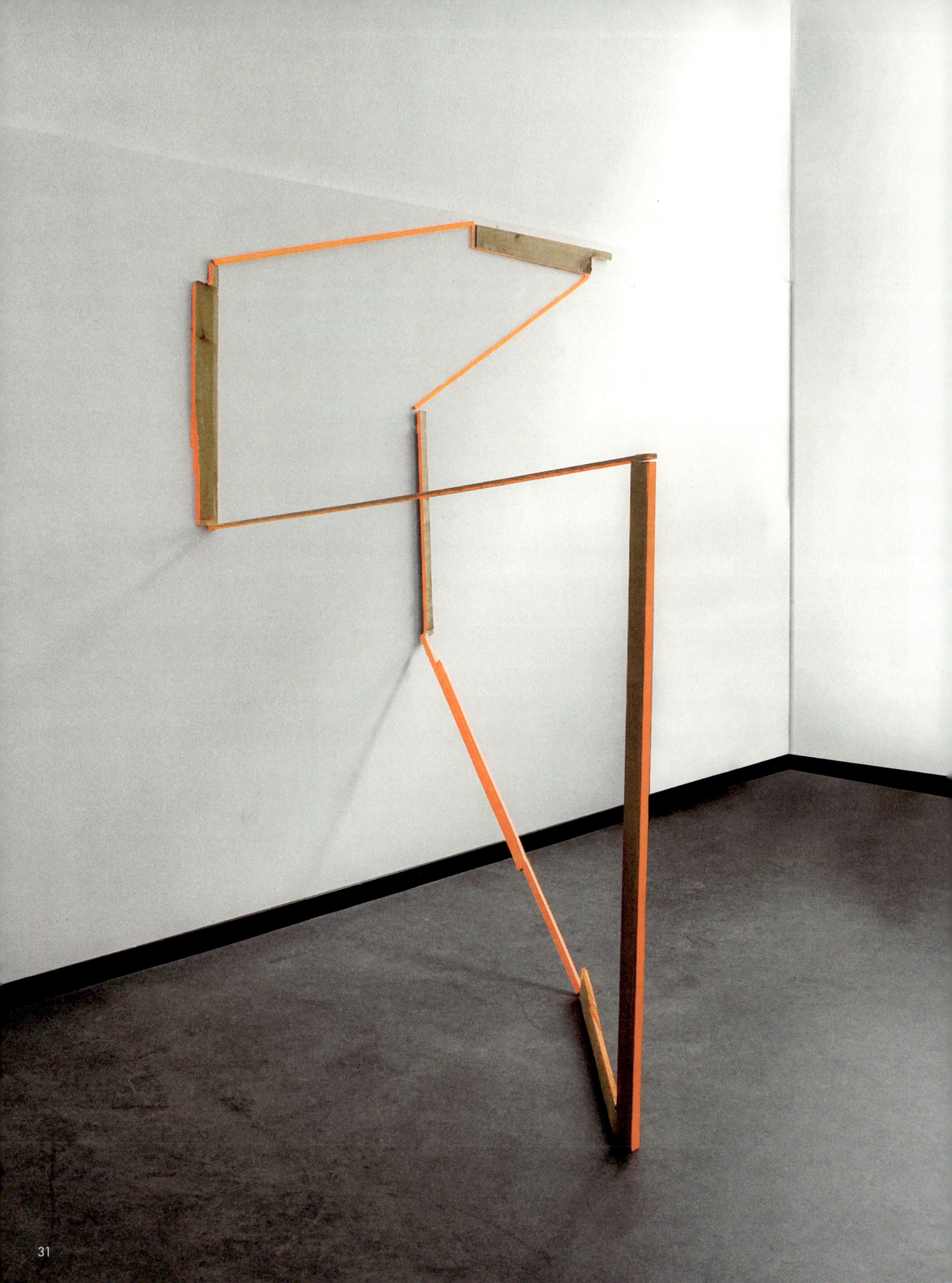

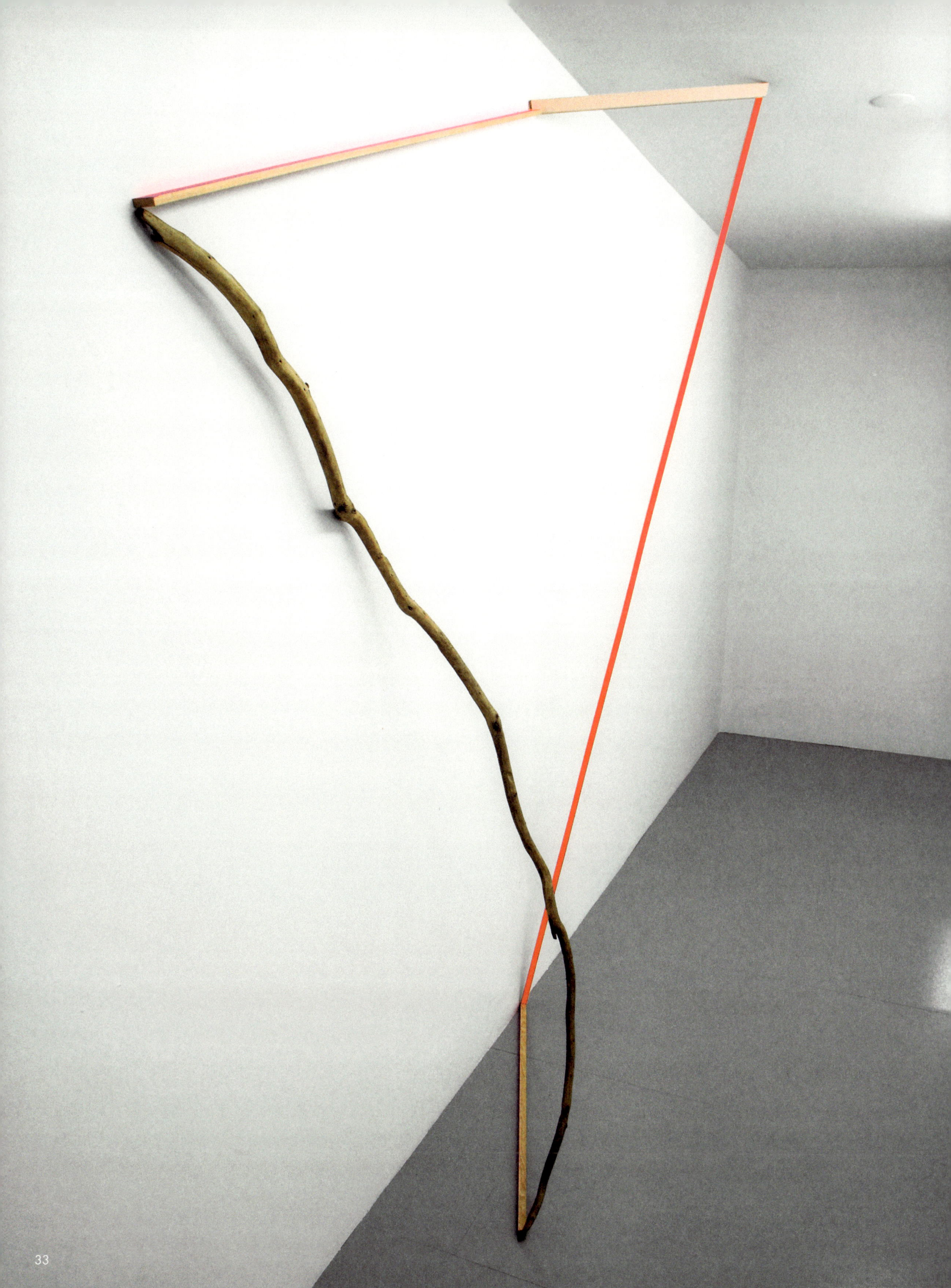

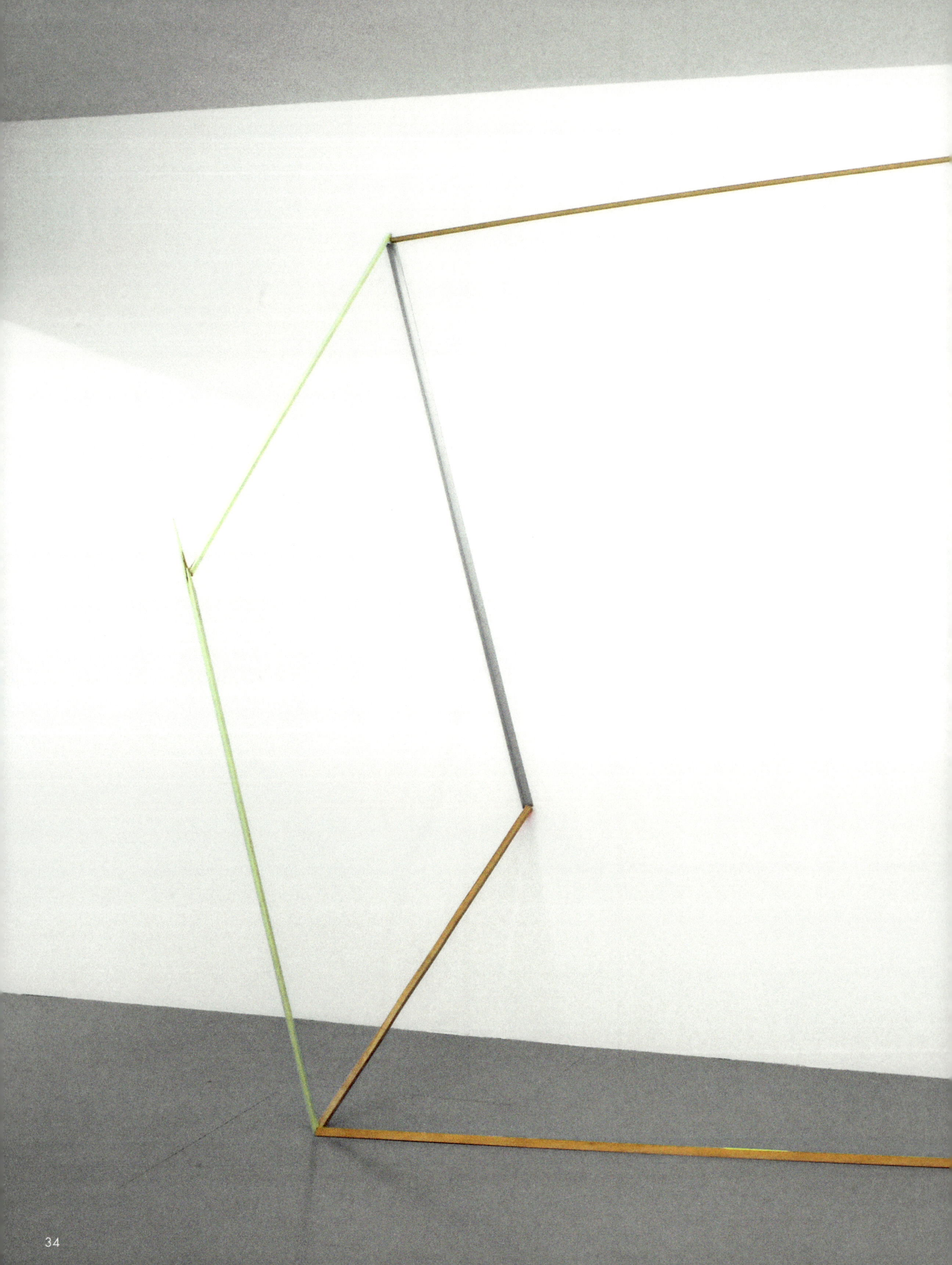

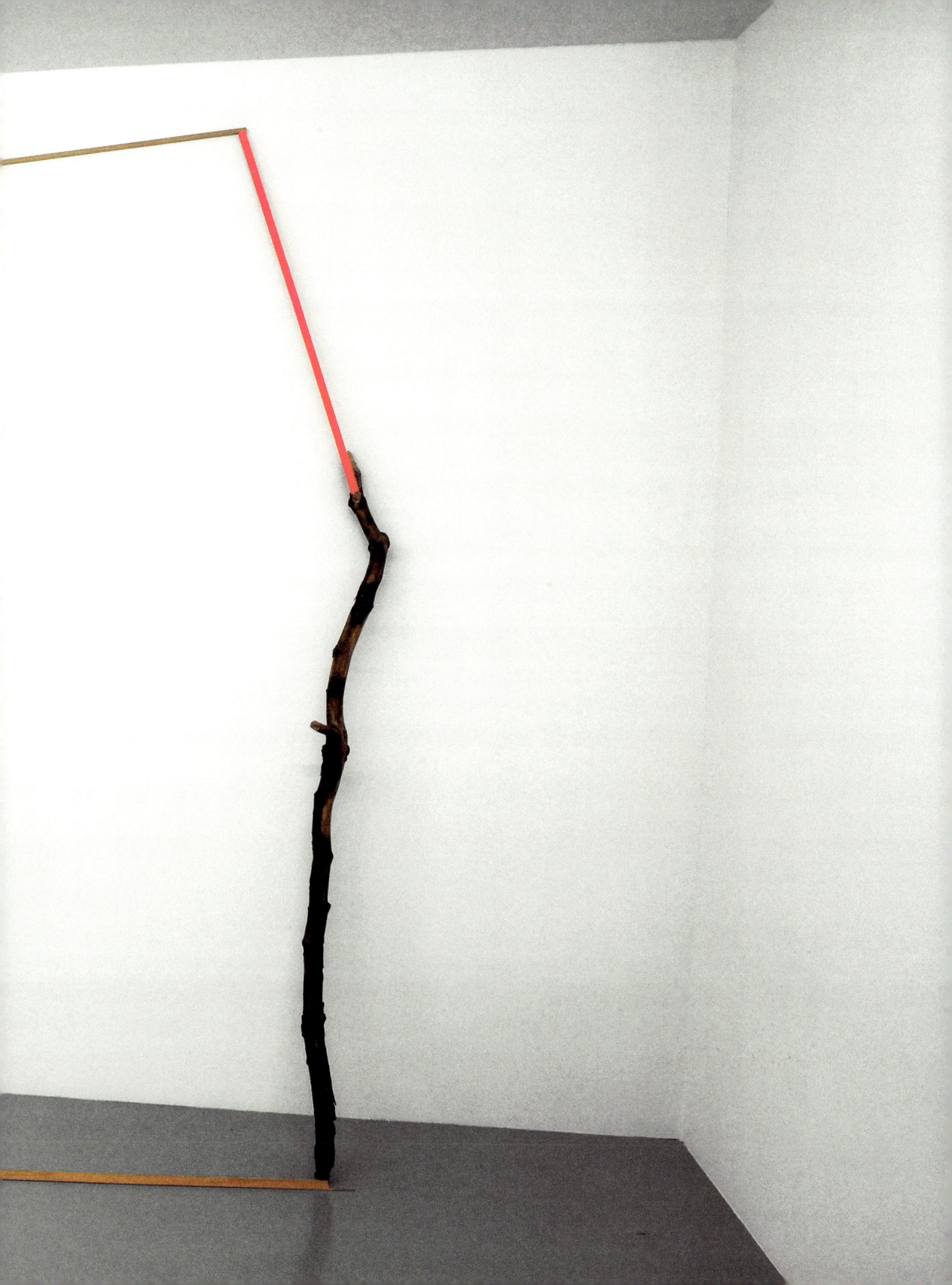

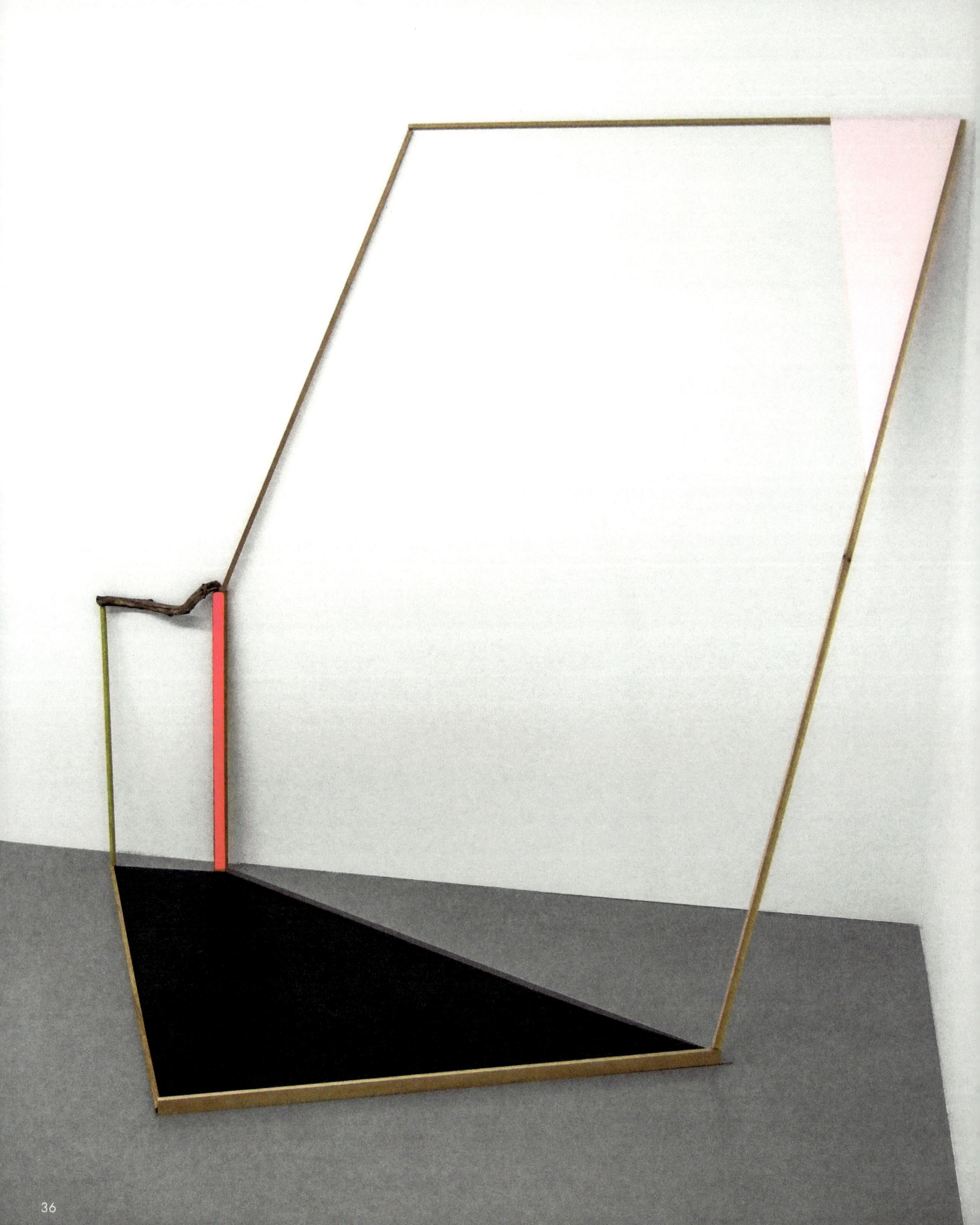

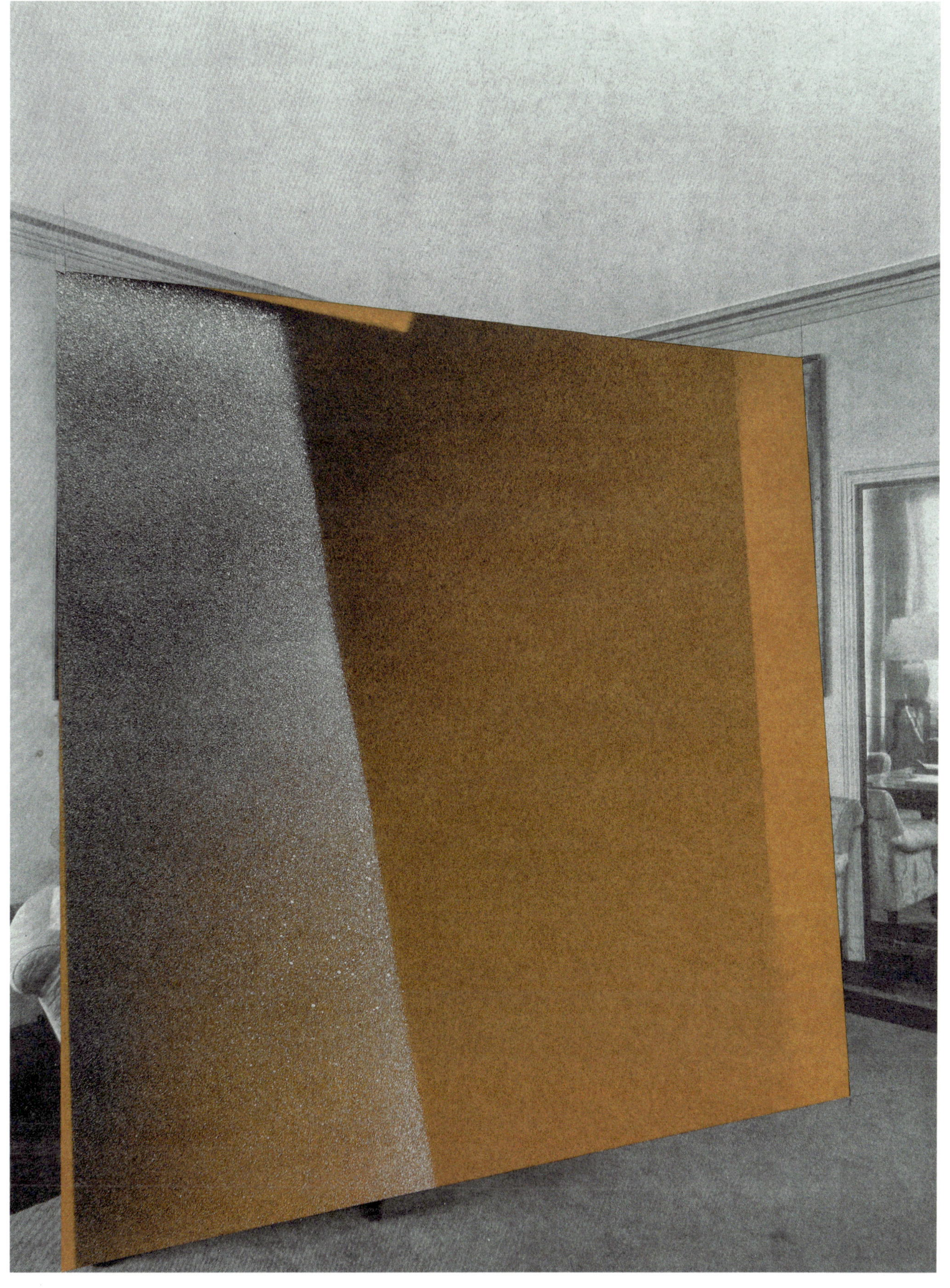

HIMMEL

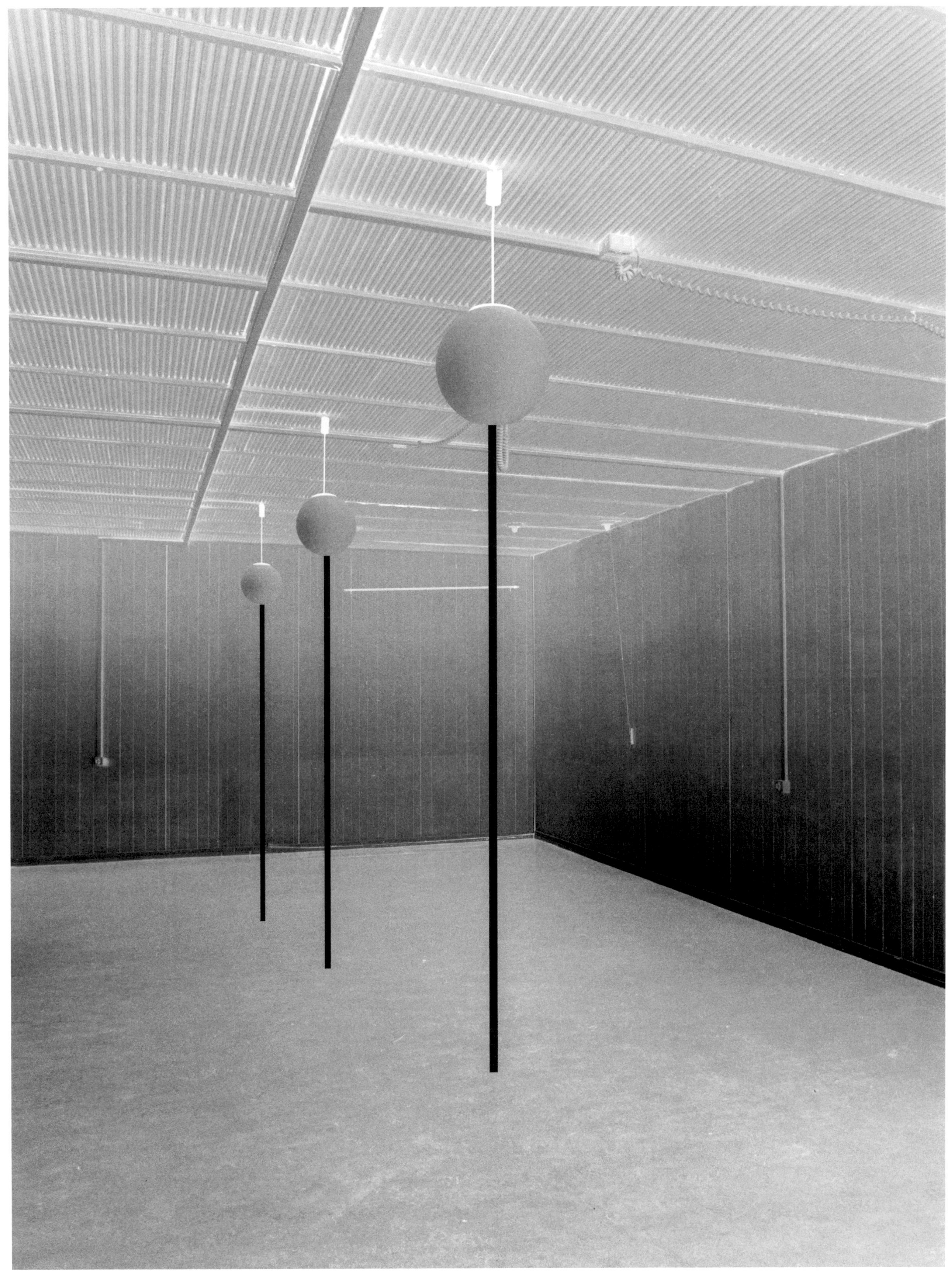

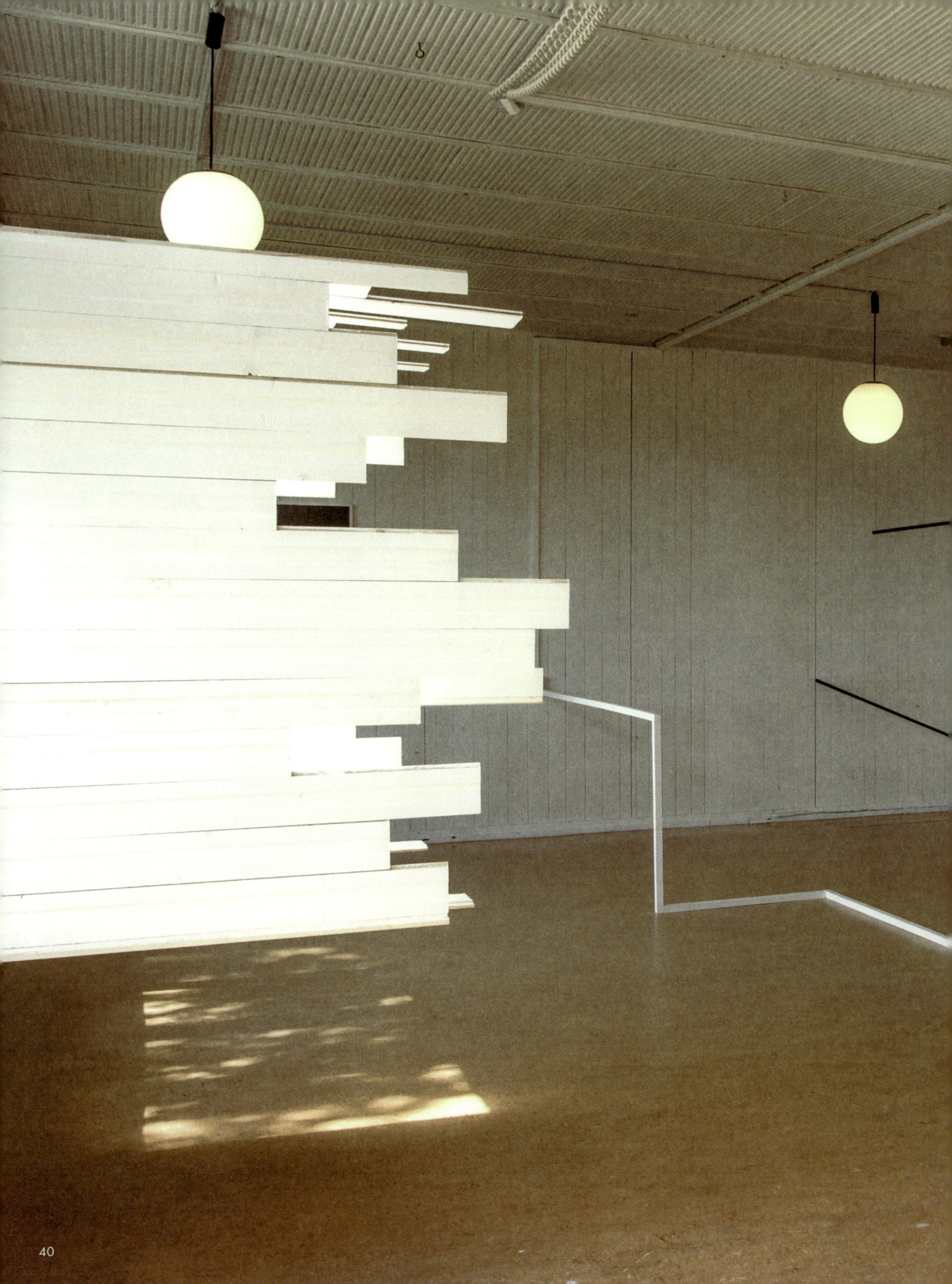

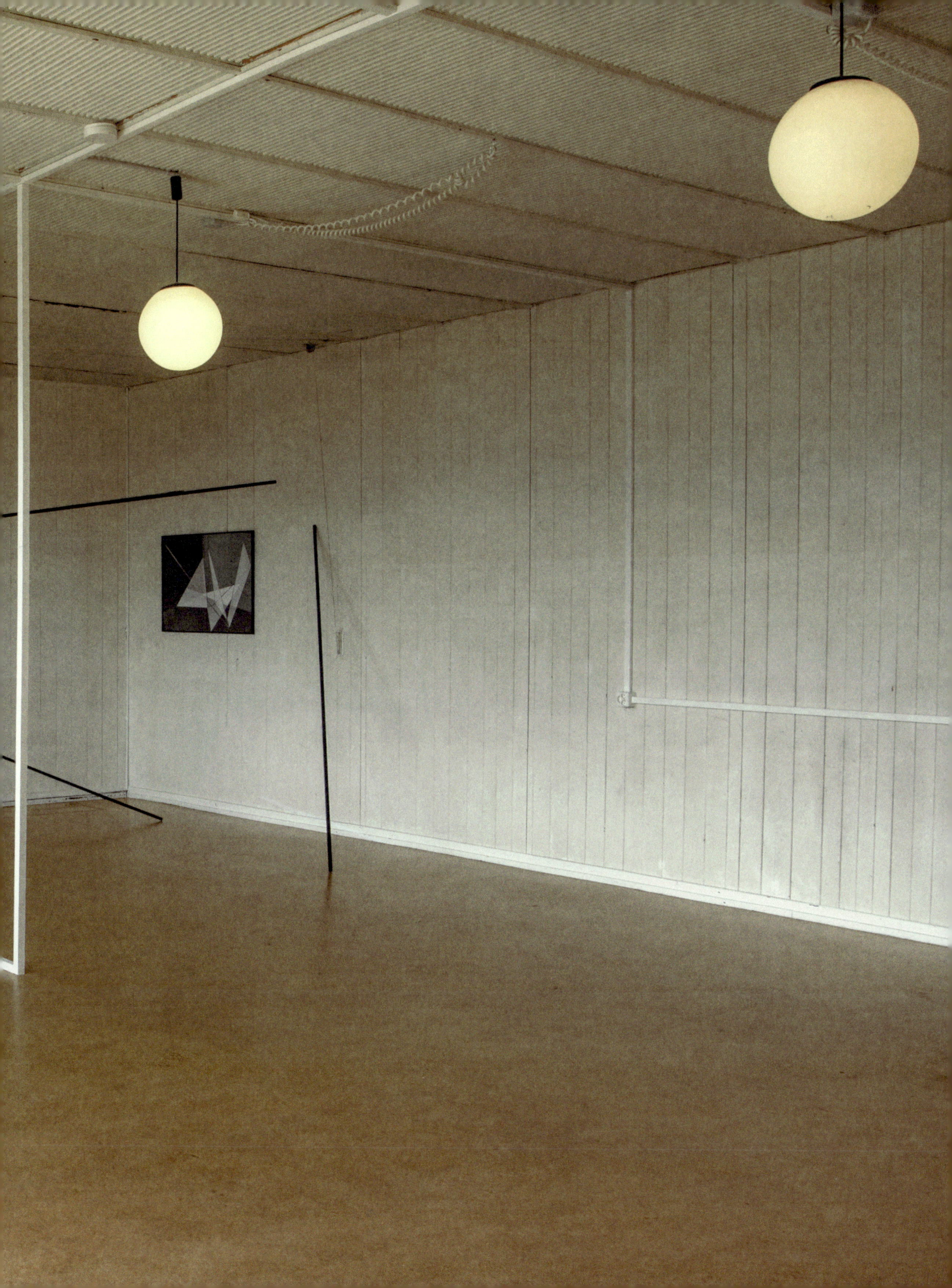

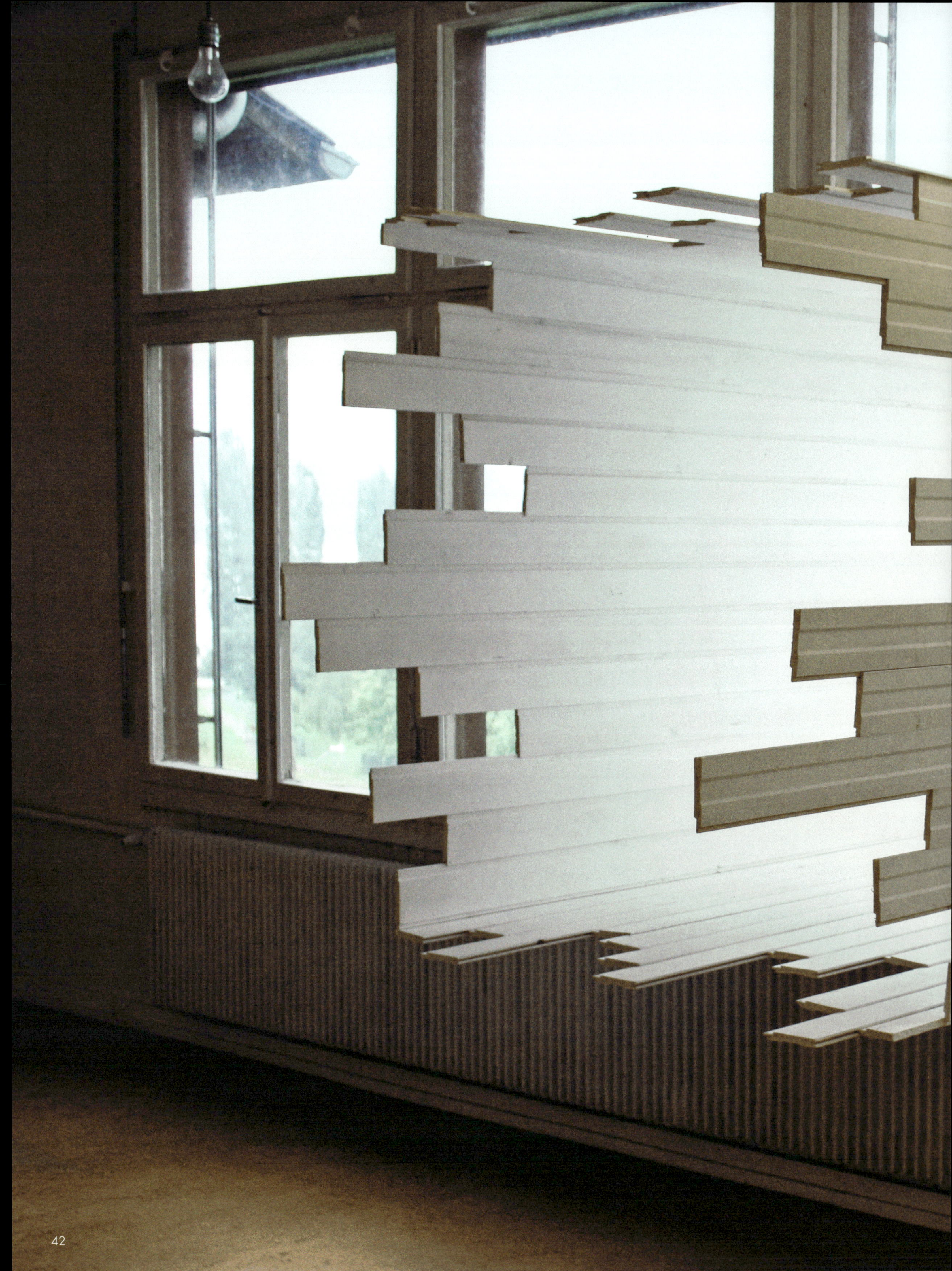

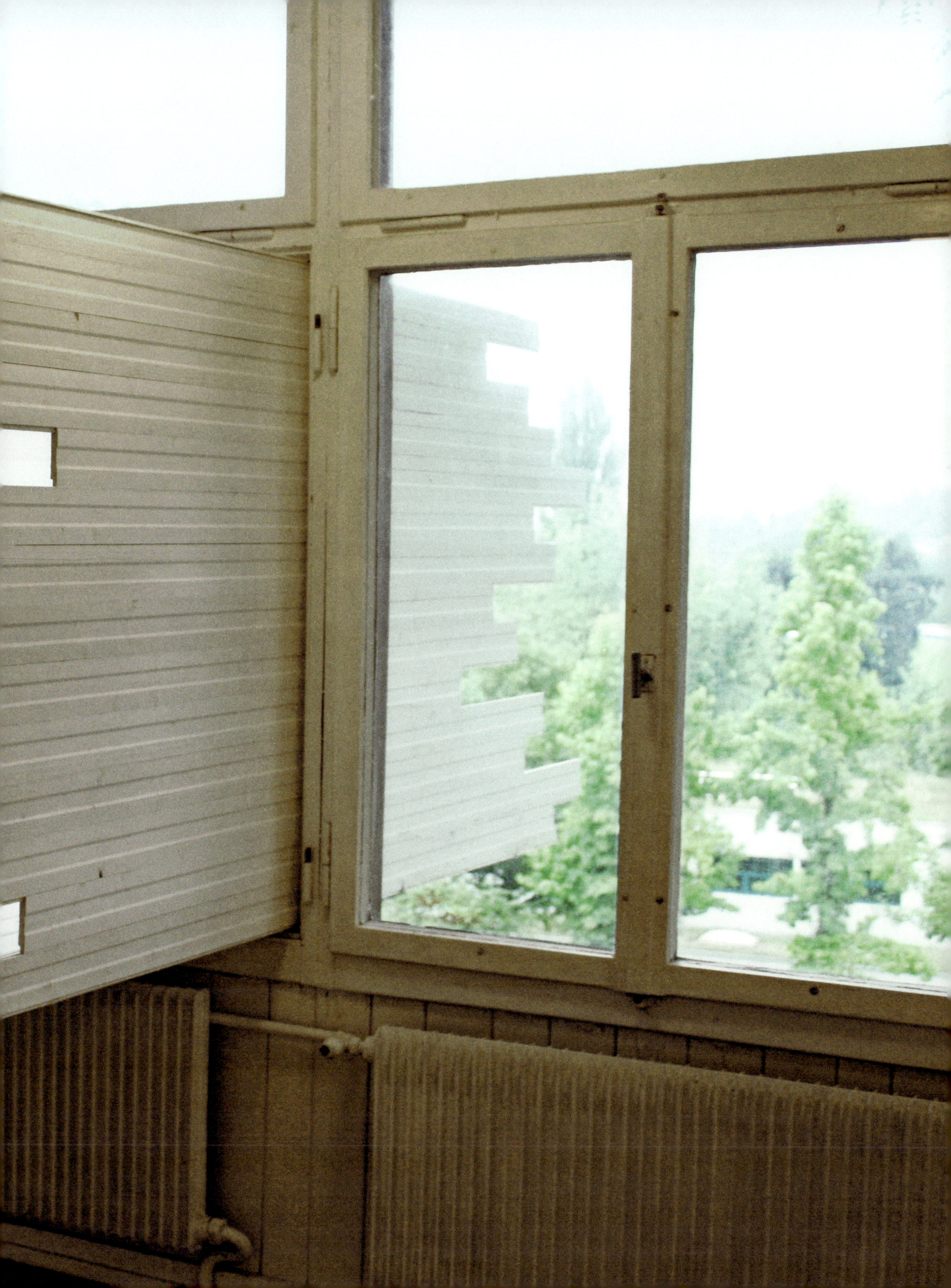

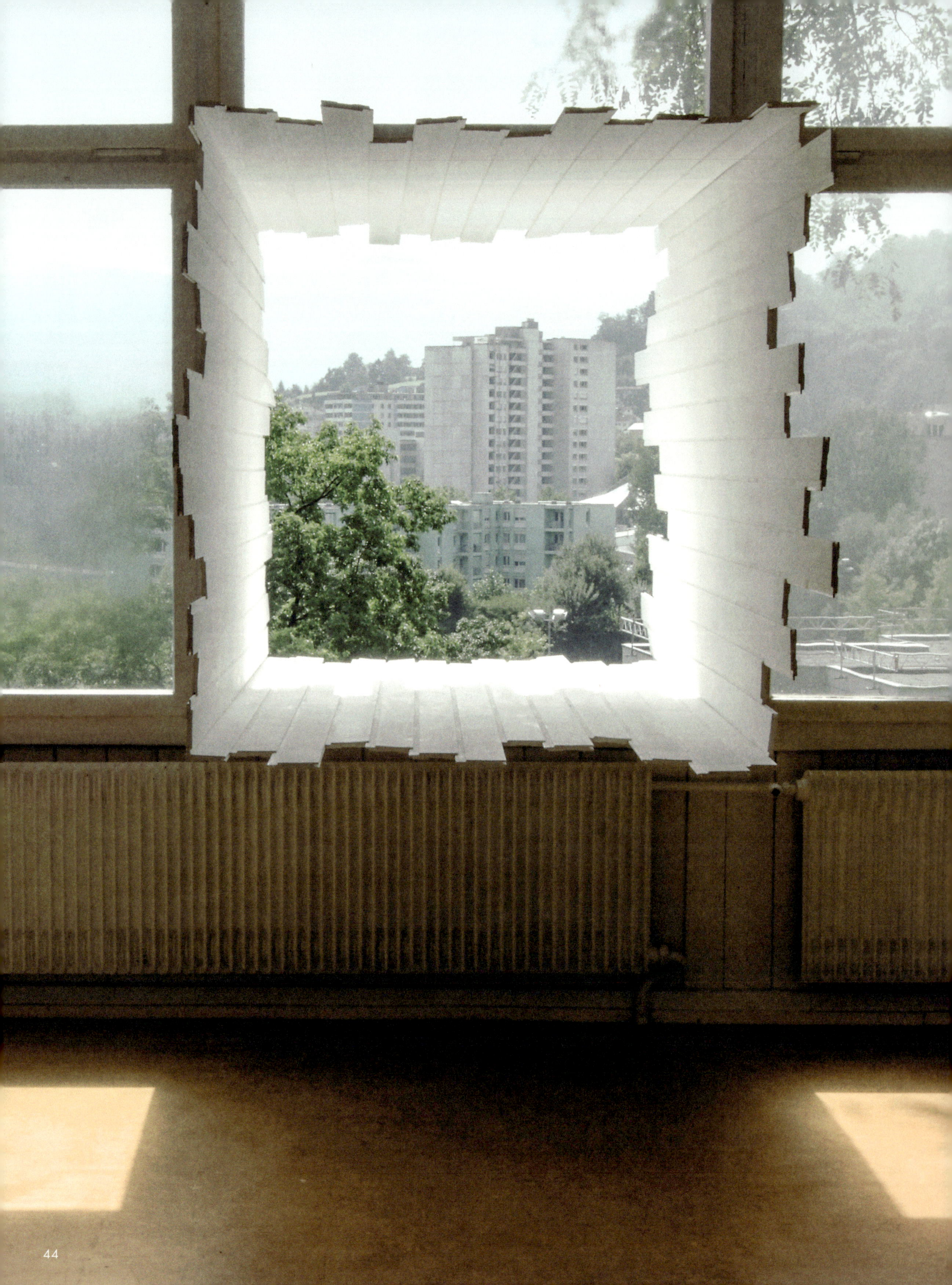

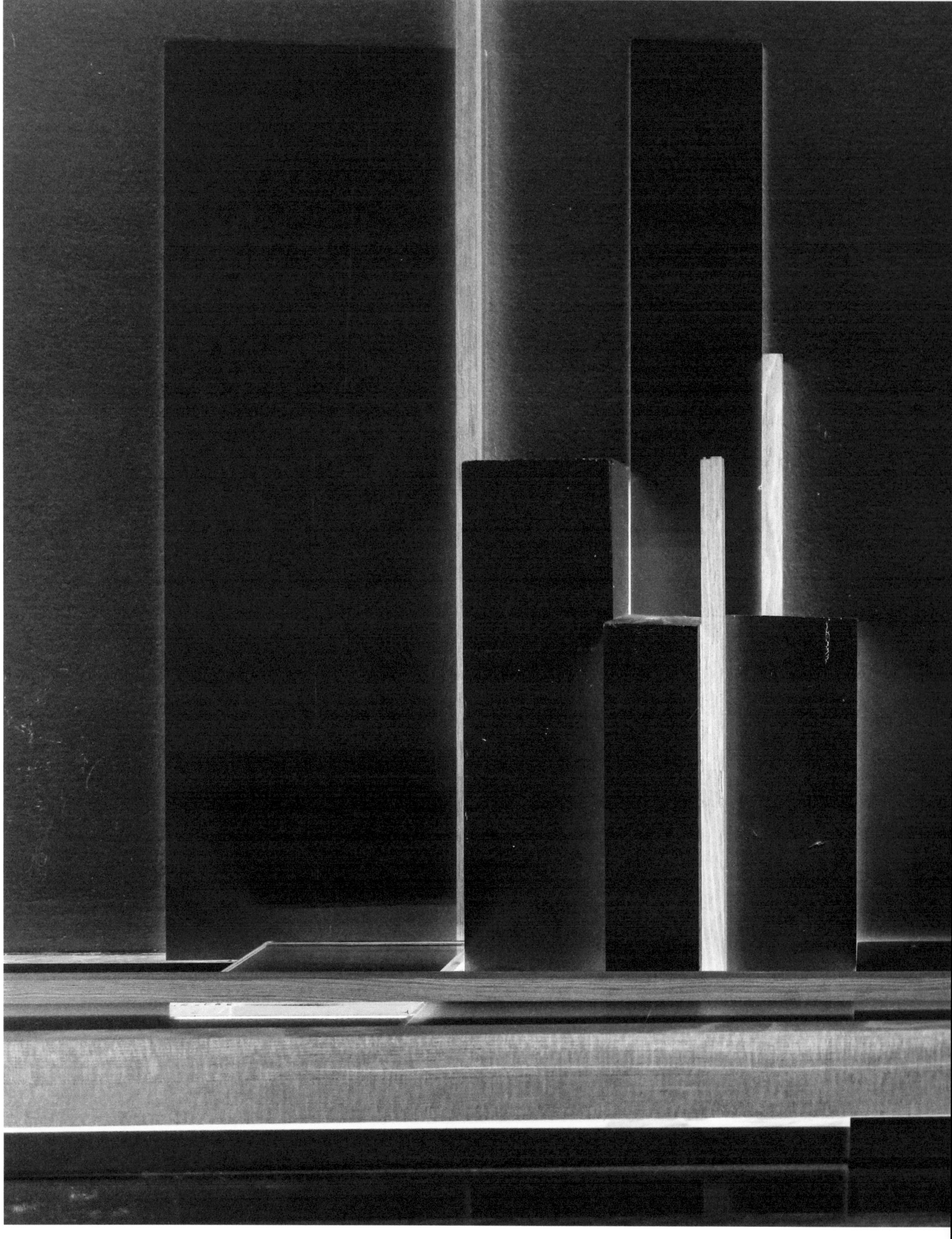

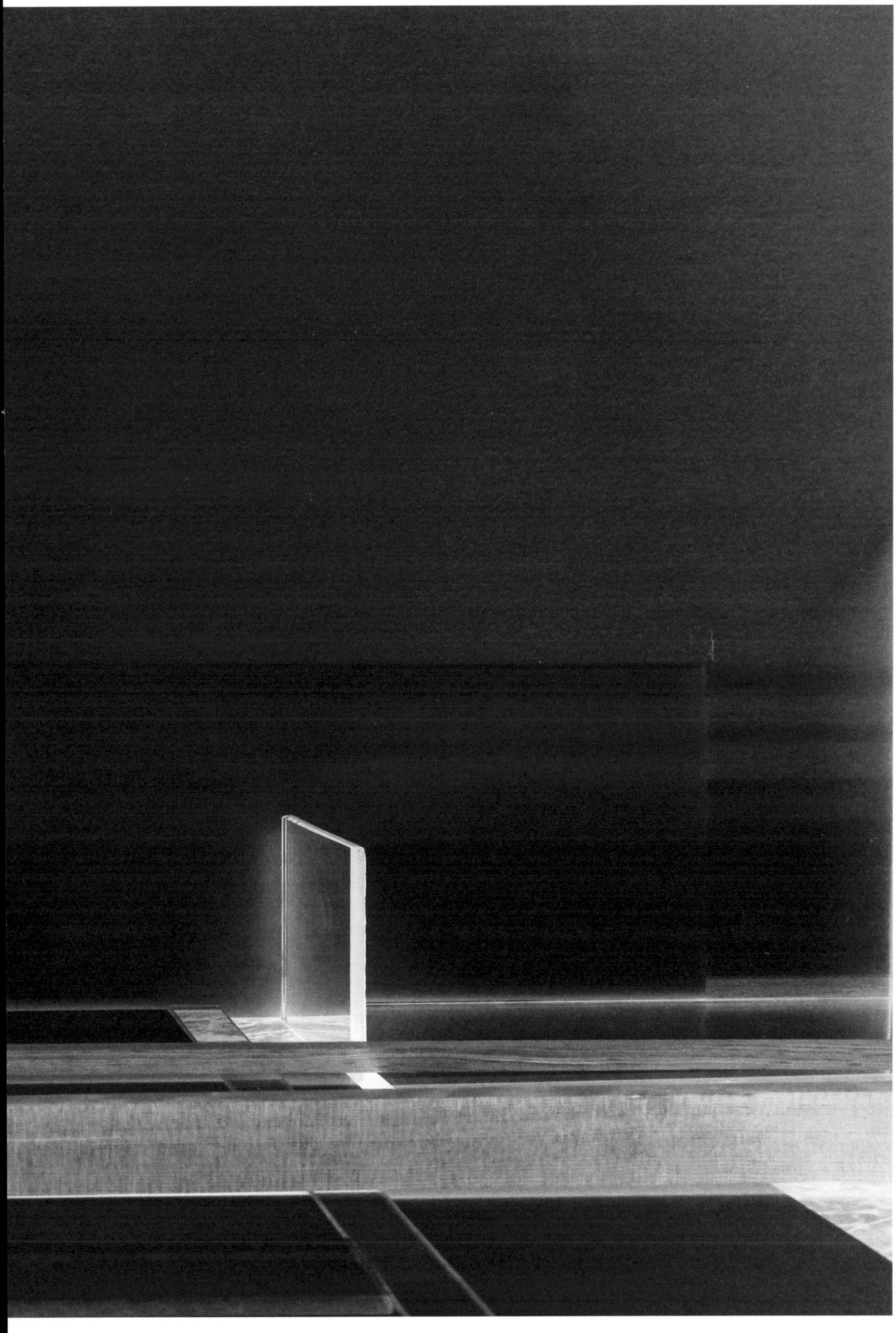

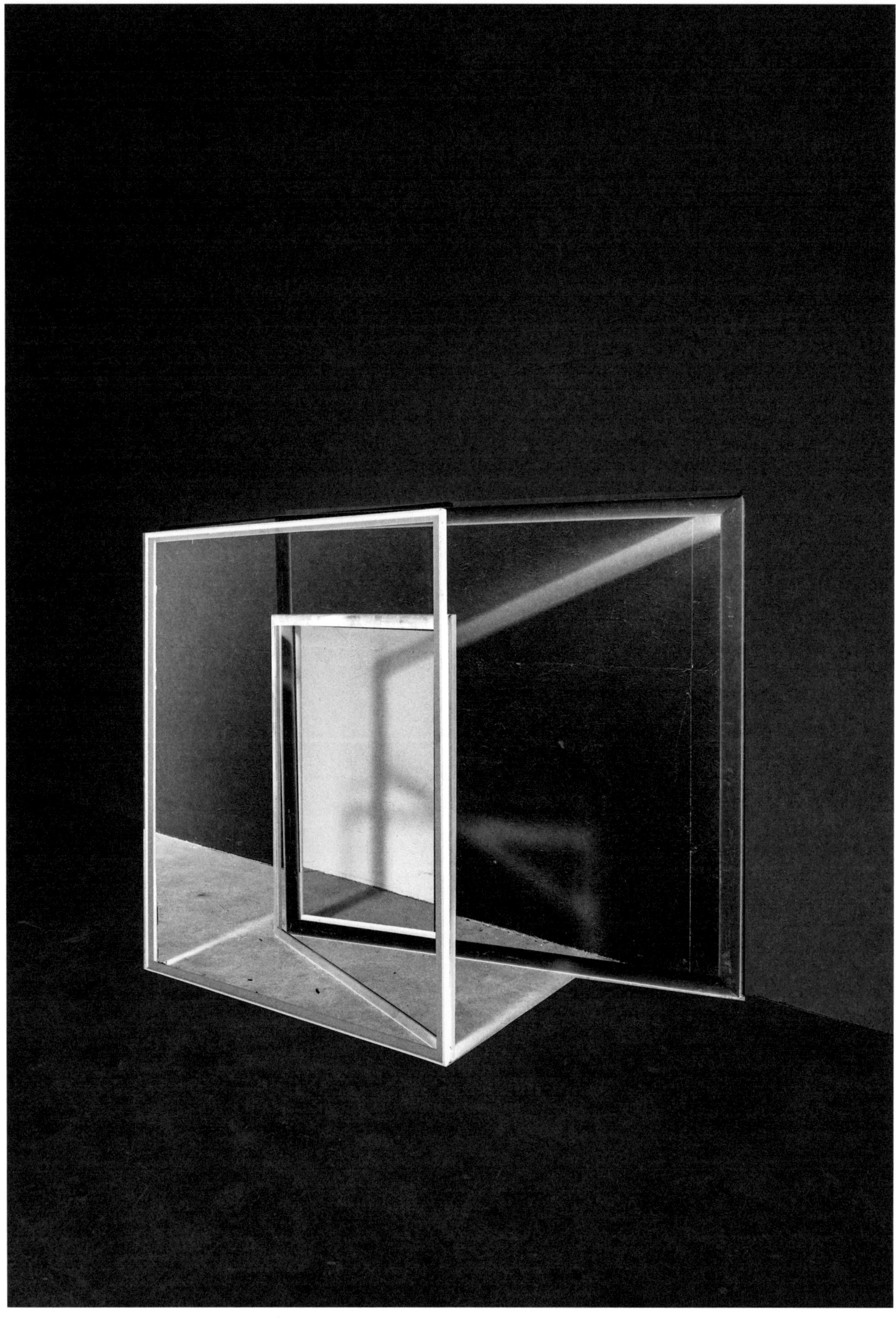

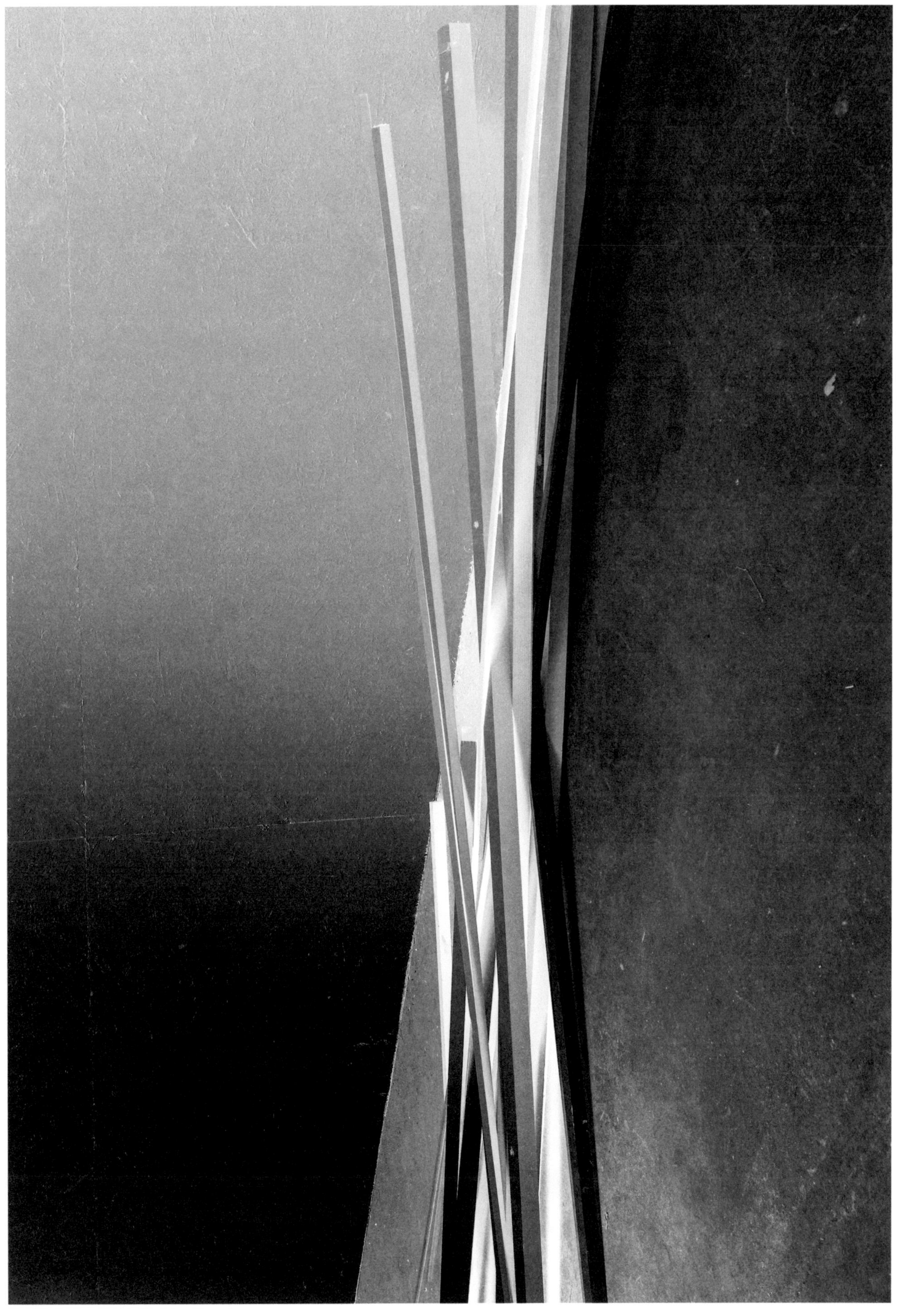

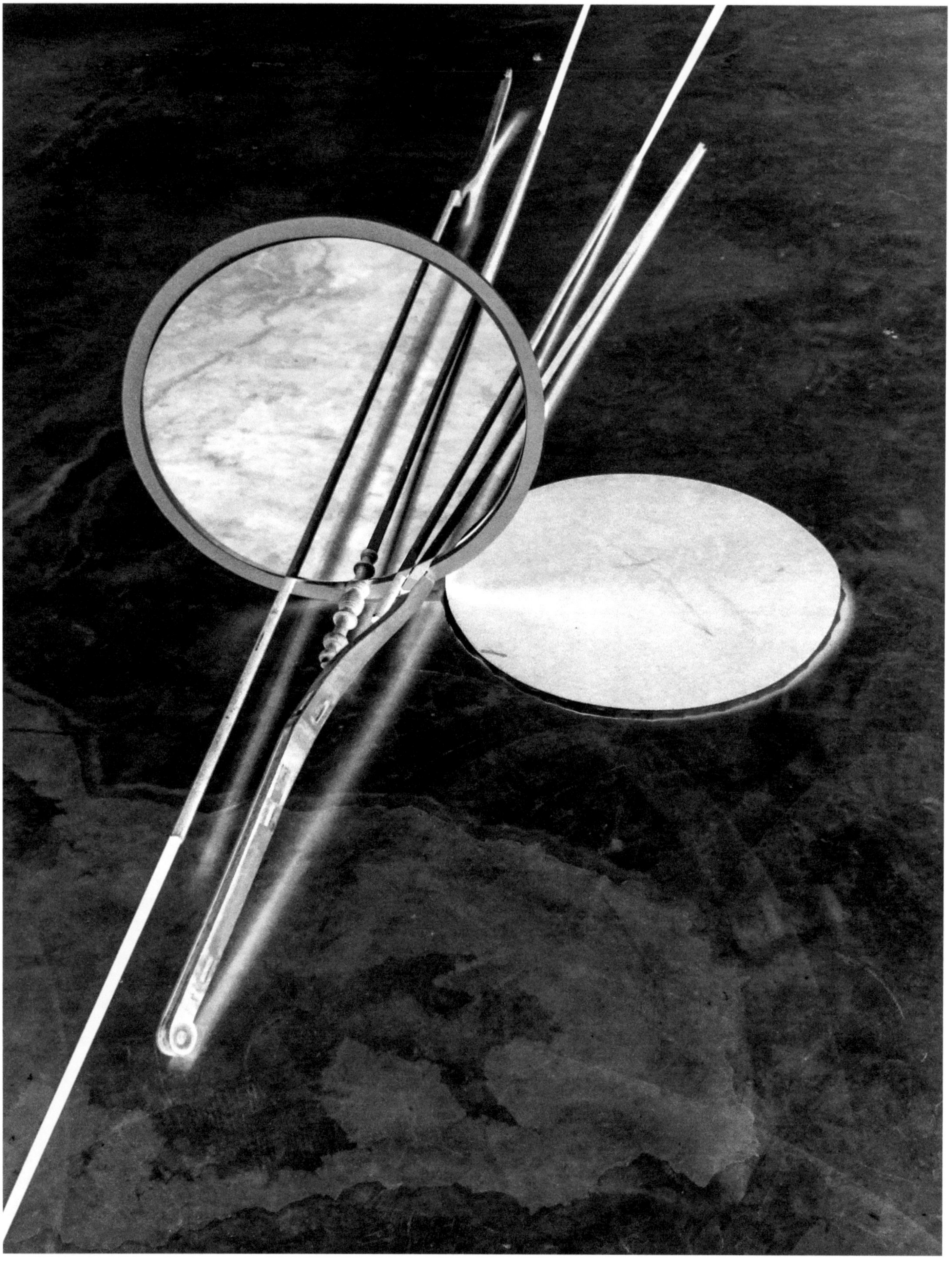

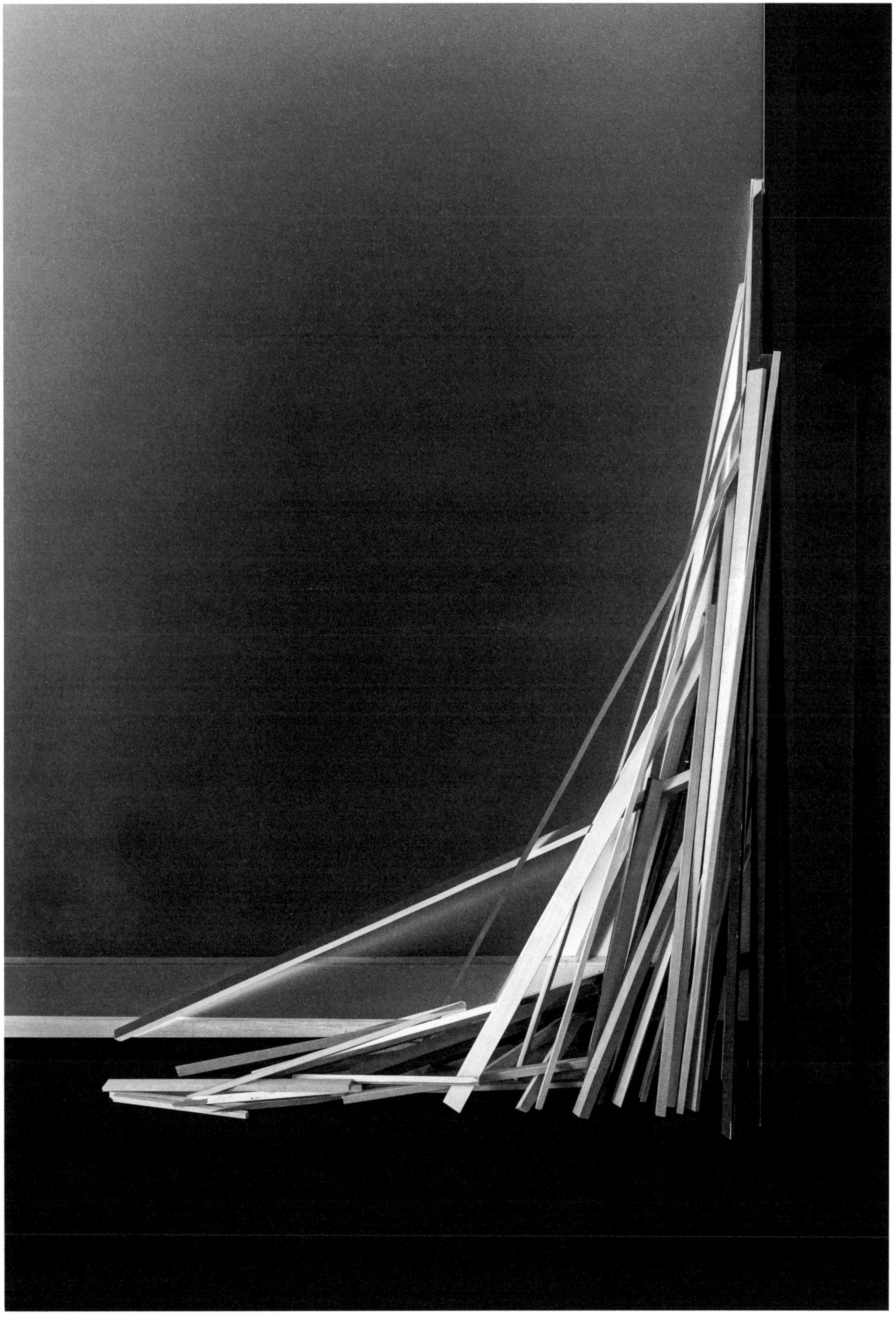

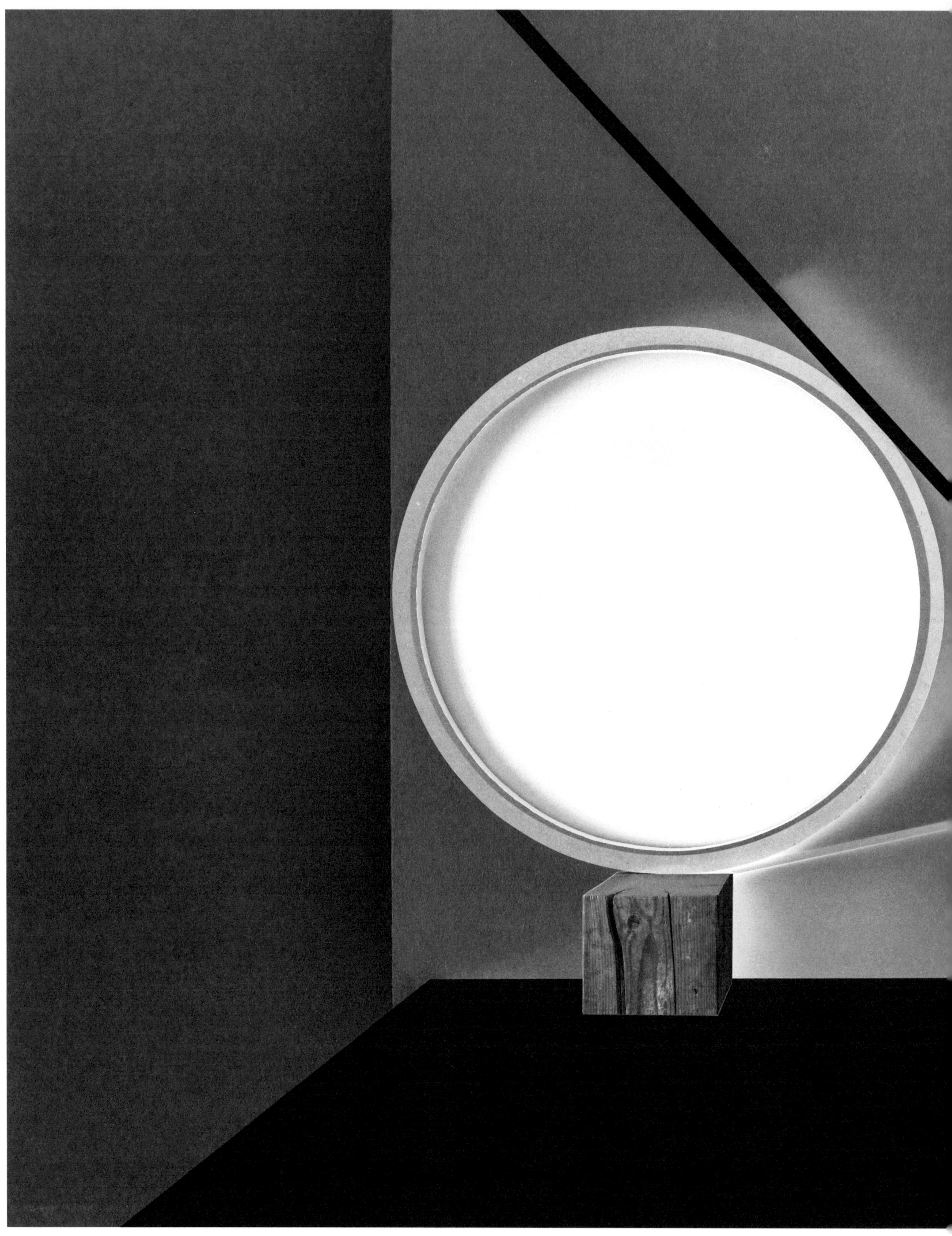

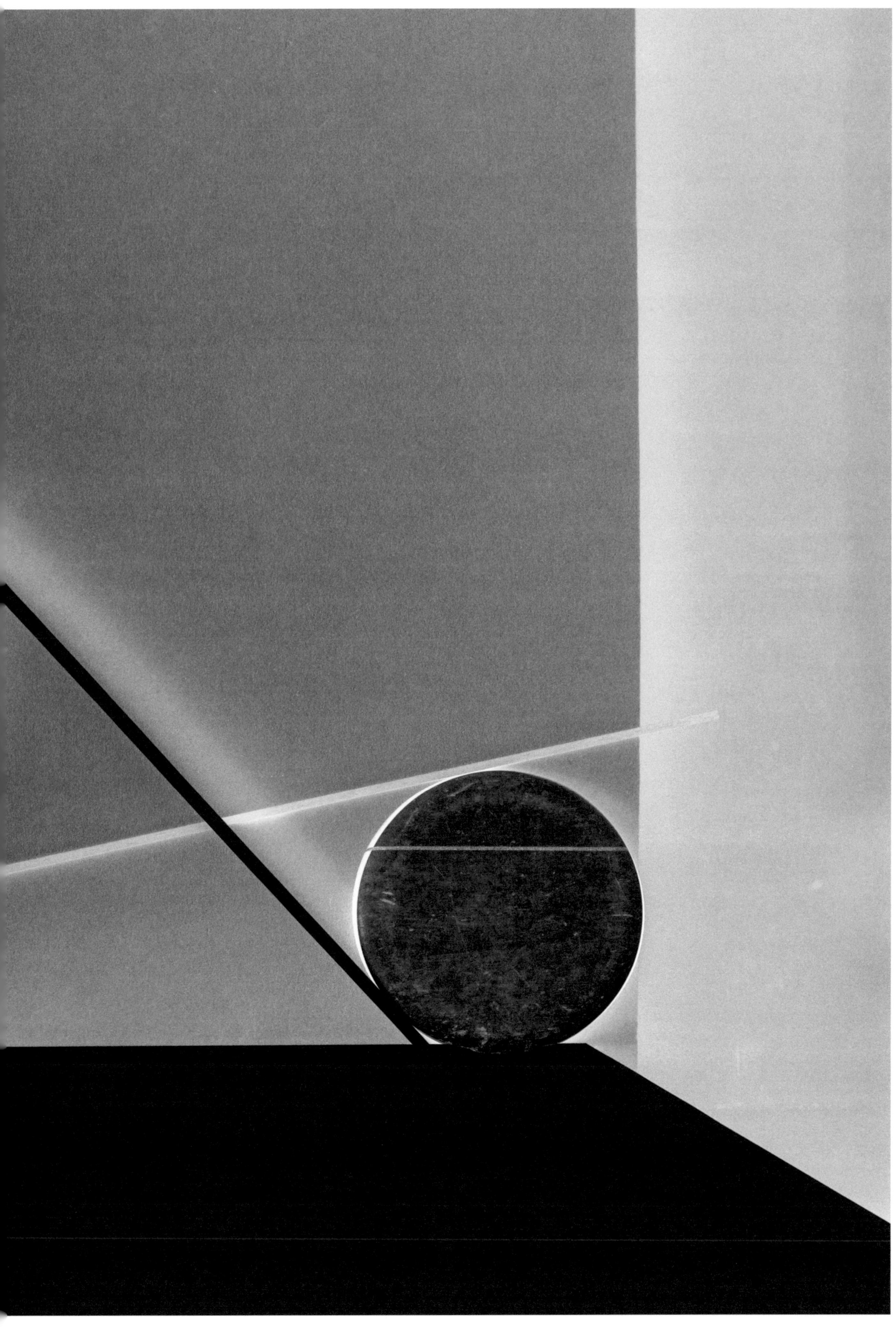

STRATEGY

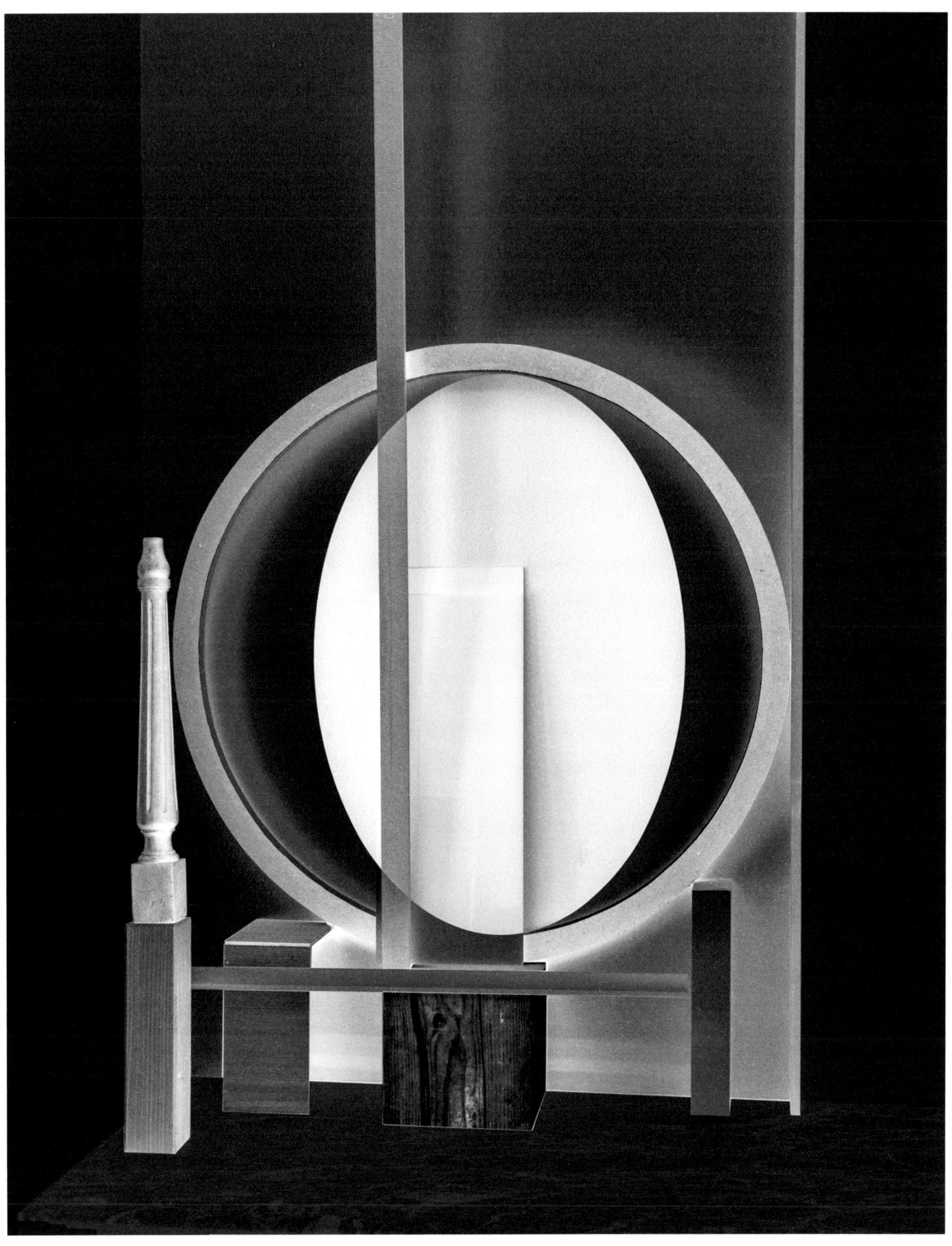

OPPOSITE A

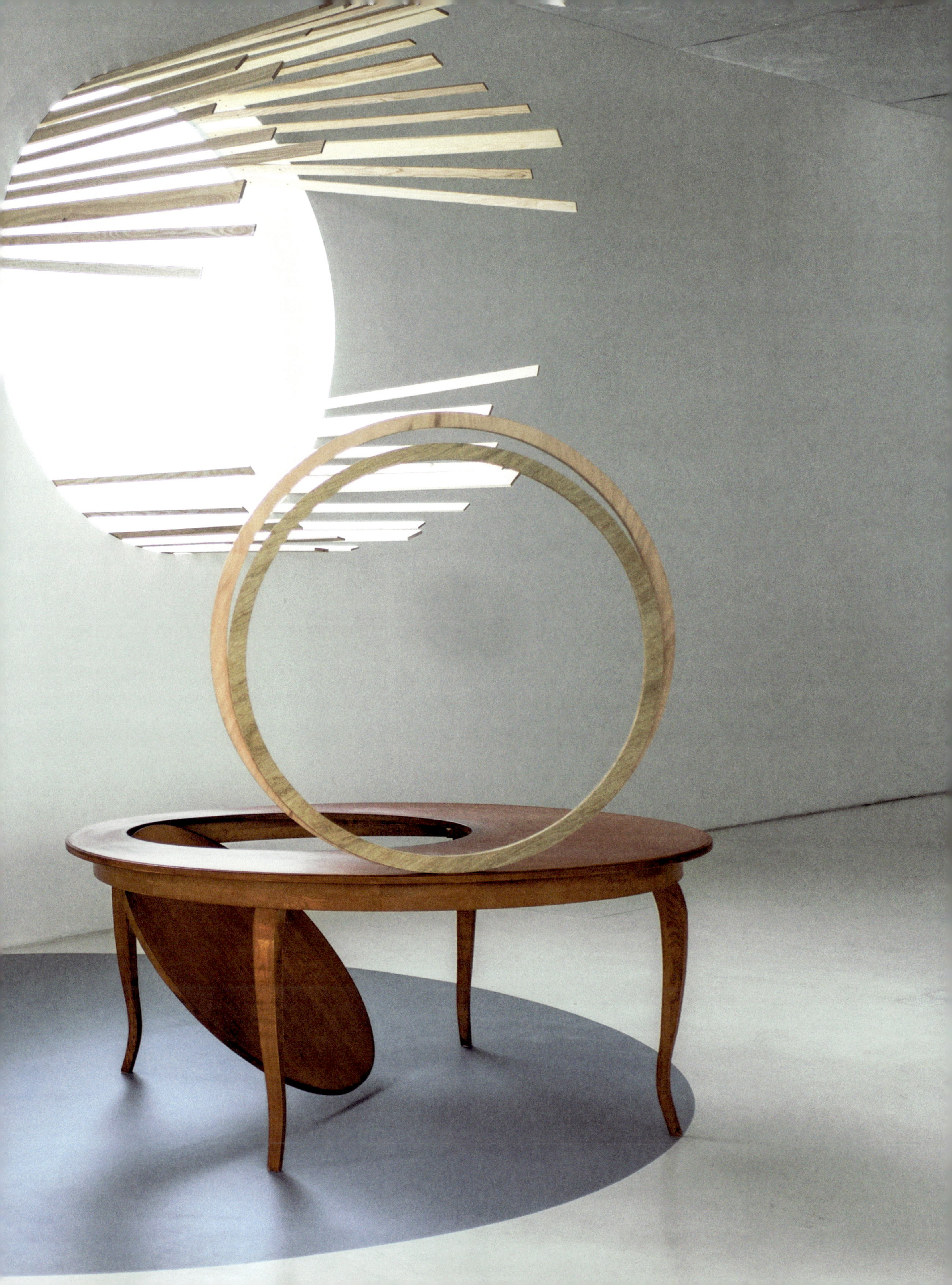

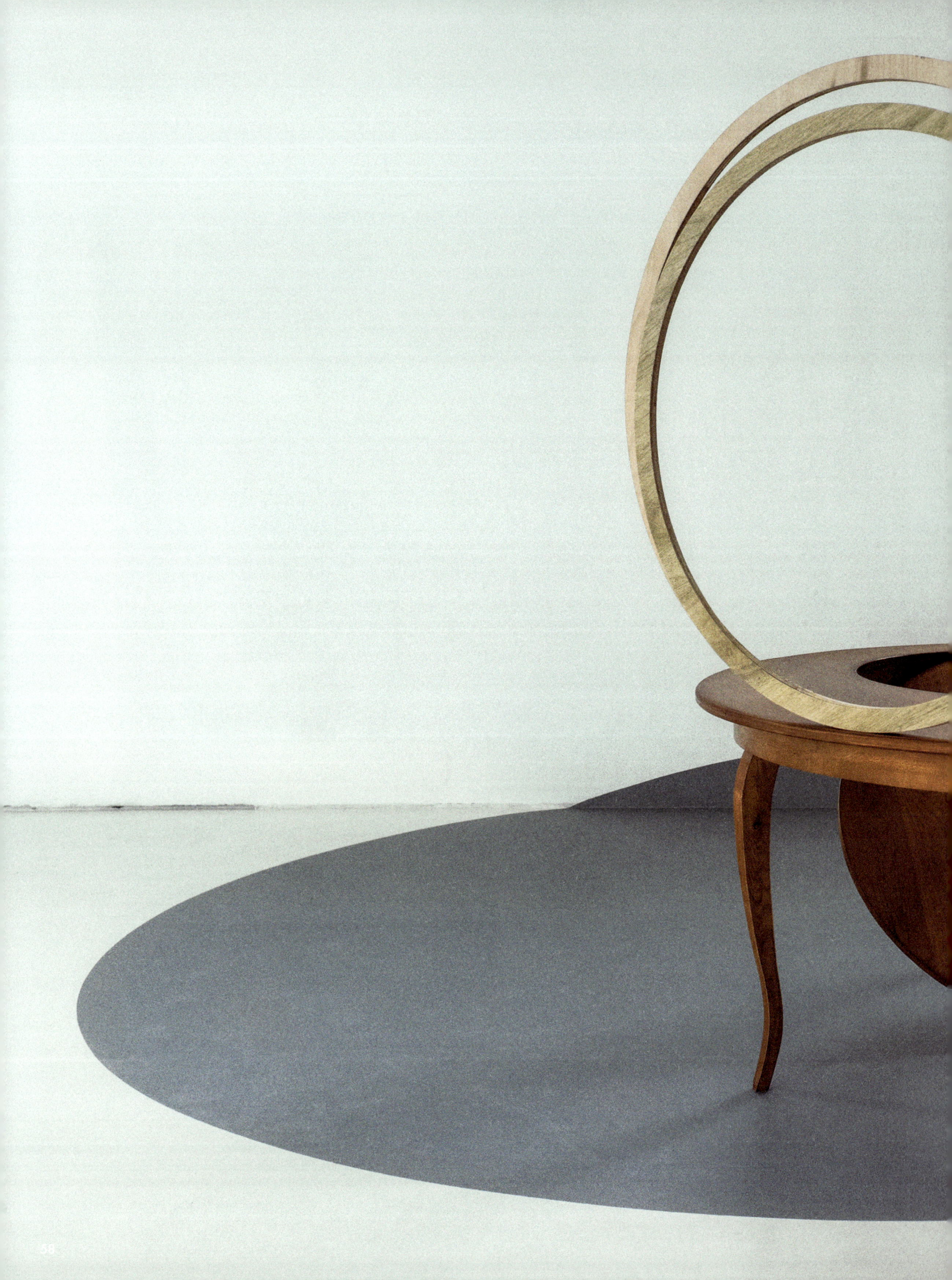

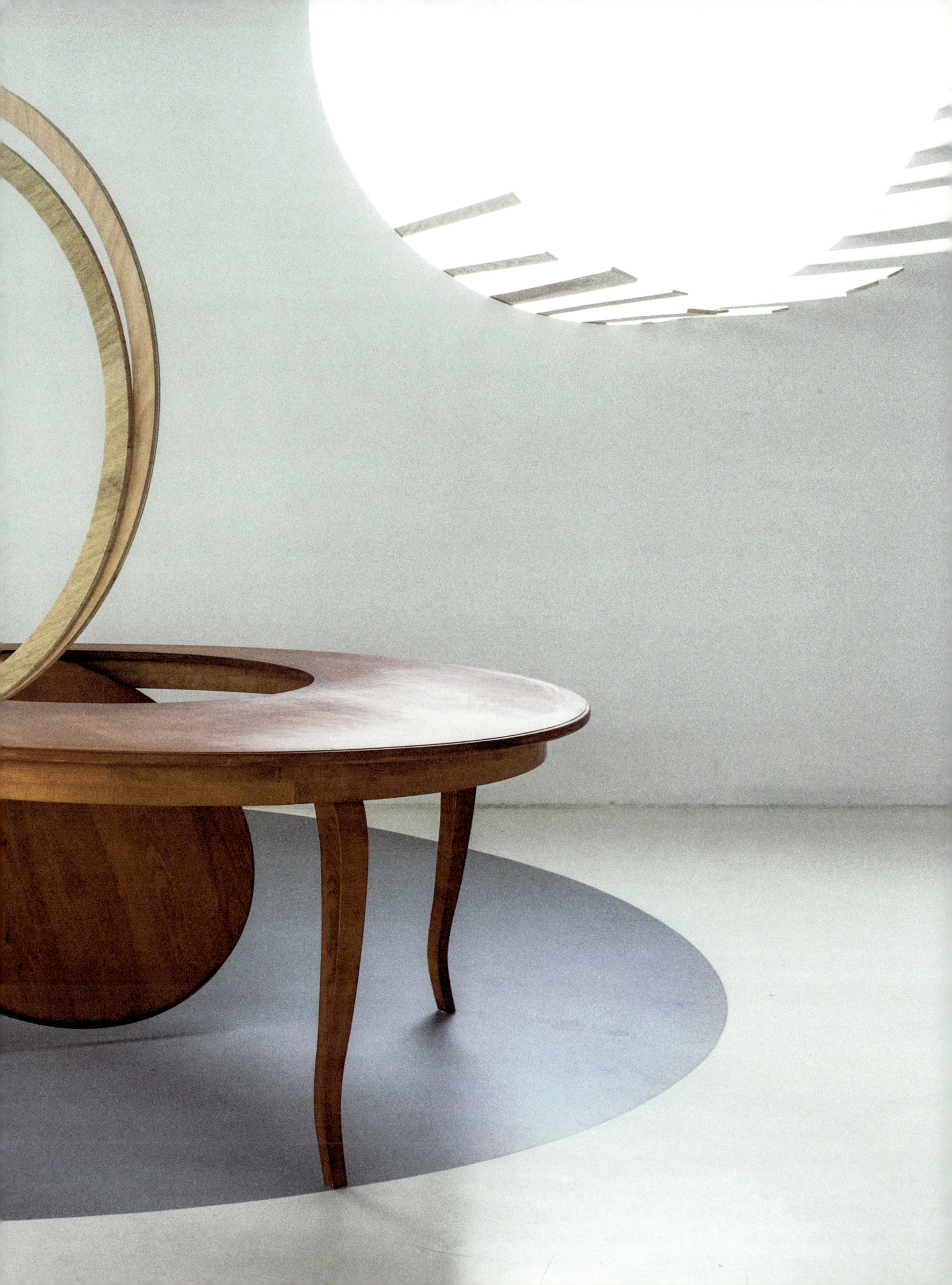

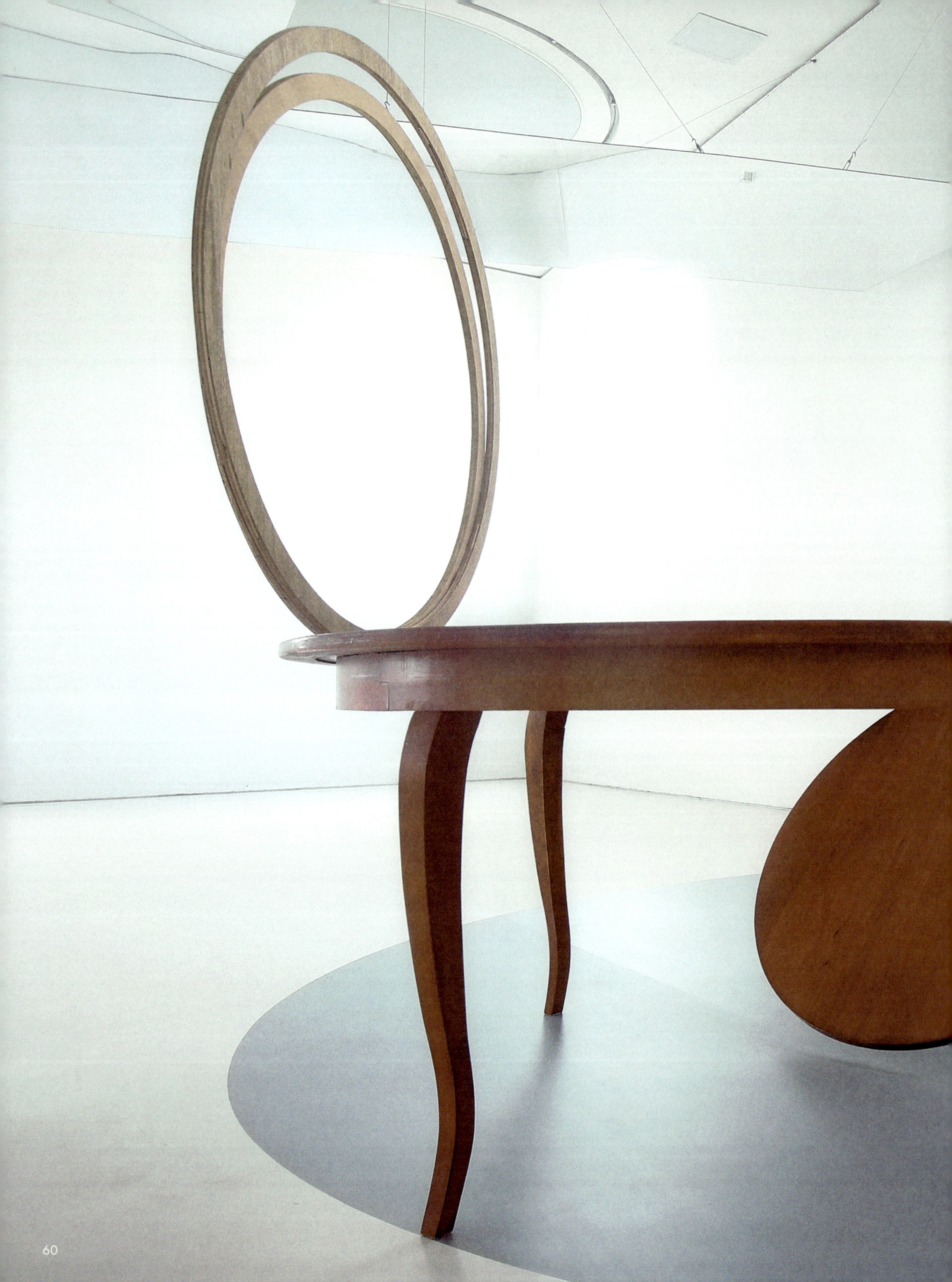

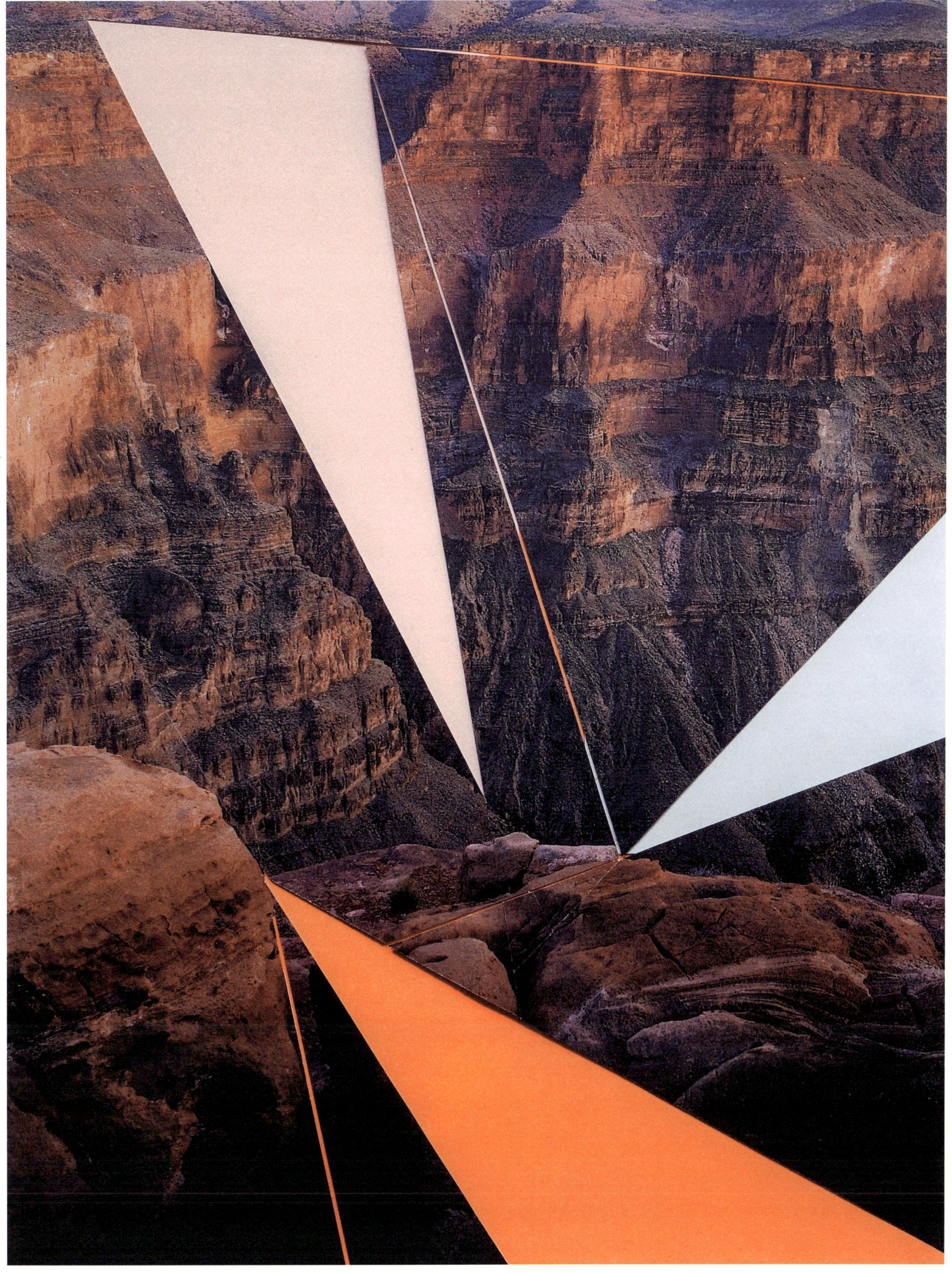

GRAND CANYON

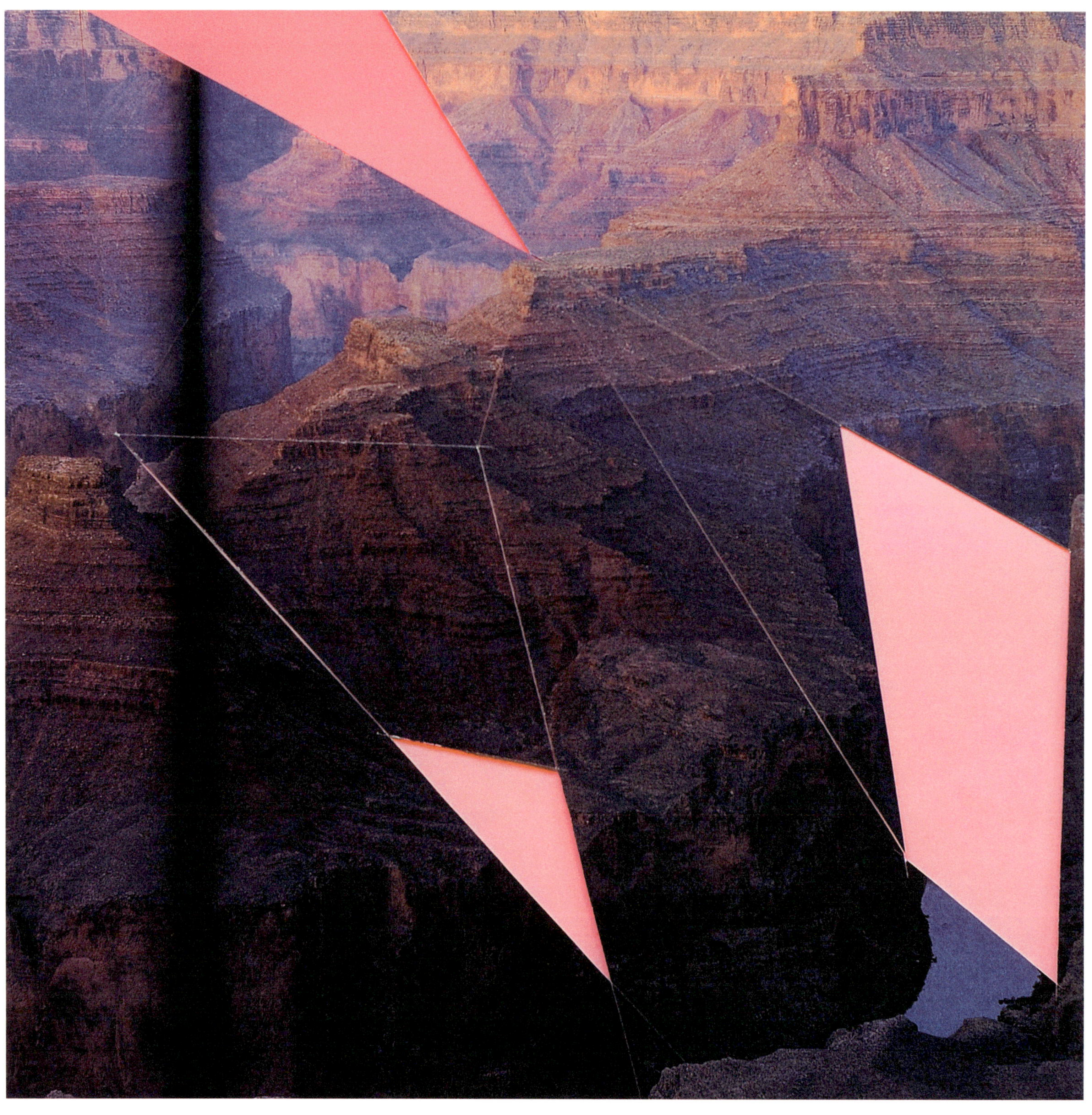

GRAND CANYON

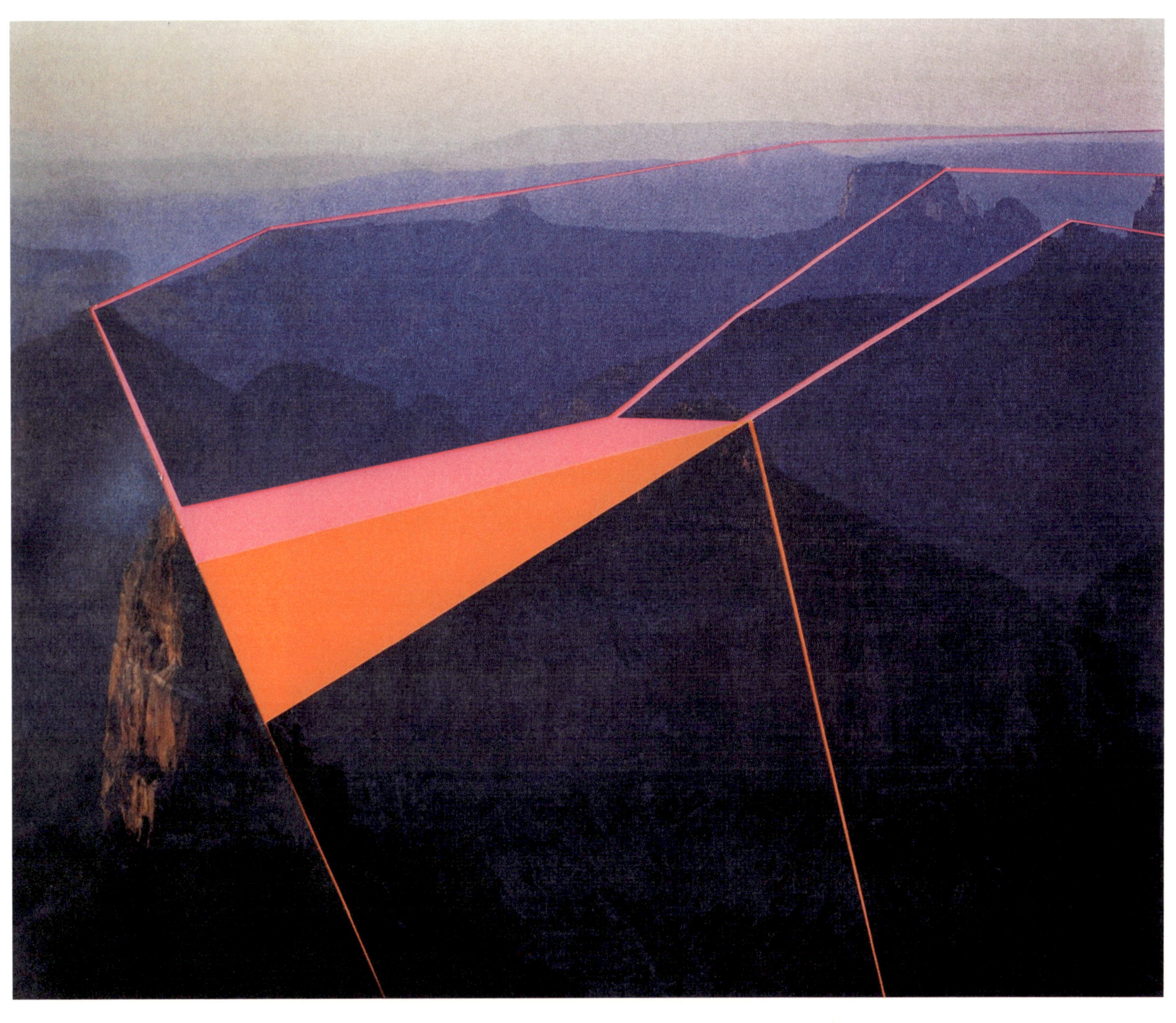

GRAND CANYON

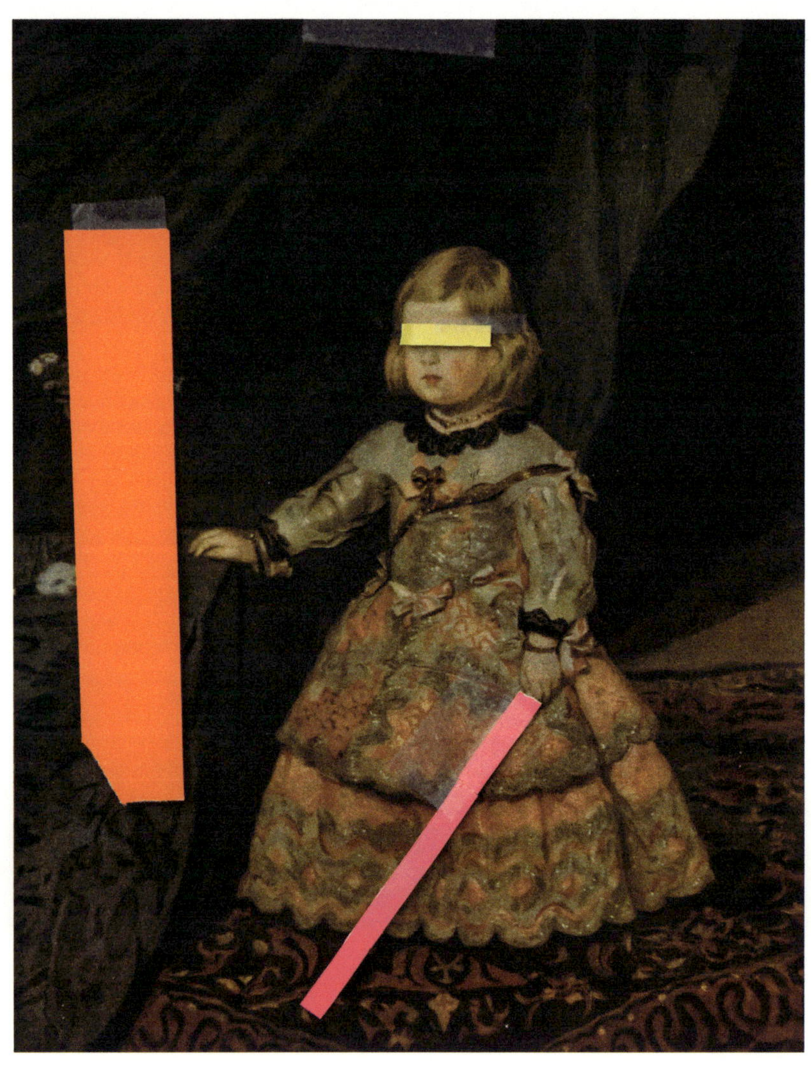

 INFANTA MARGARITA

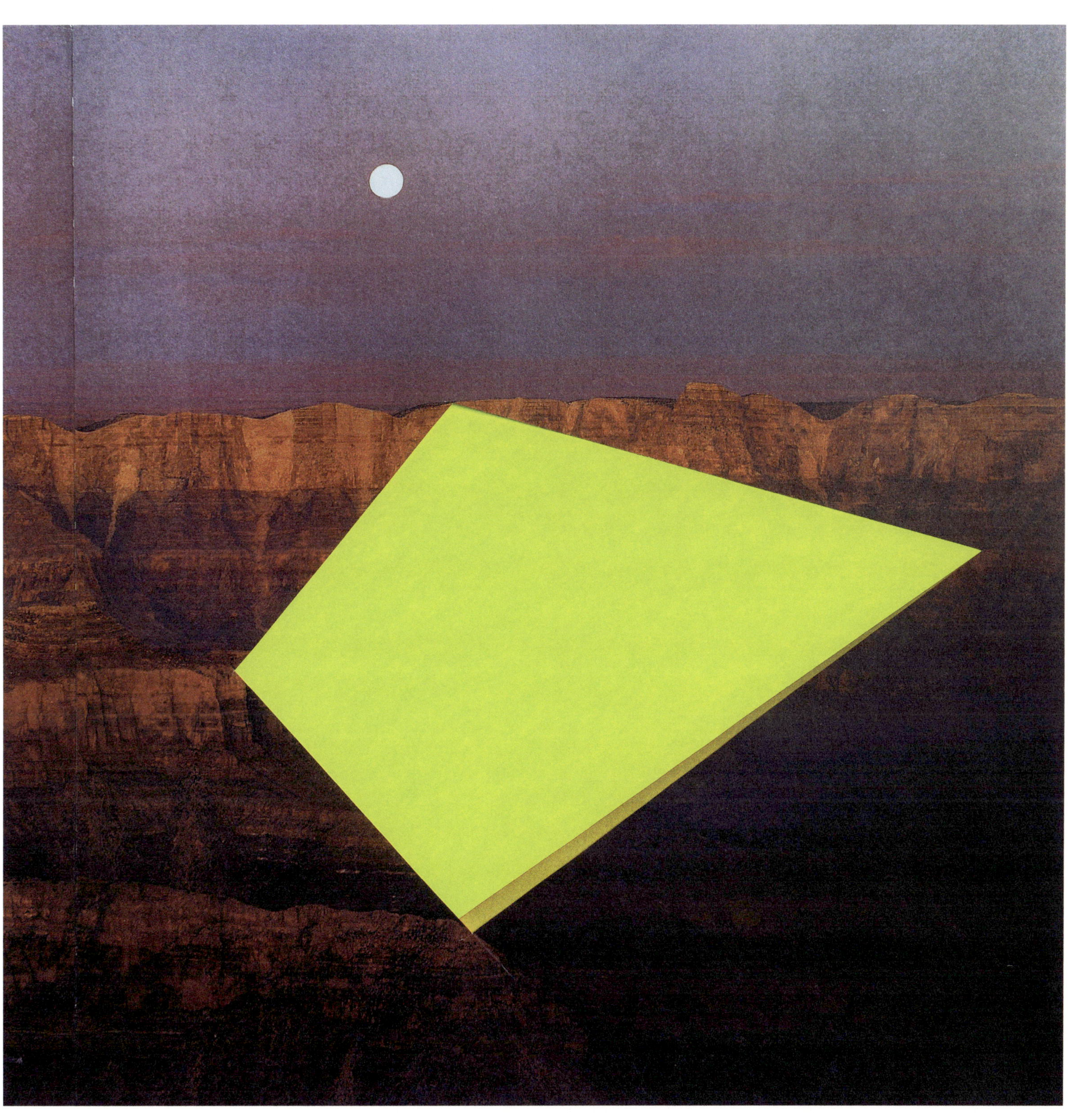

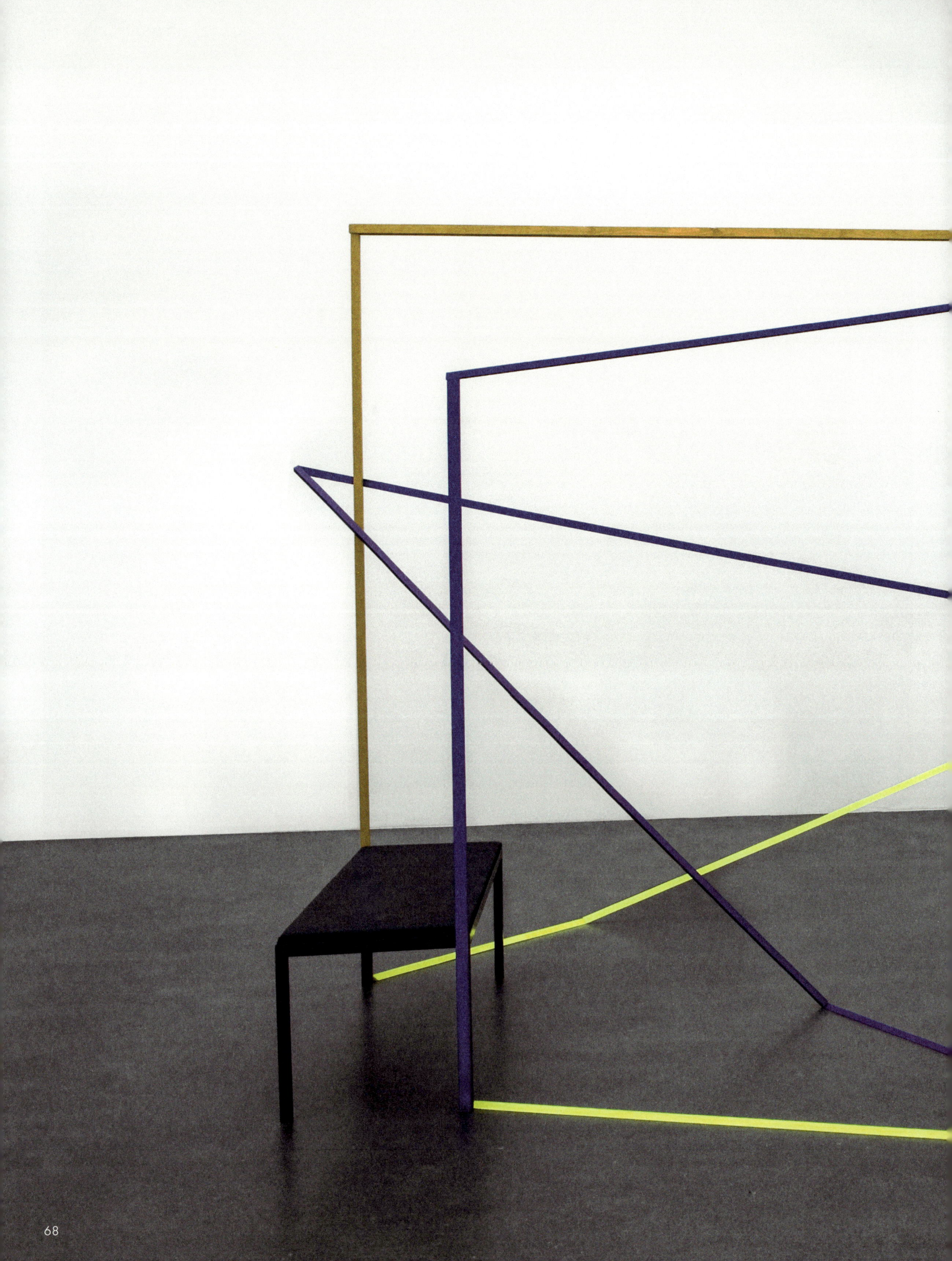

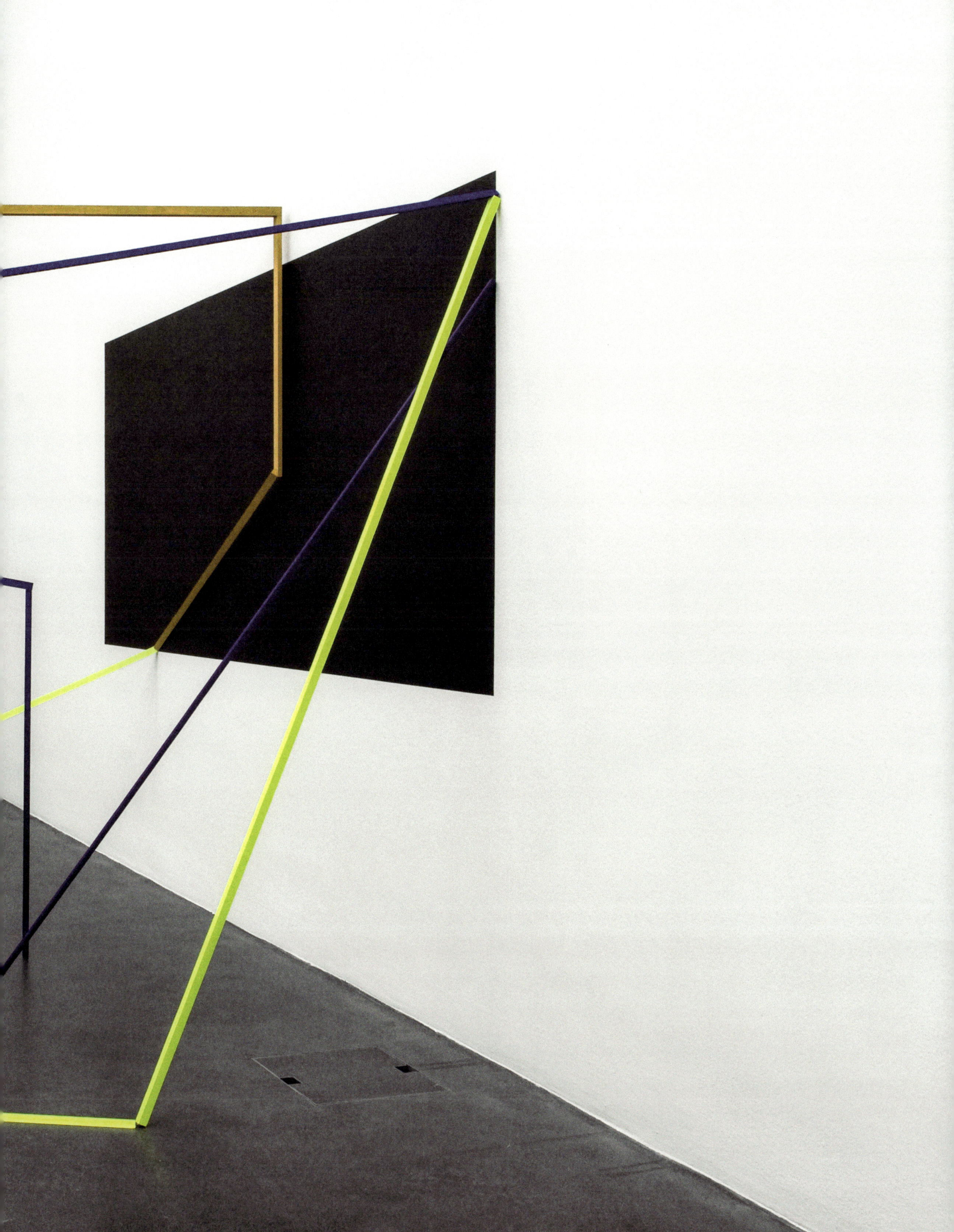

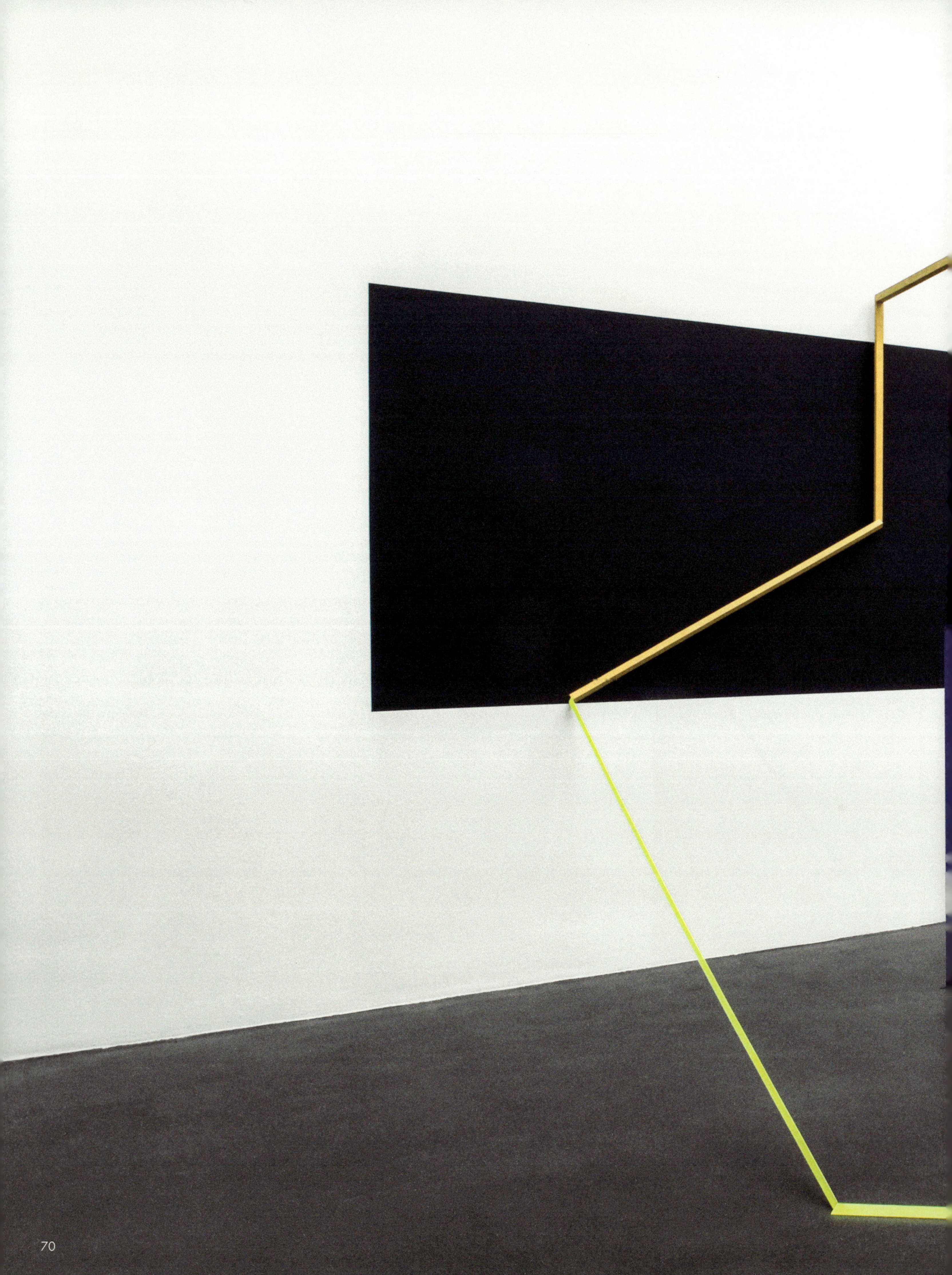

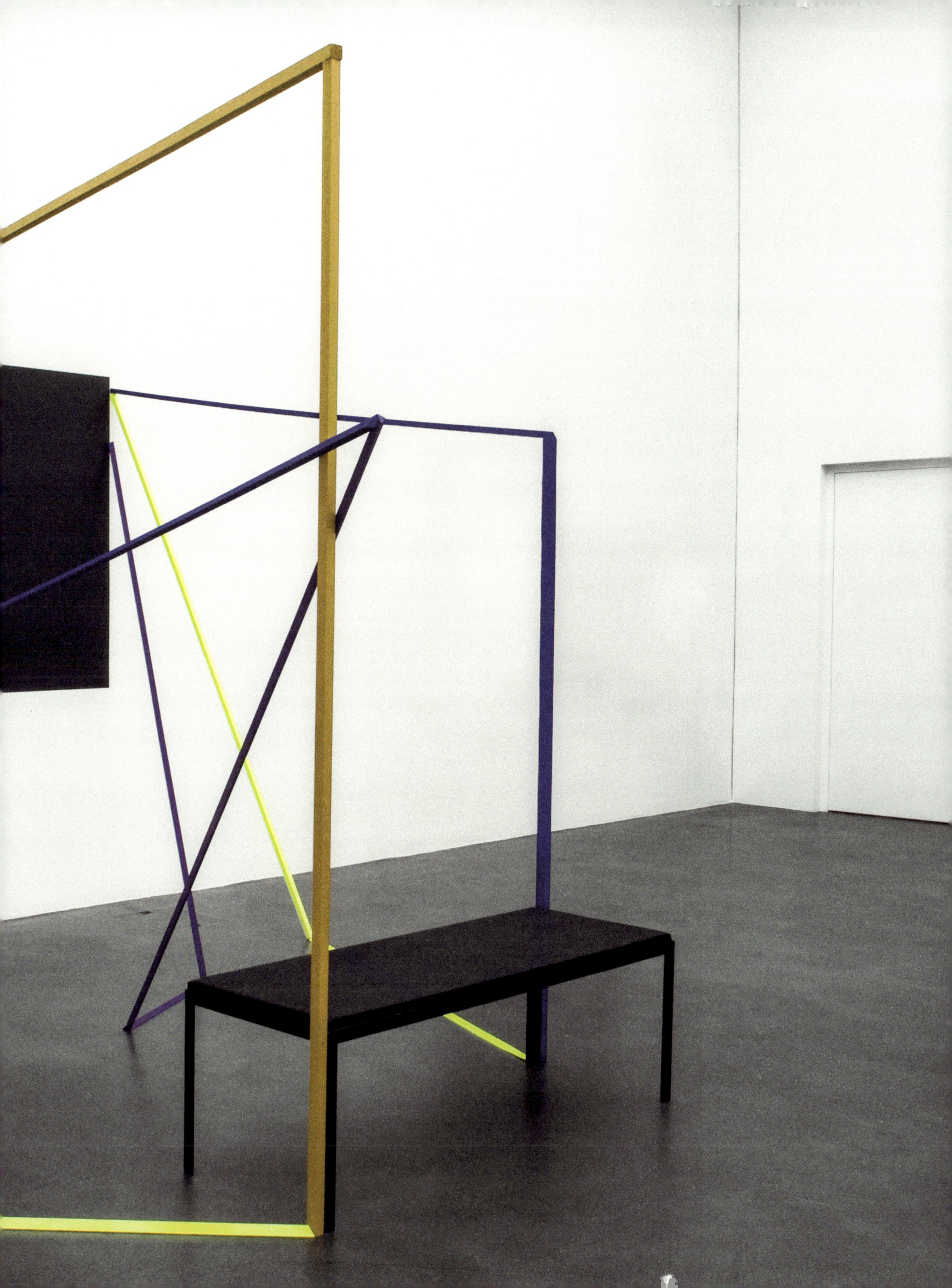

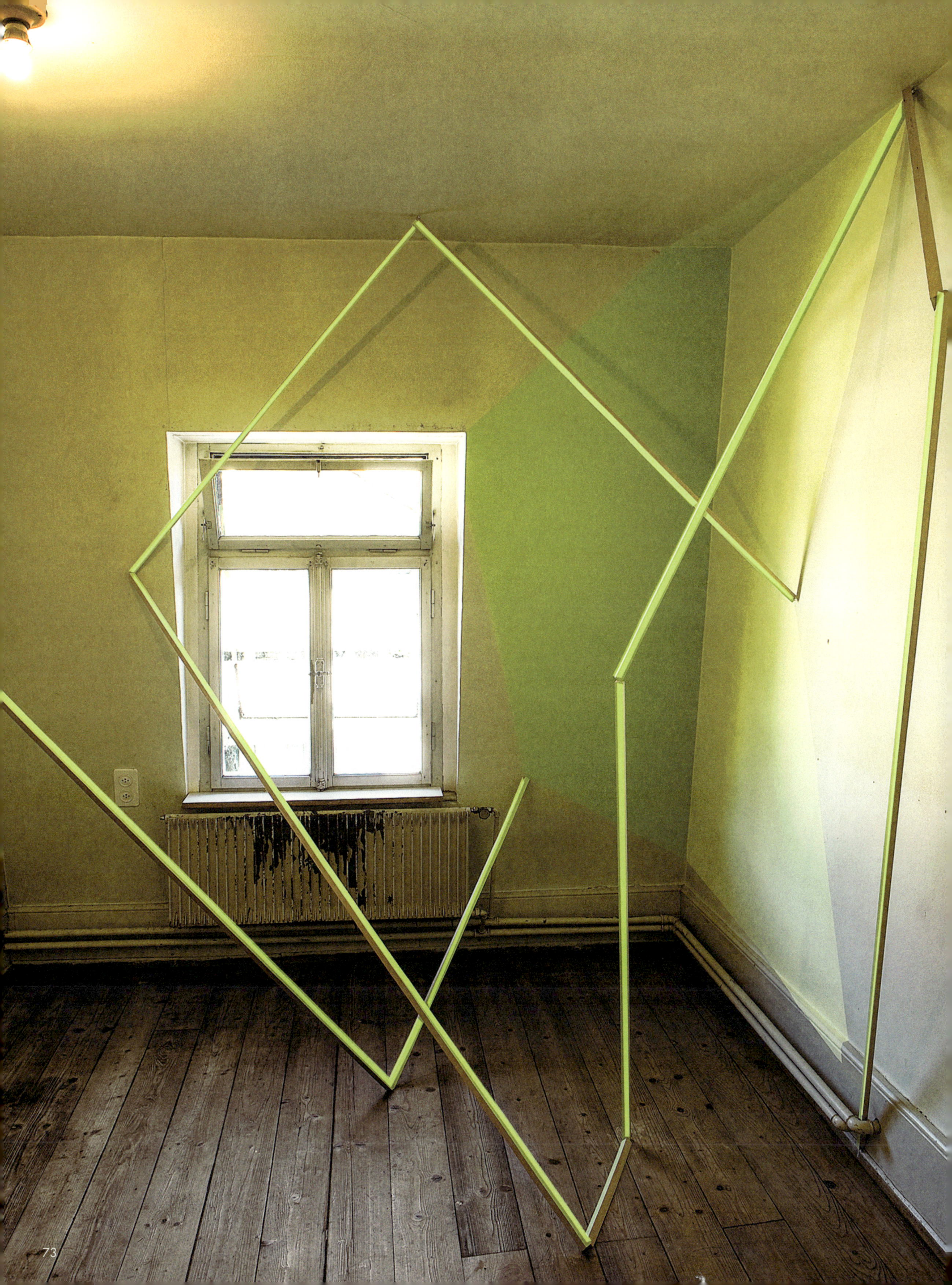

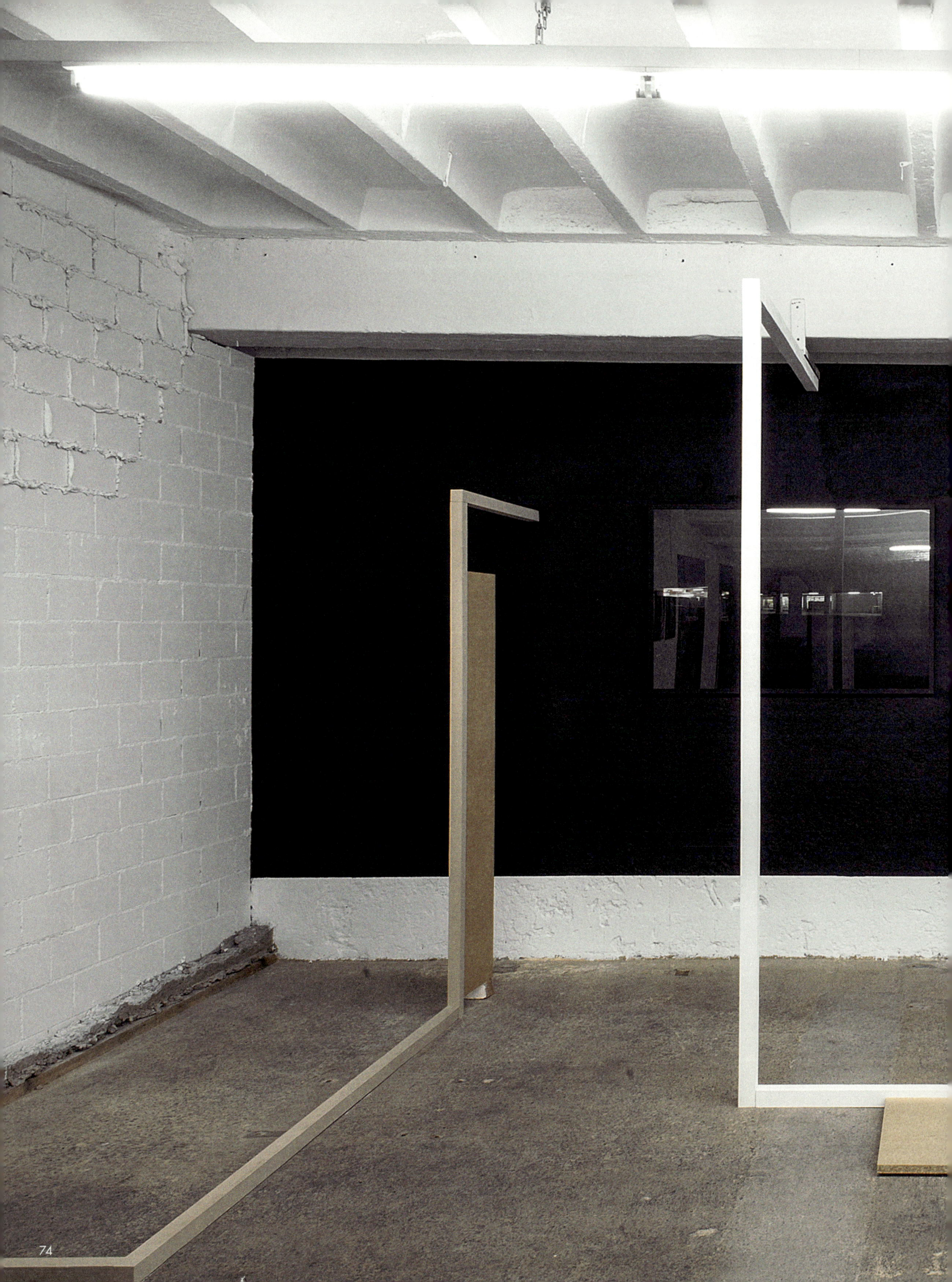

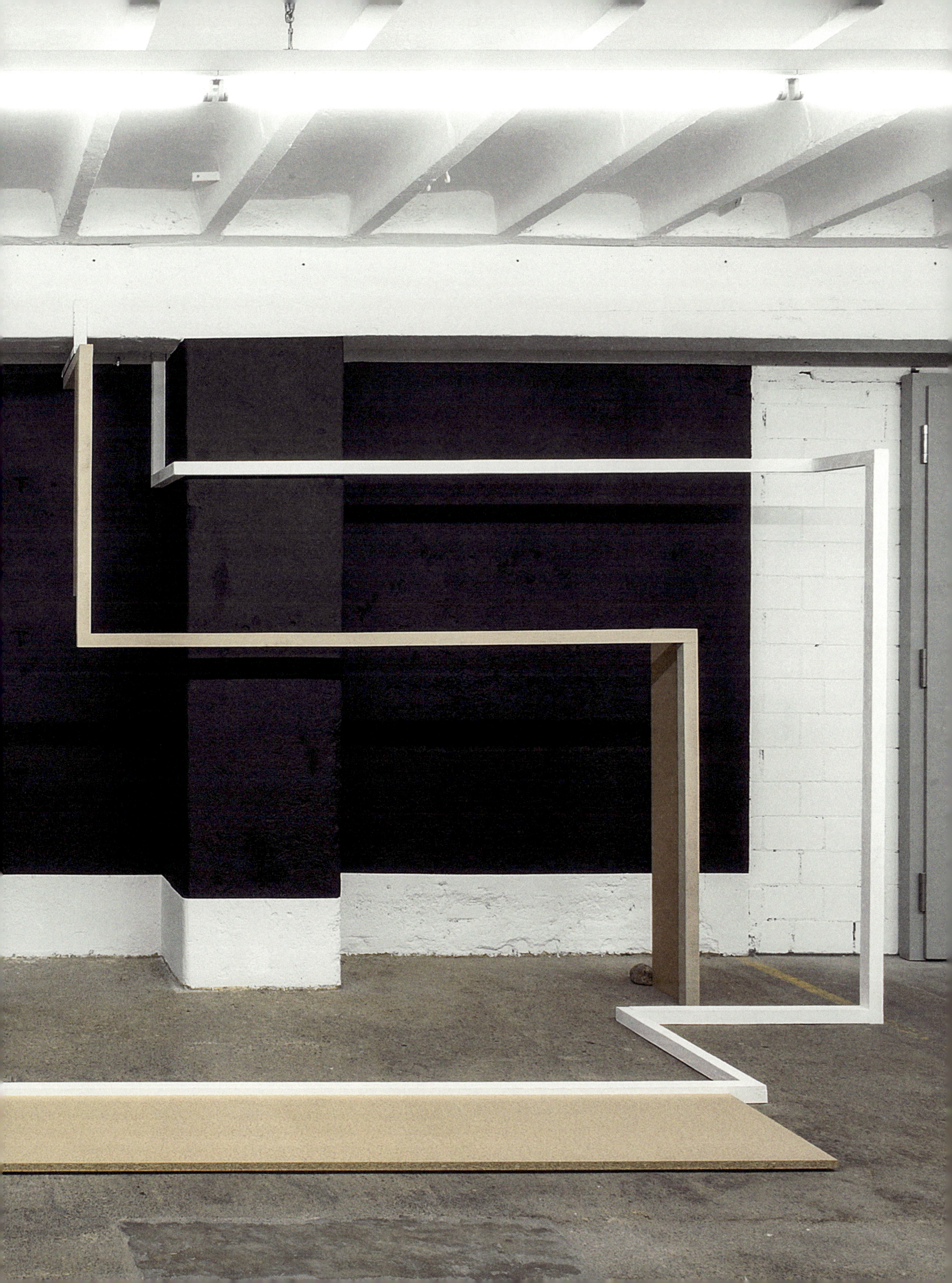

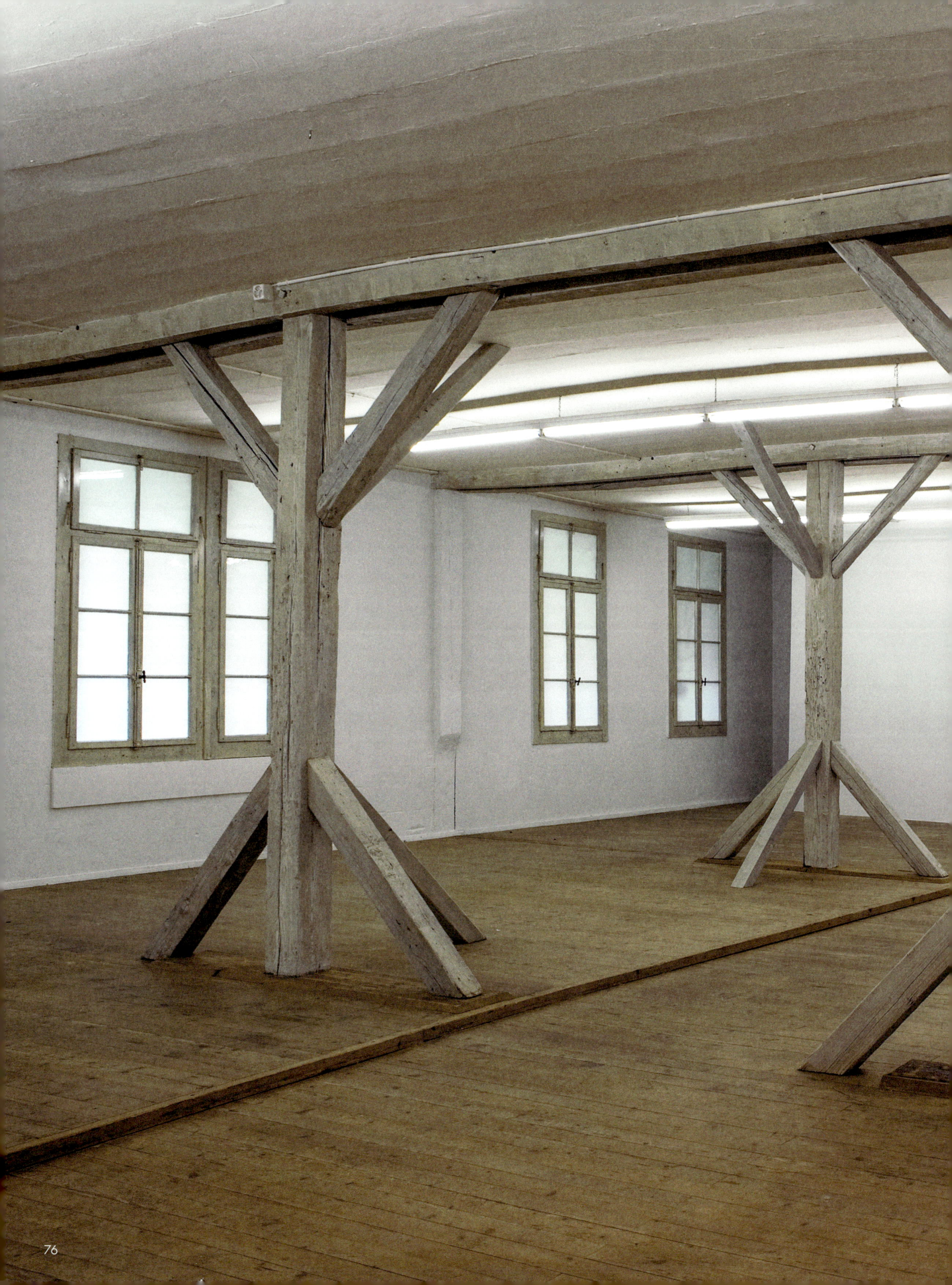

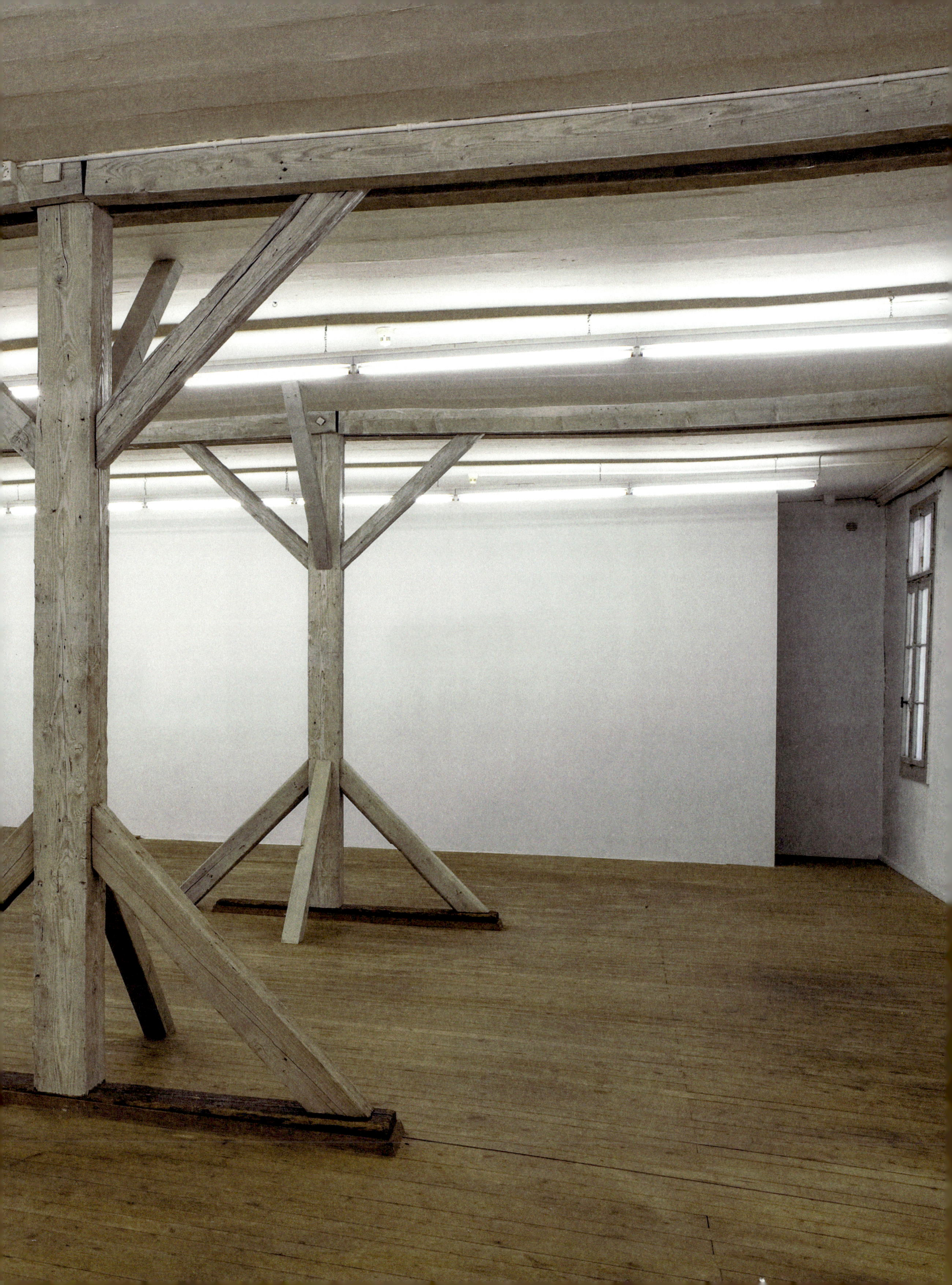

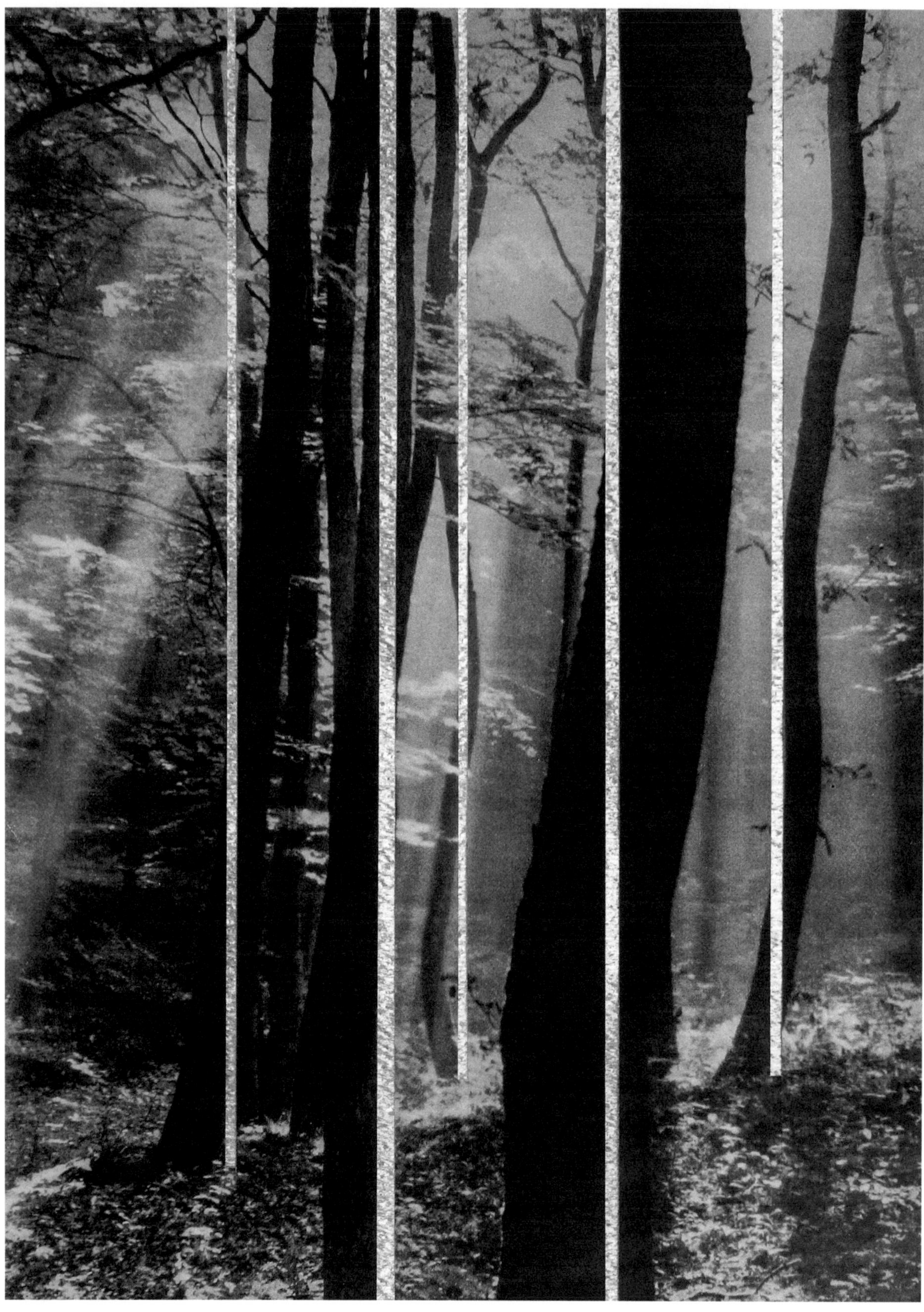

WALD

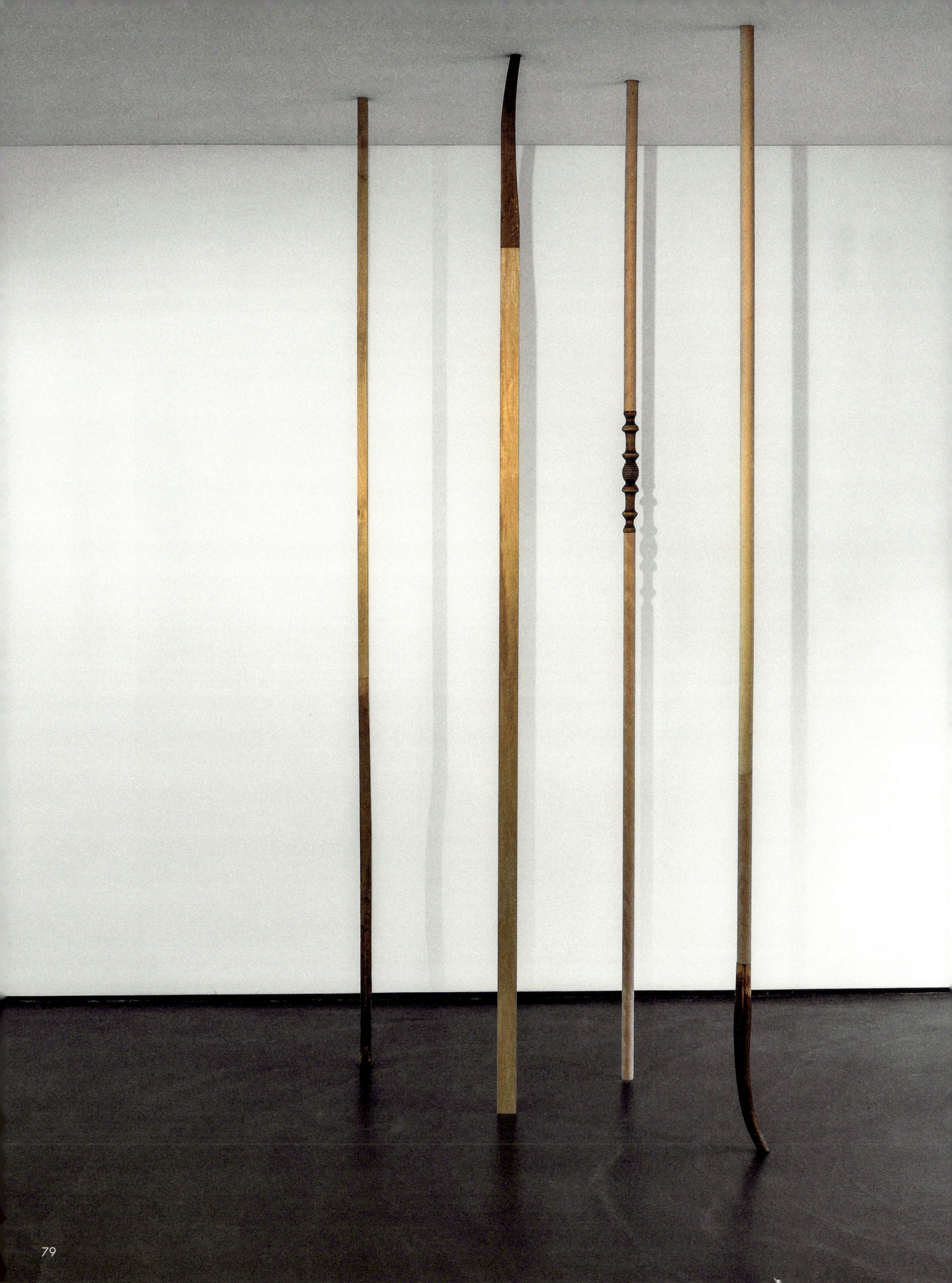

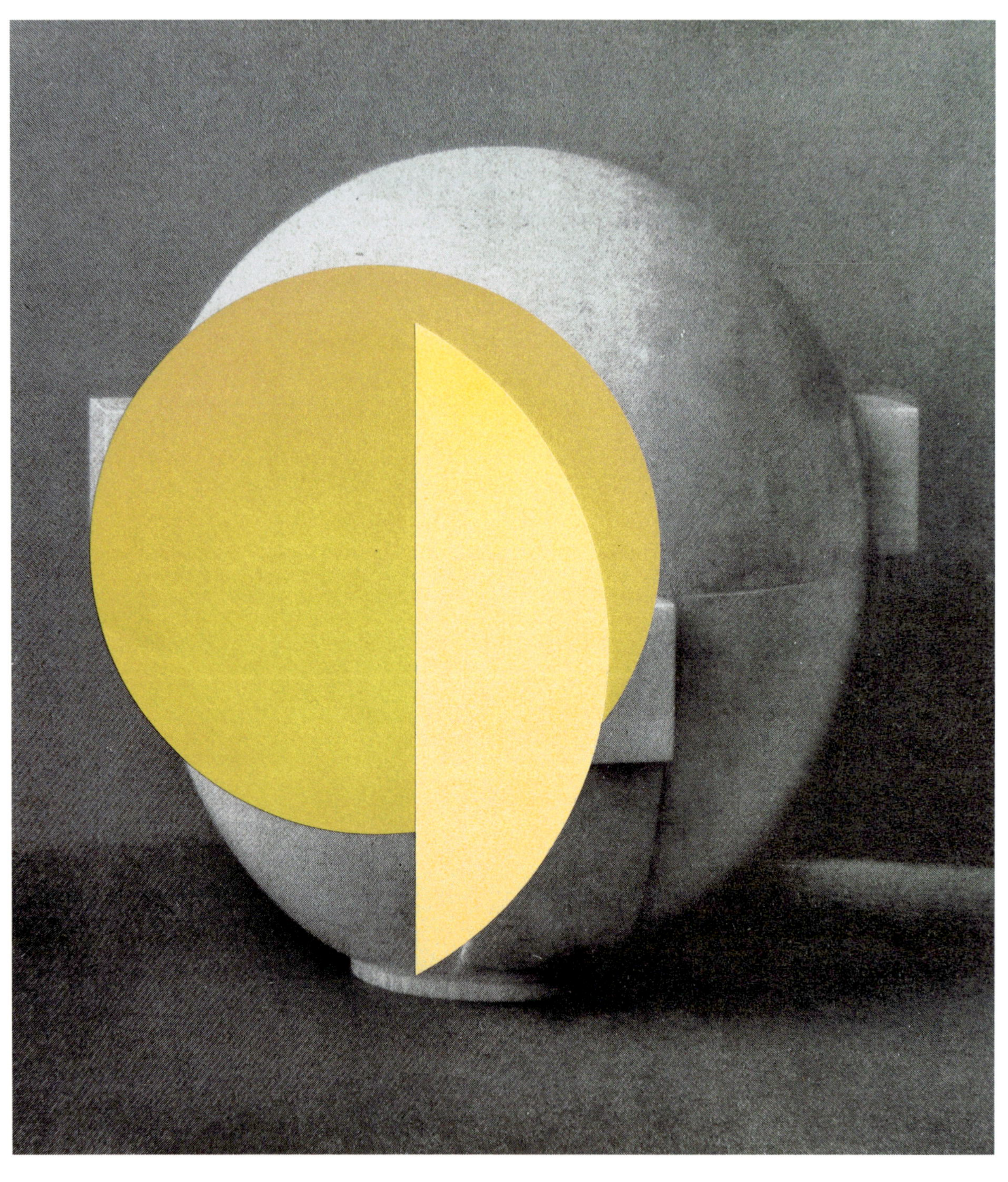

PHANTOM

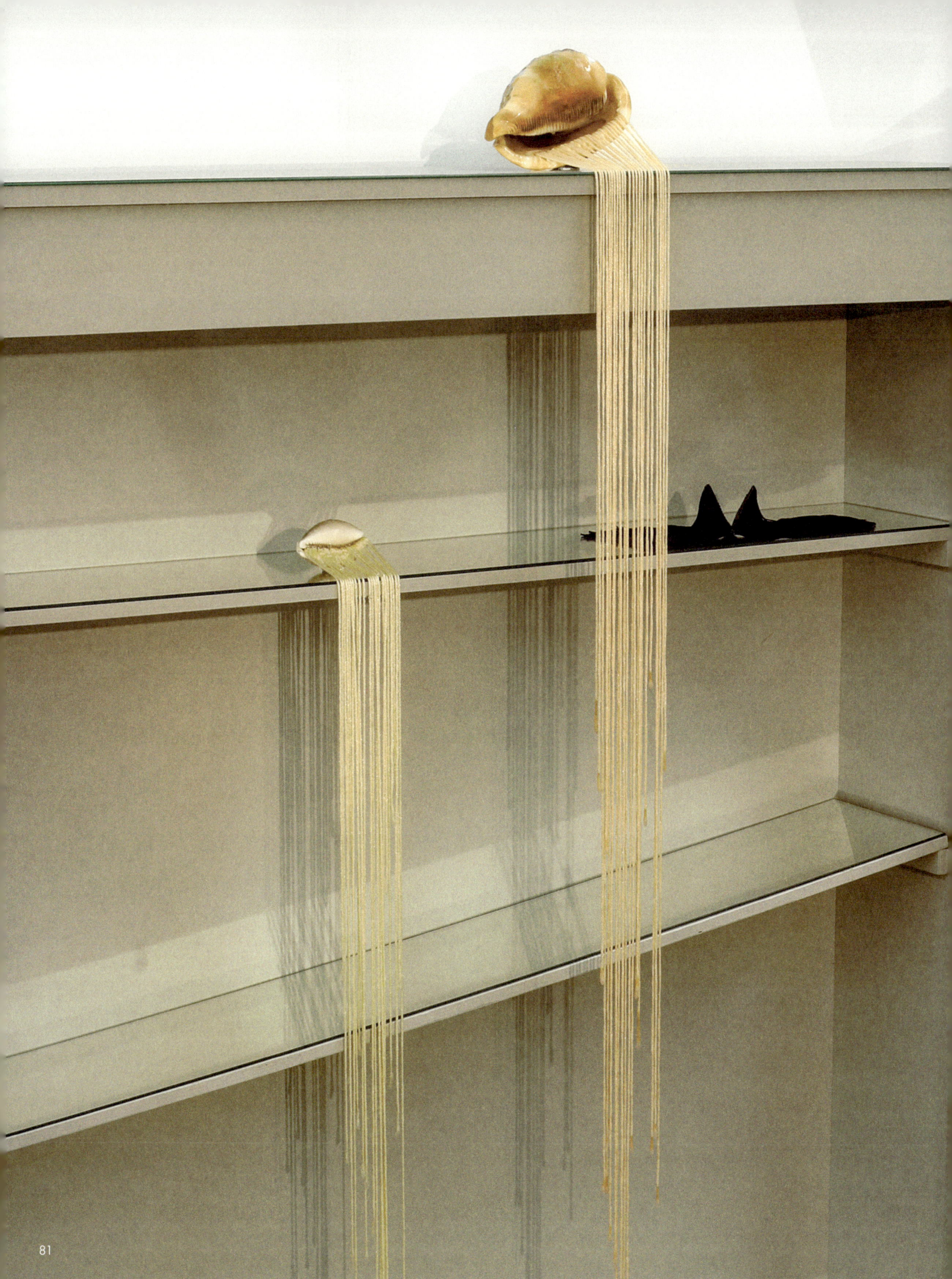

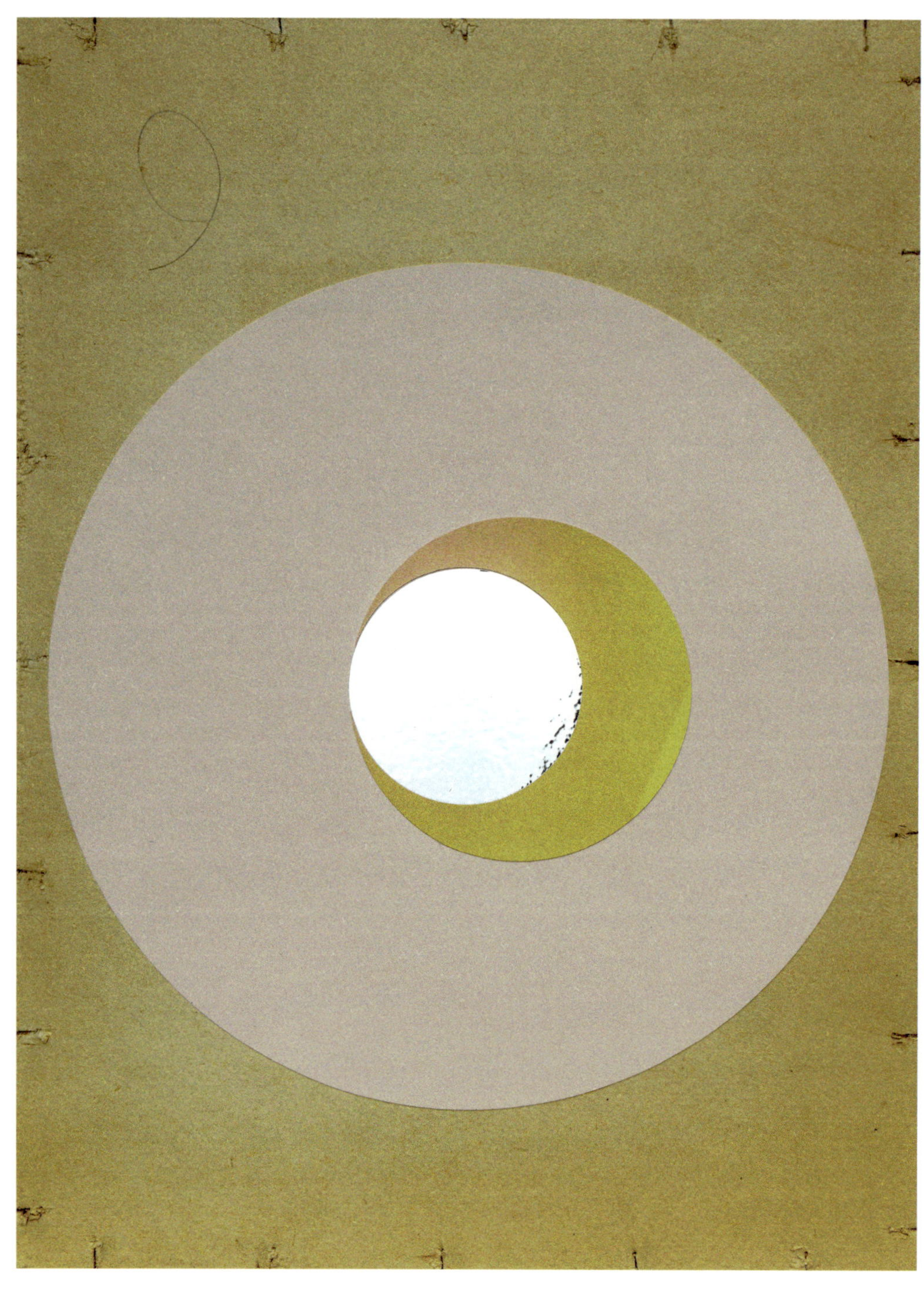

4 KREISE

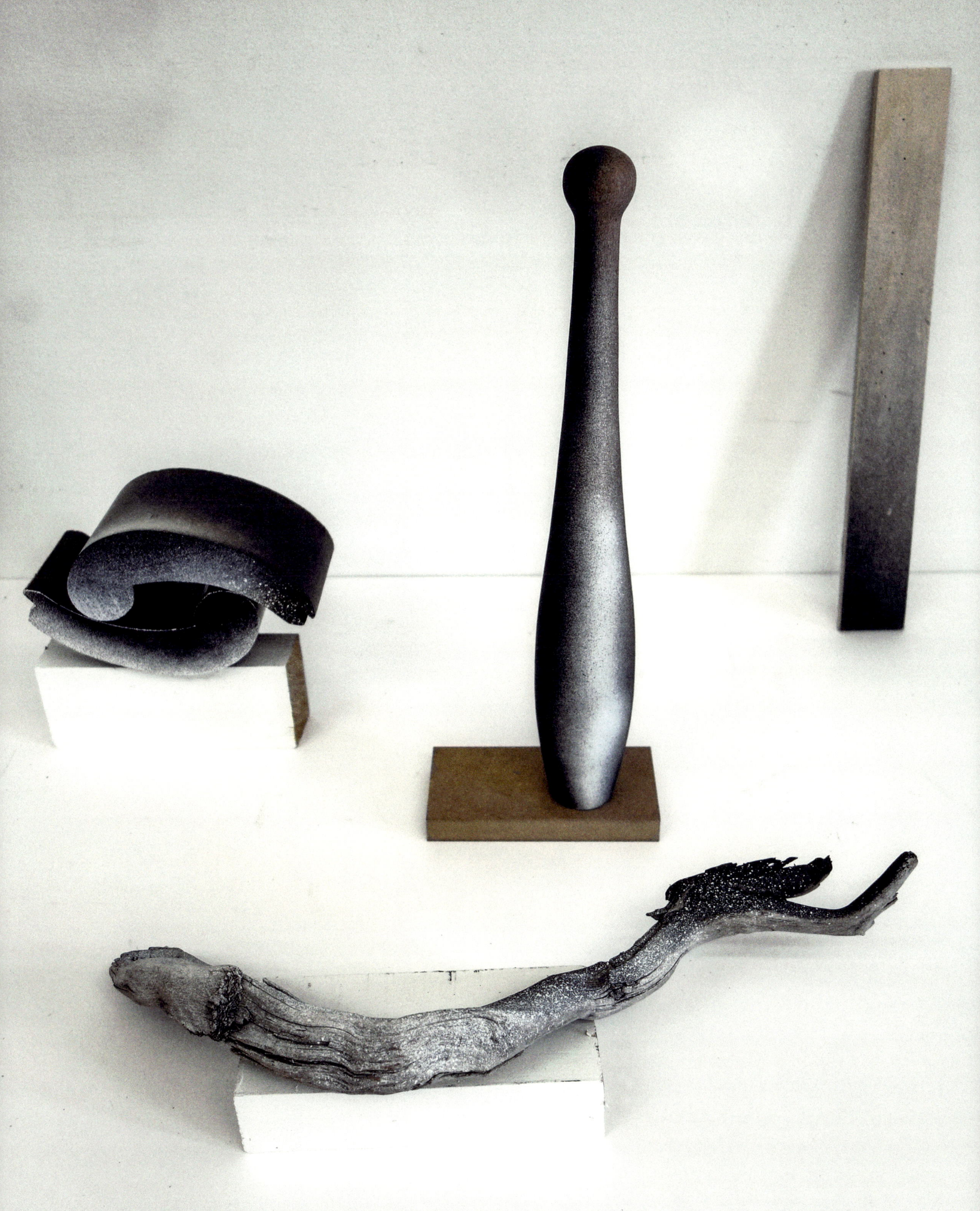

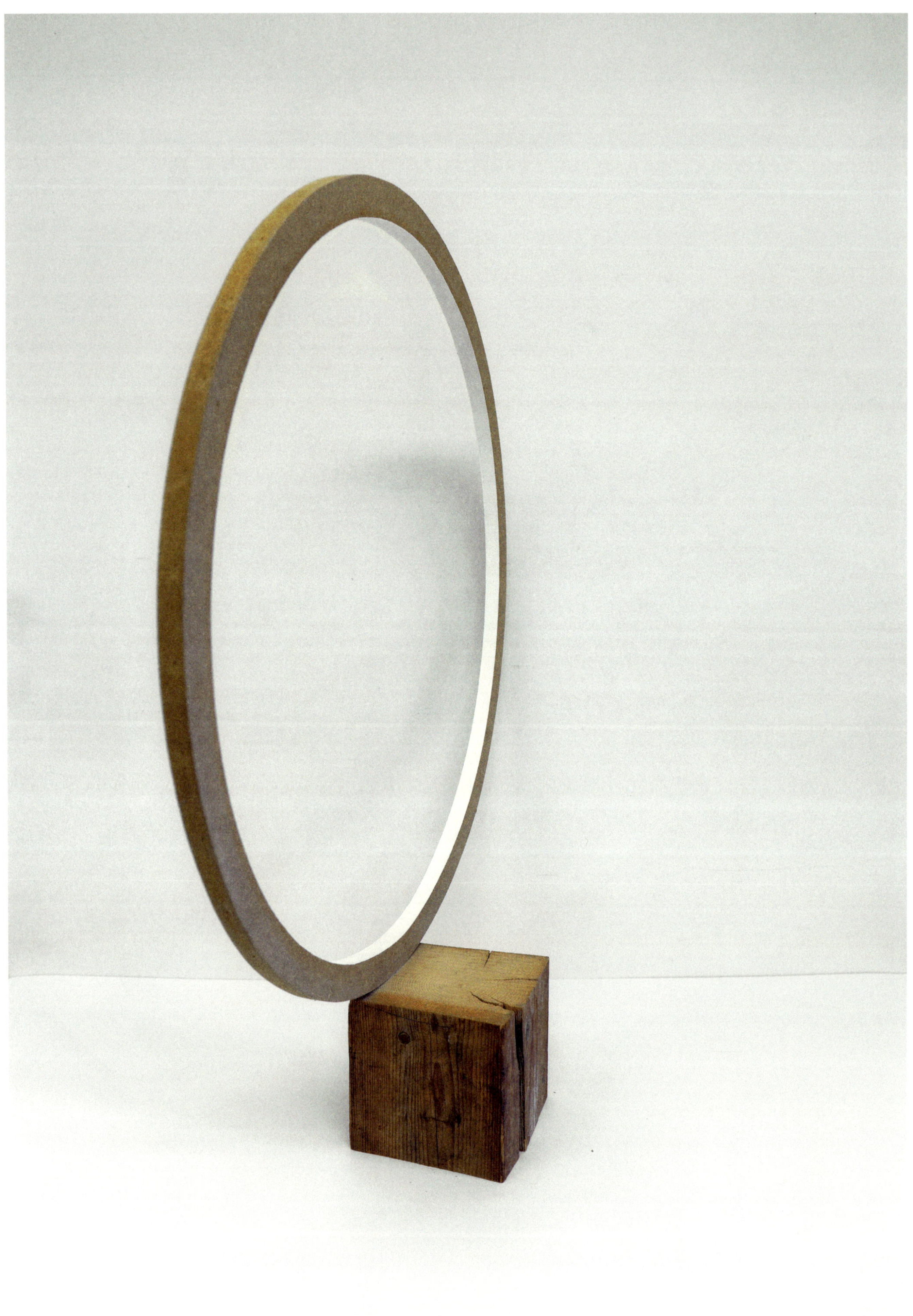

KREIS AUF KUBUS

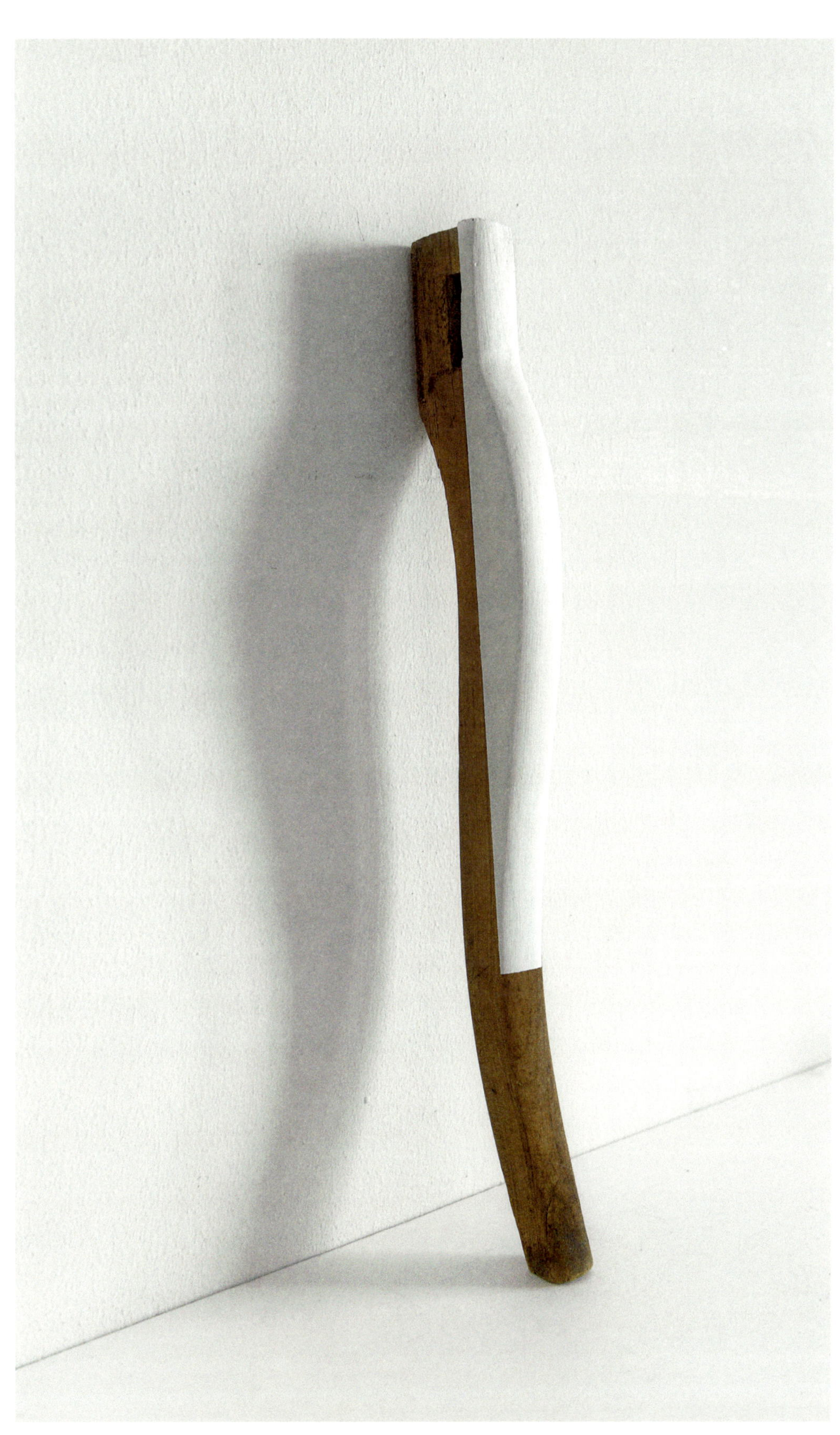

BEIN

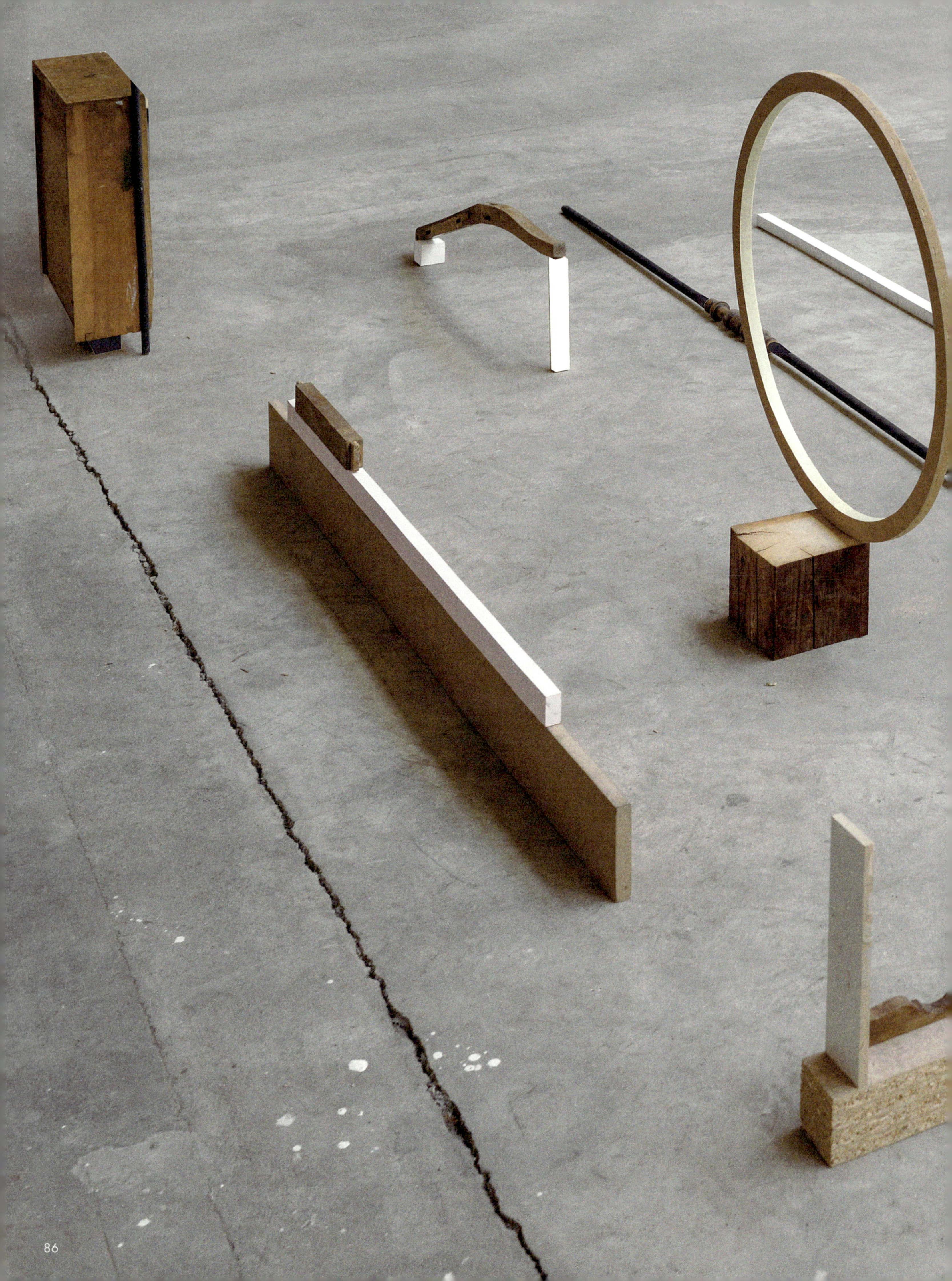

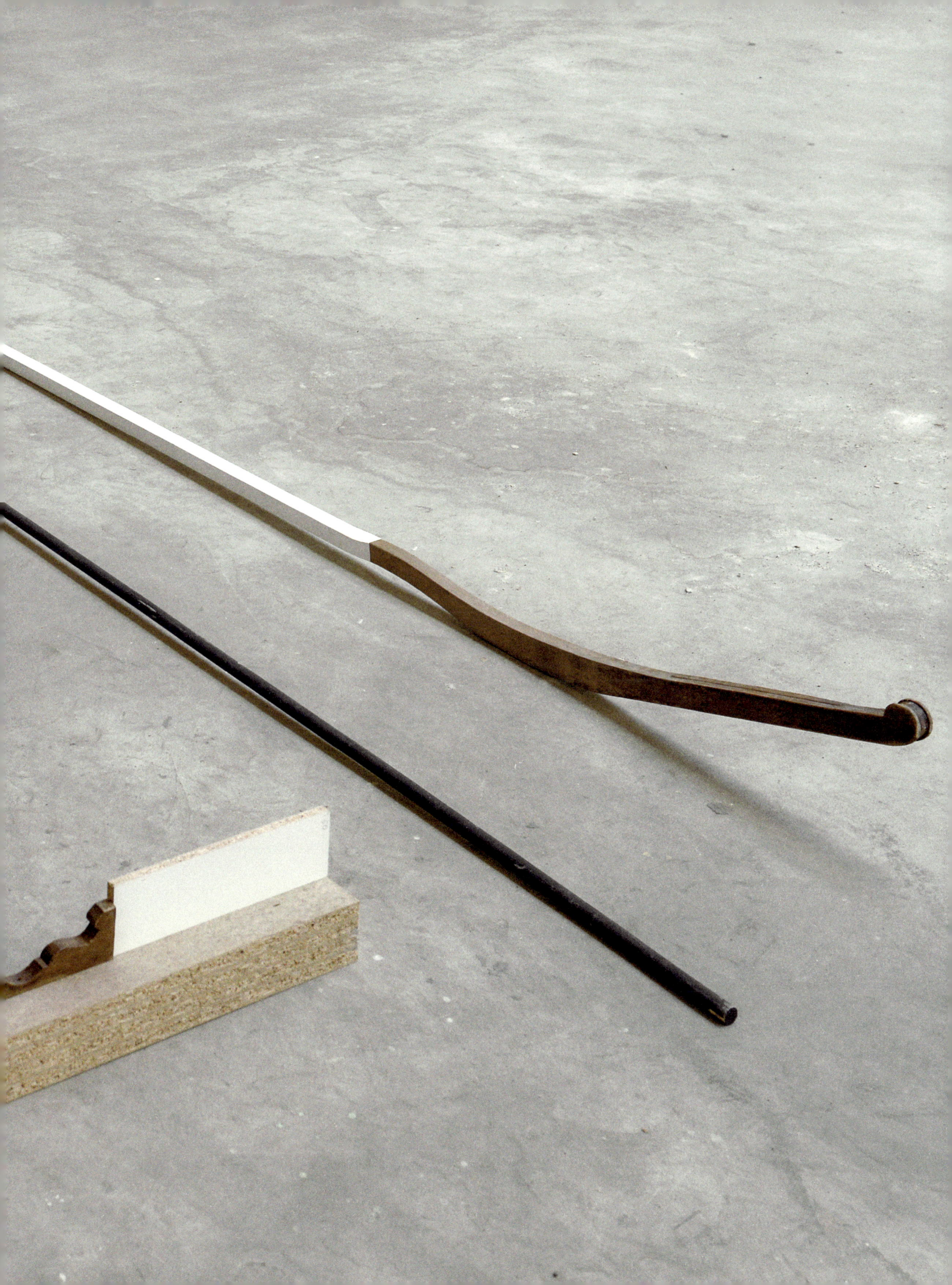

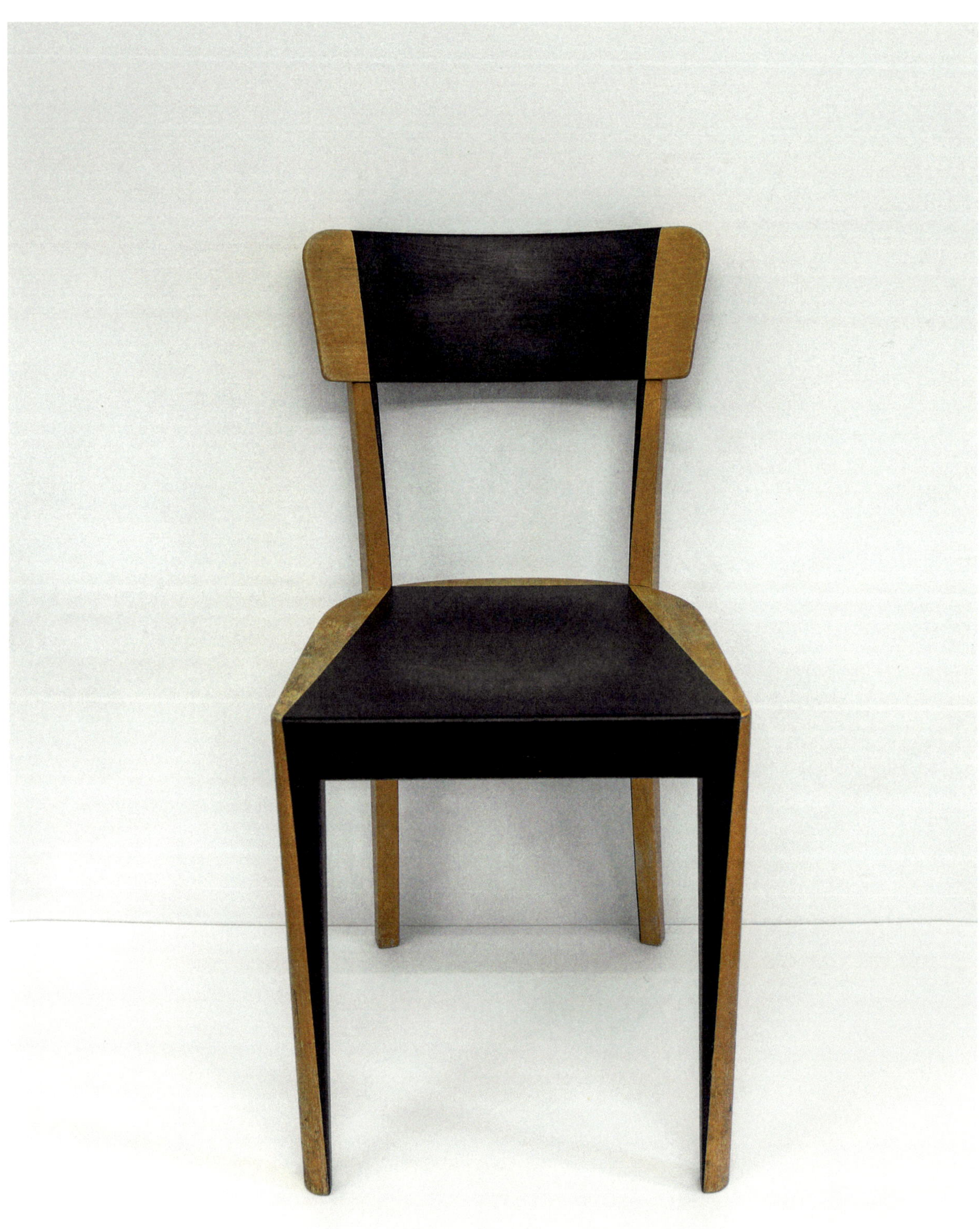

CHAIR, CHAIR

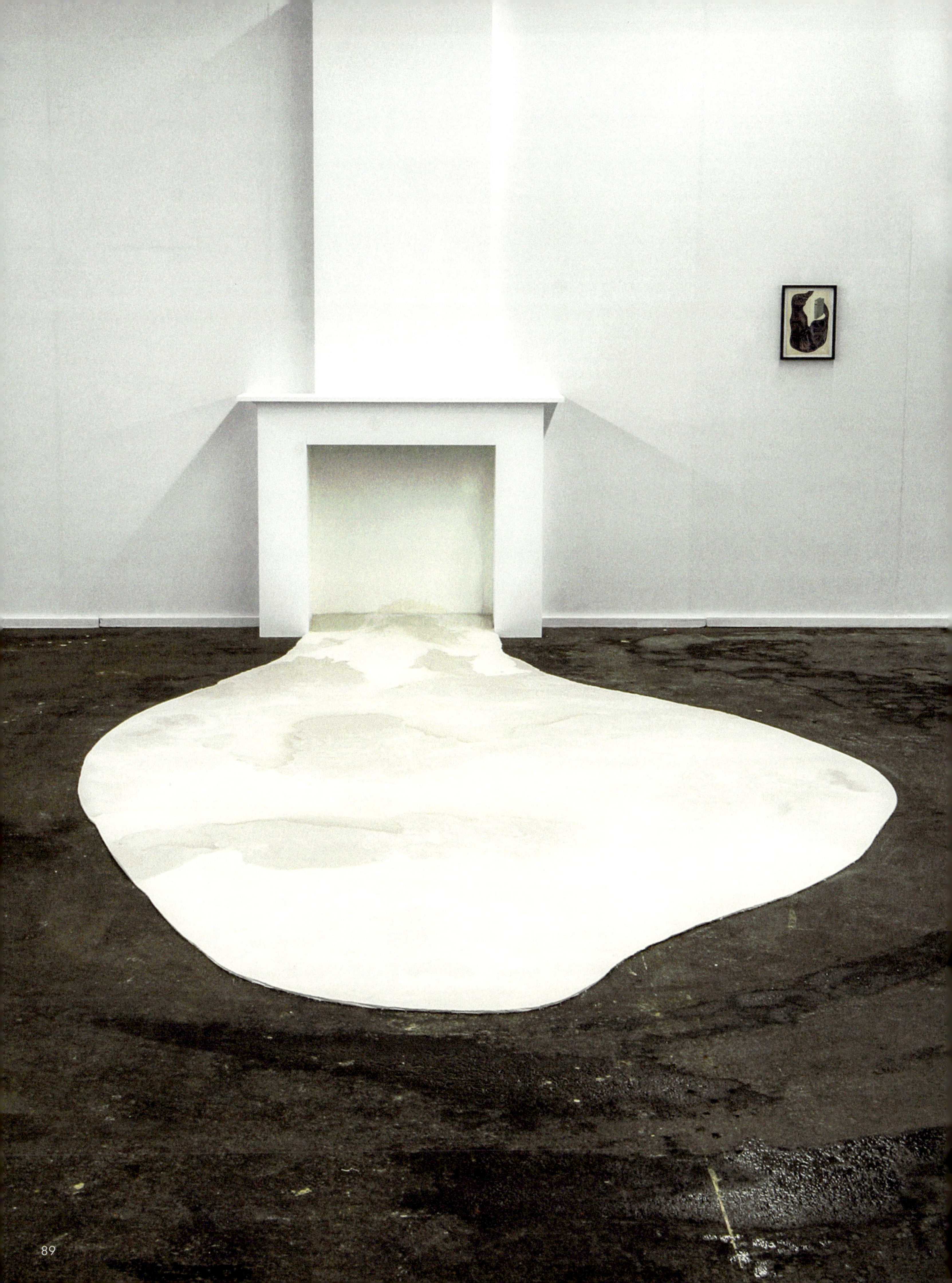

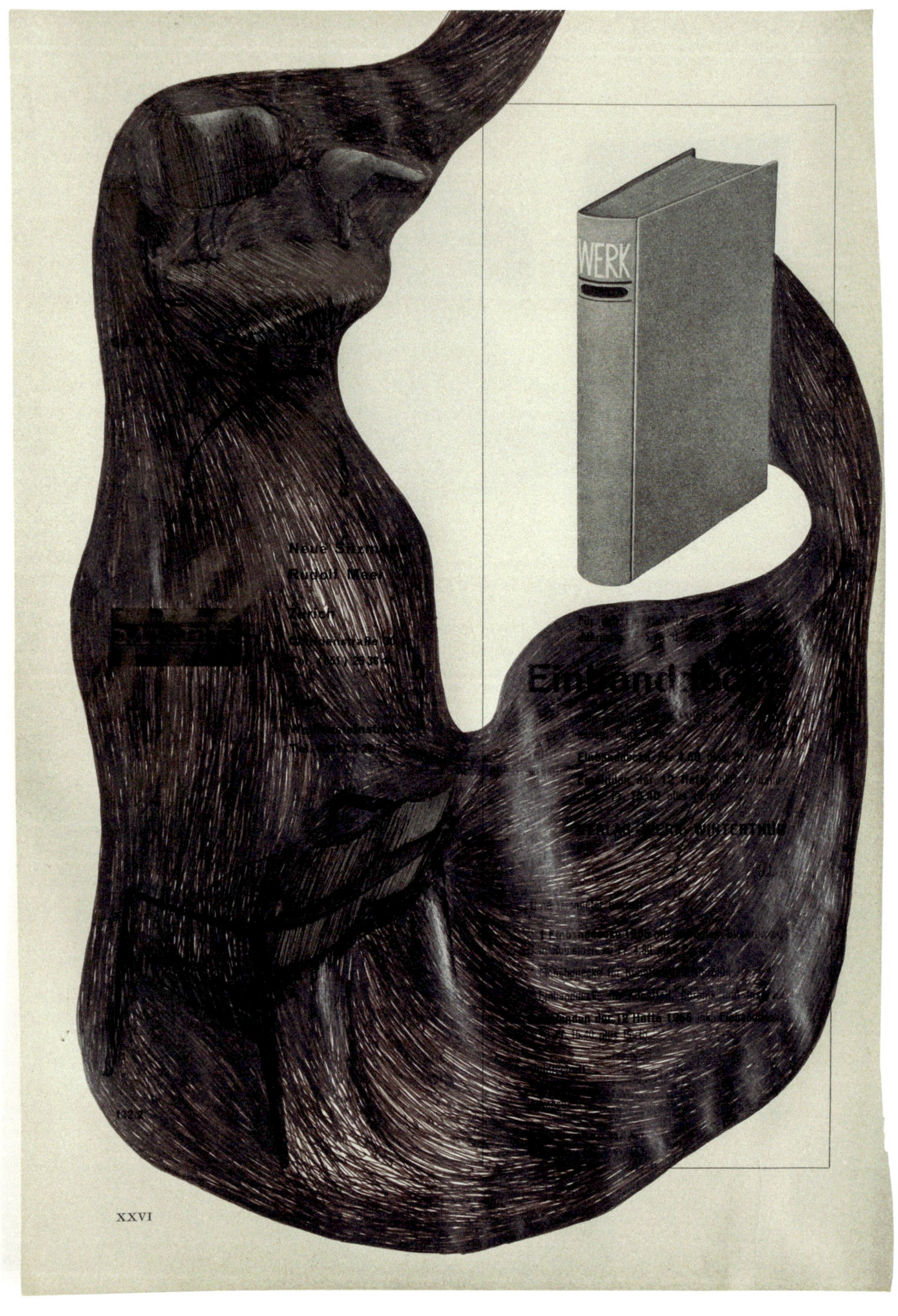

WERK
Einband-Decke

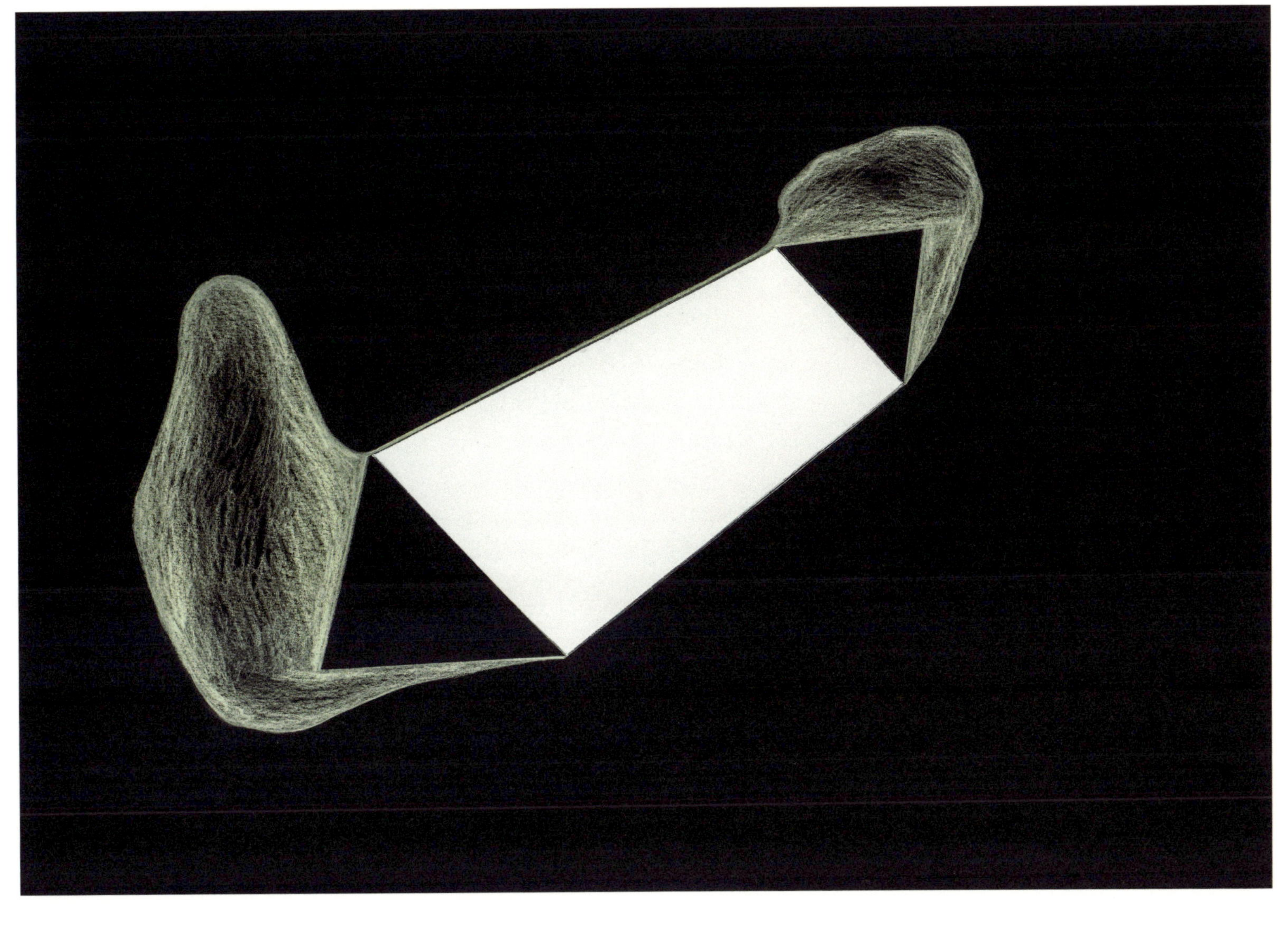

UNTITLED

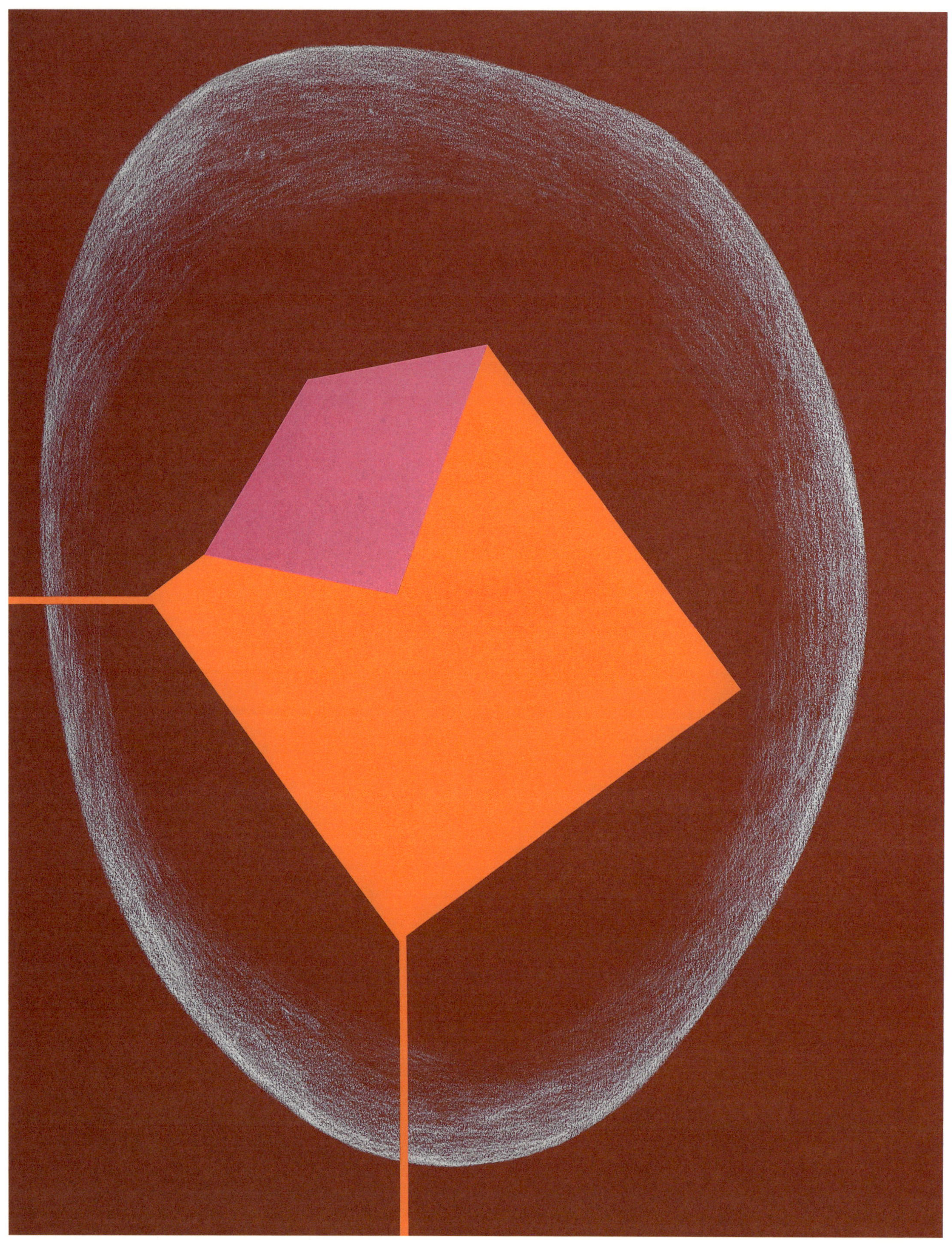

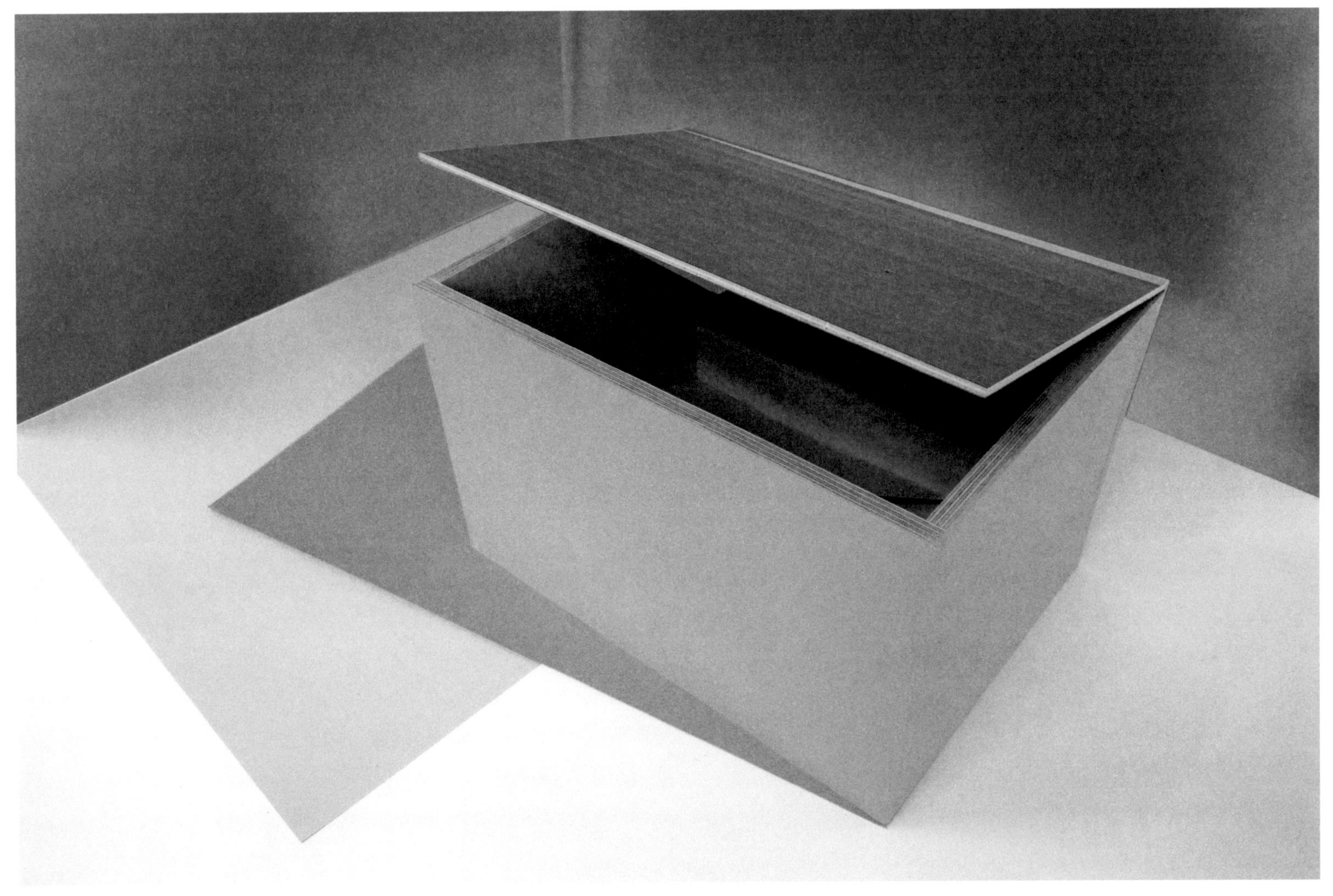

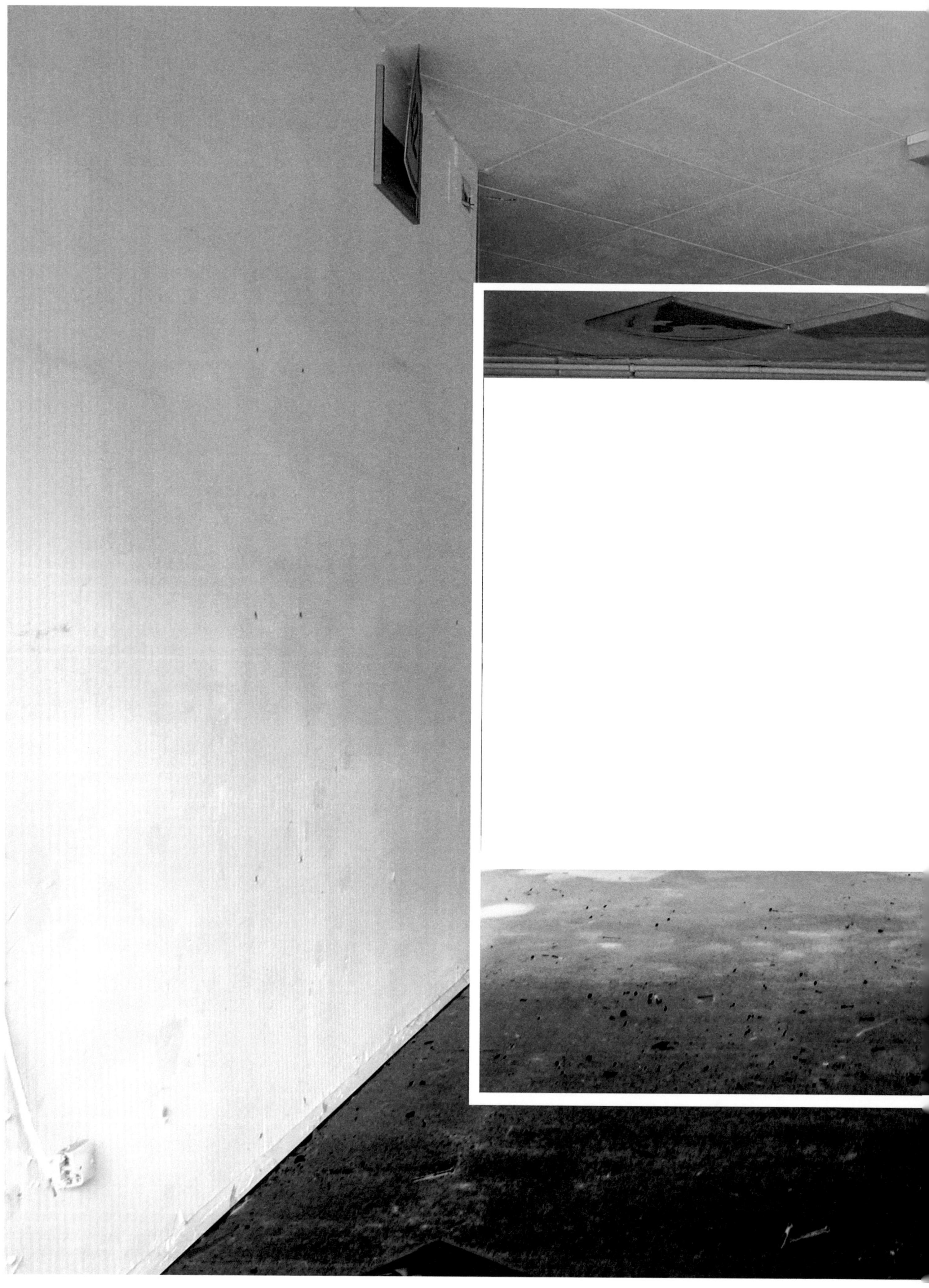

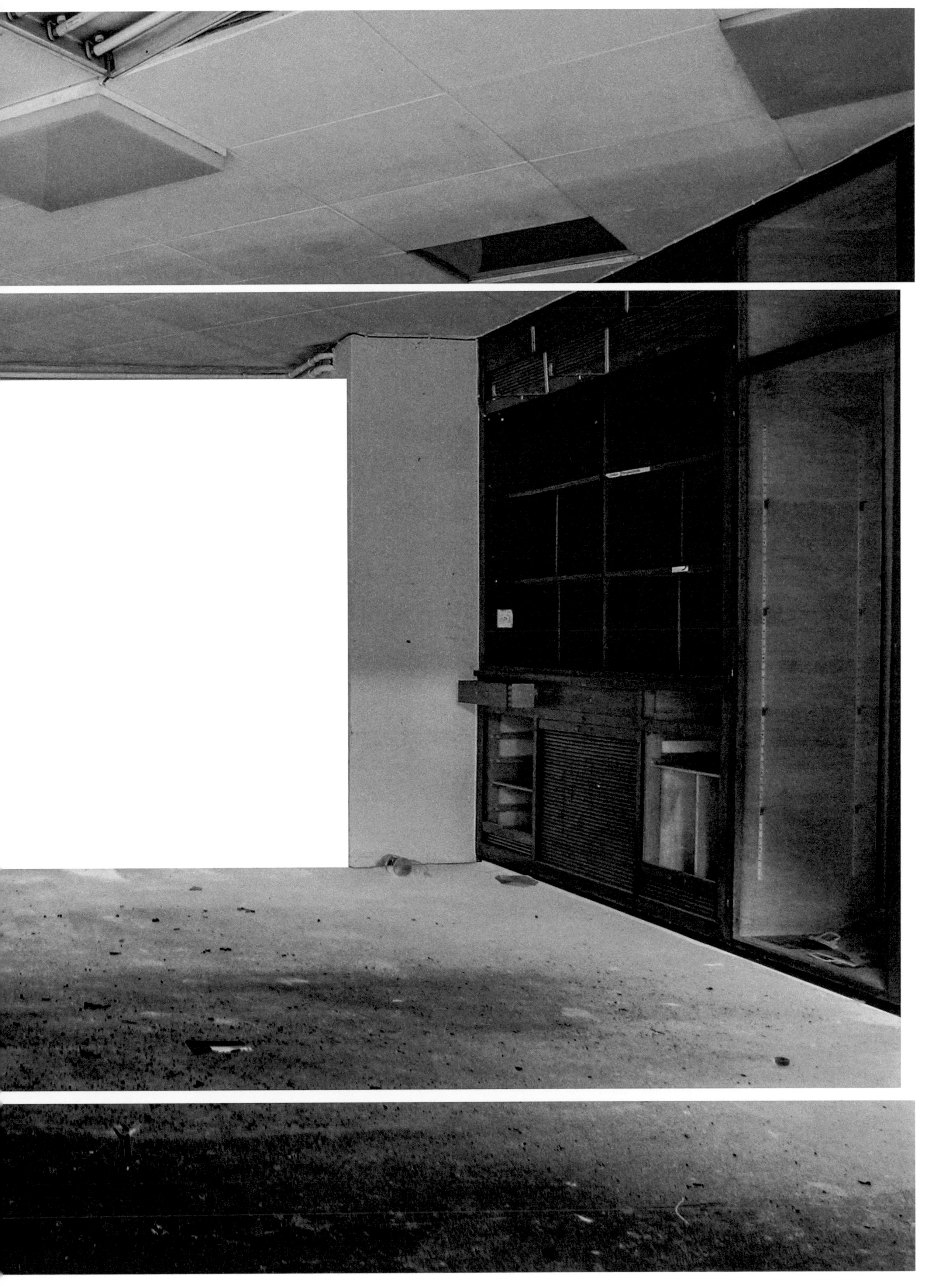

ABANDONED BOOKSTORE

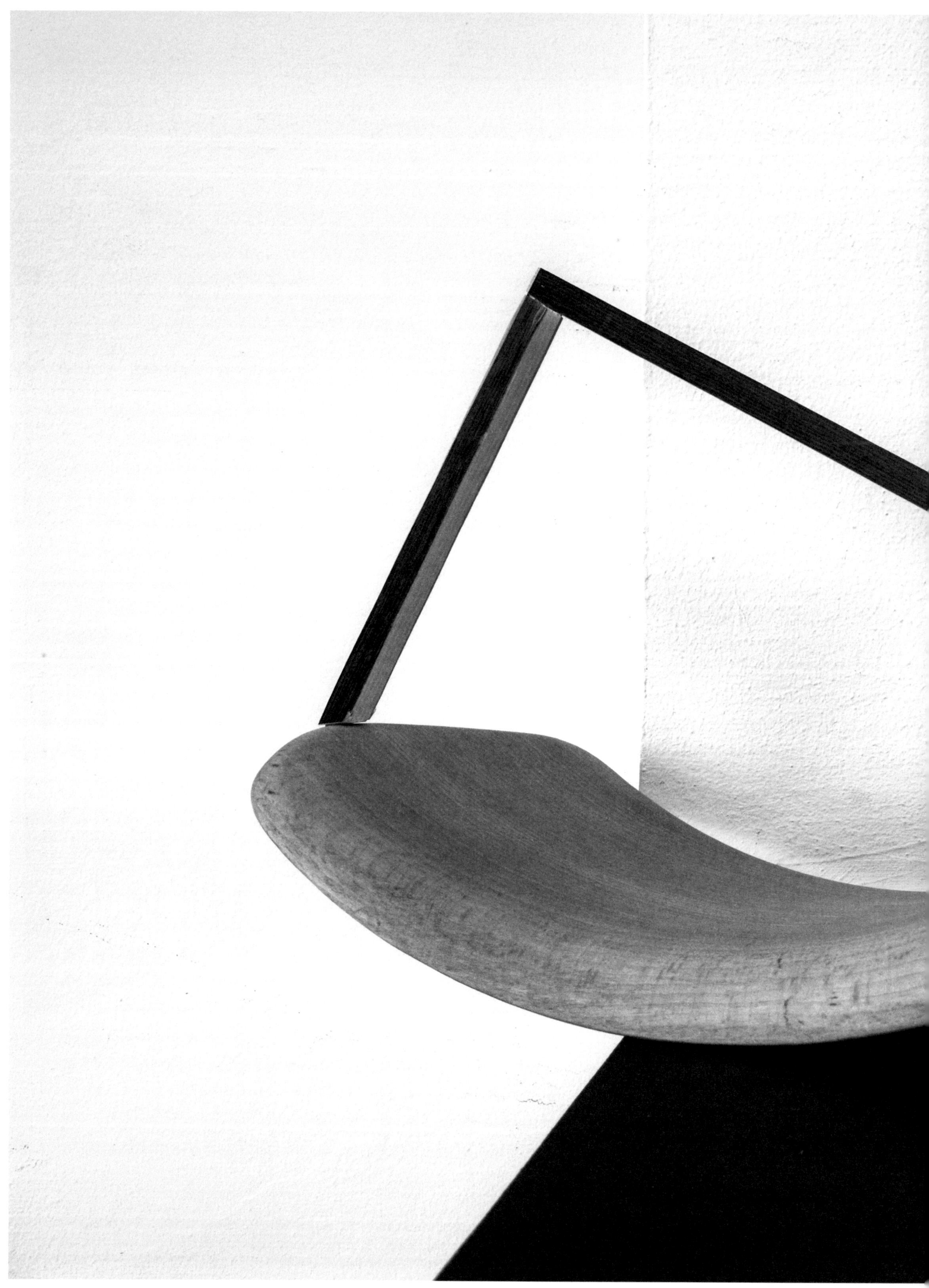

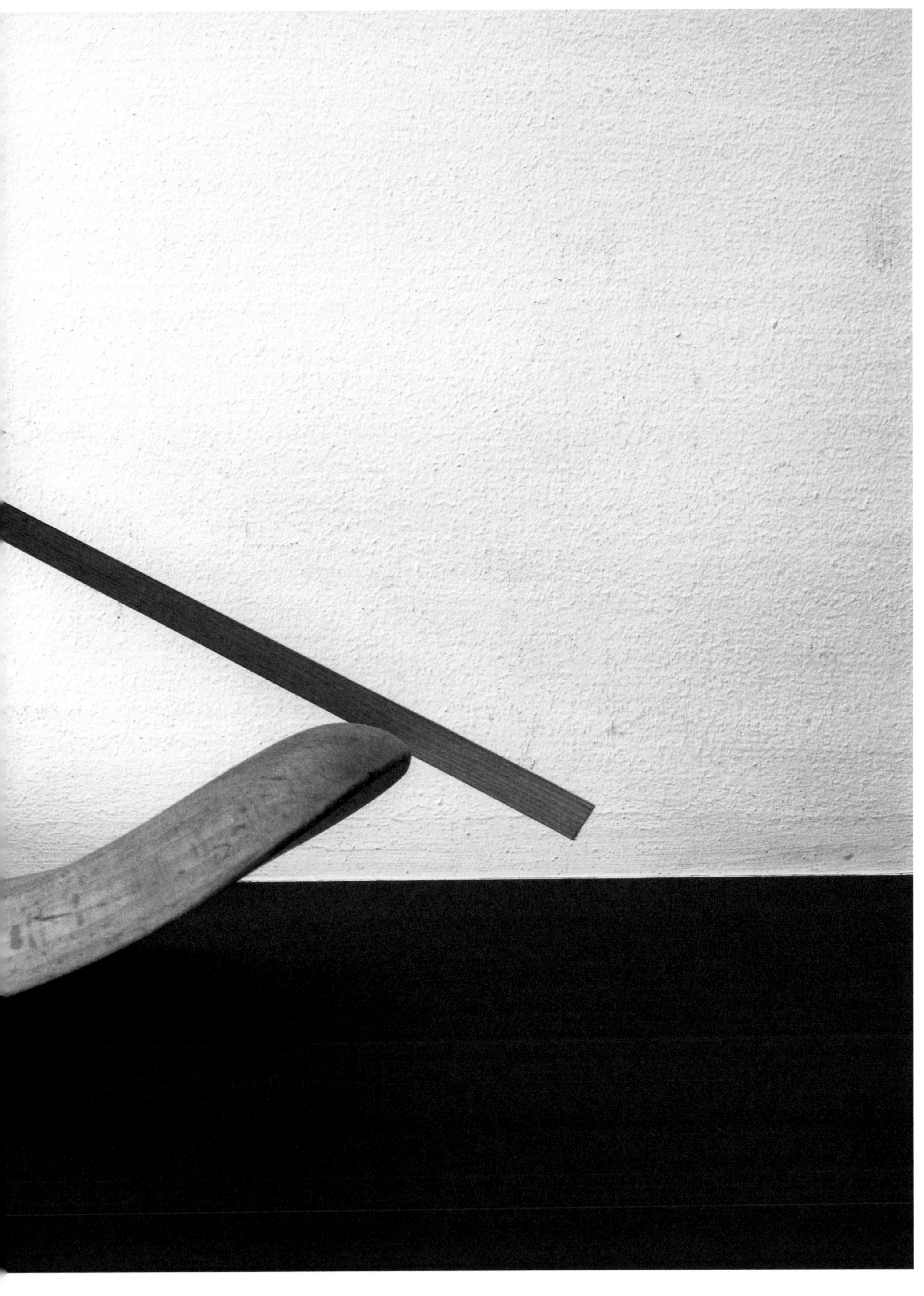

BALANCE

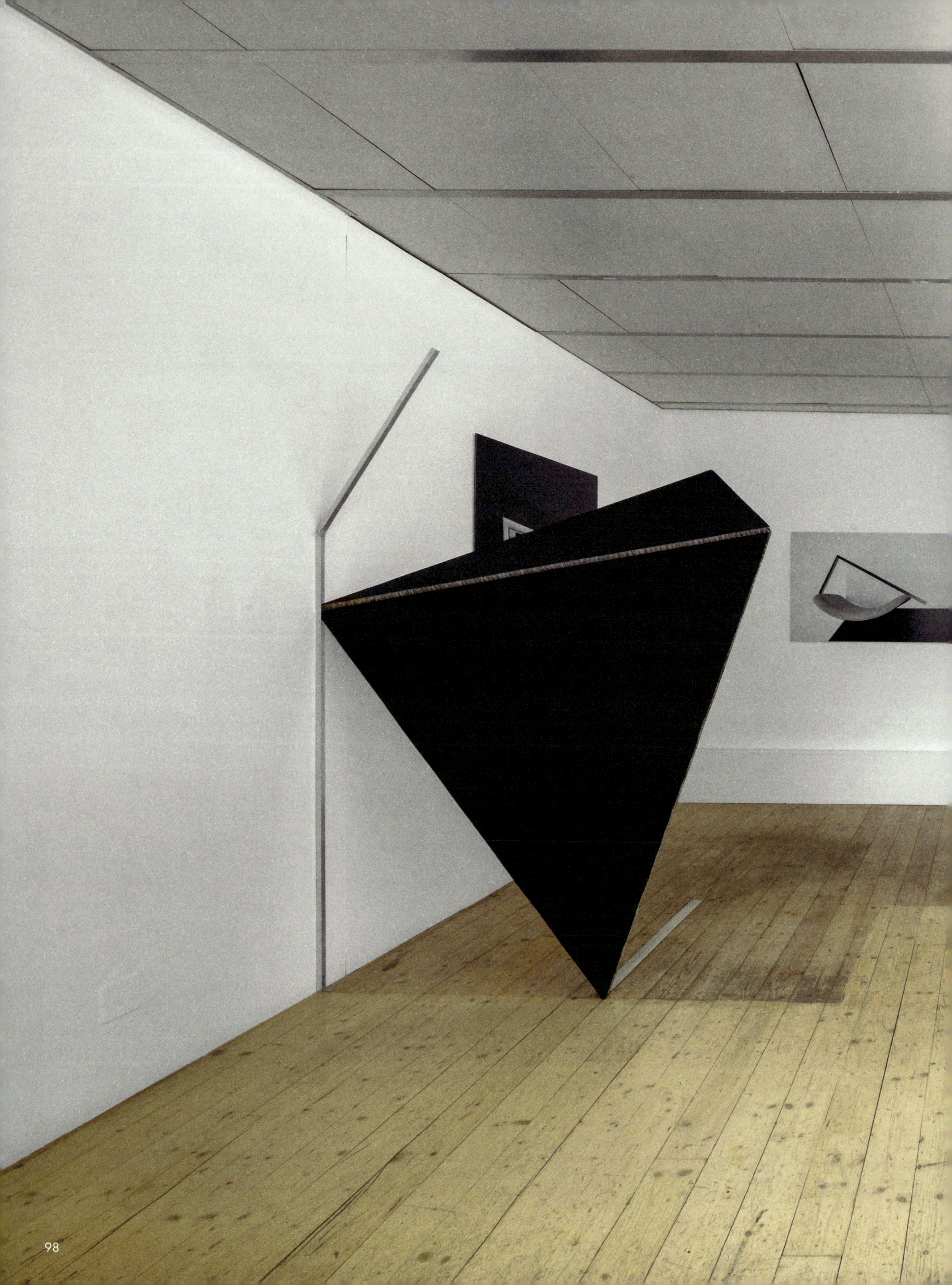

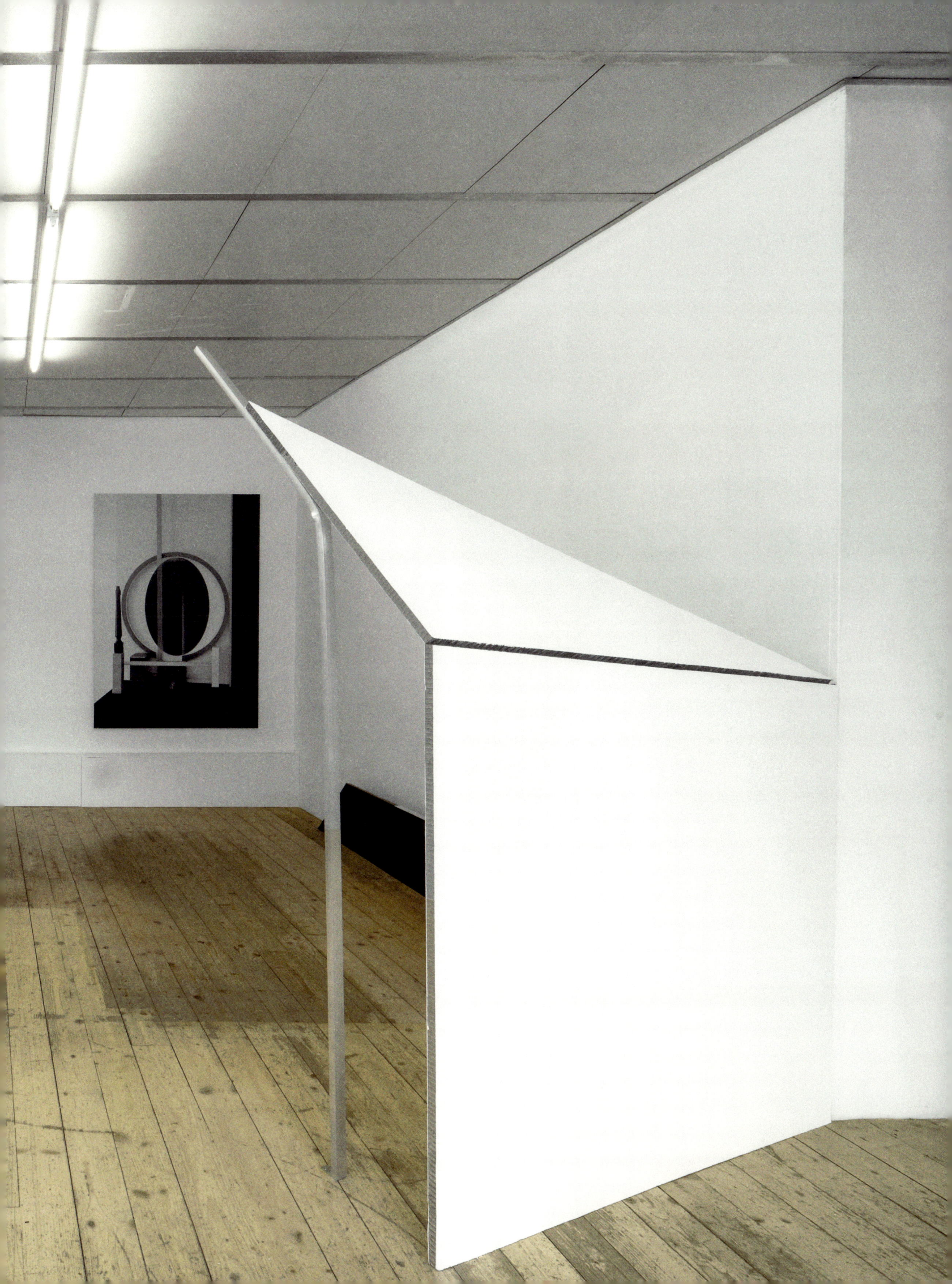

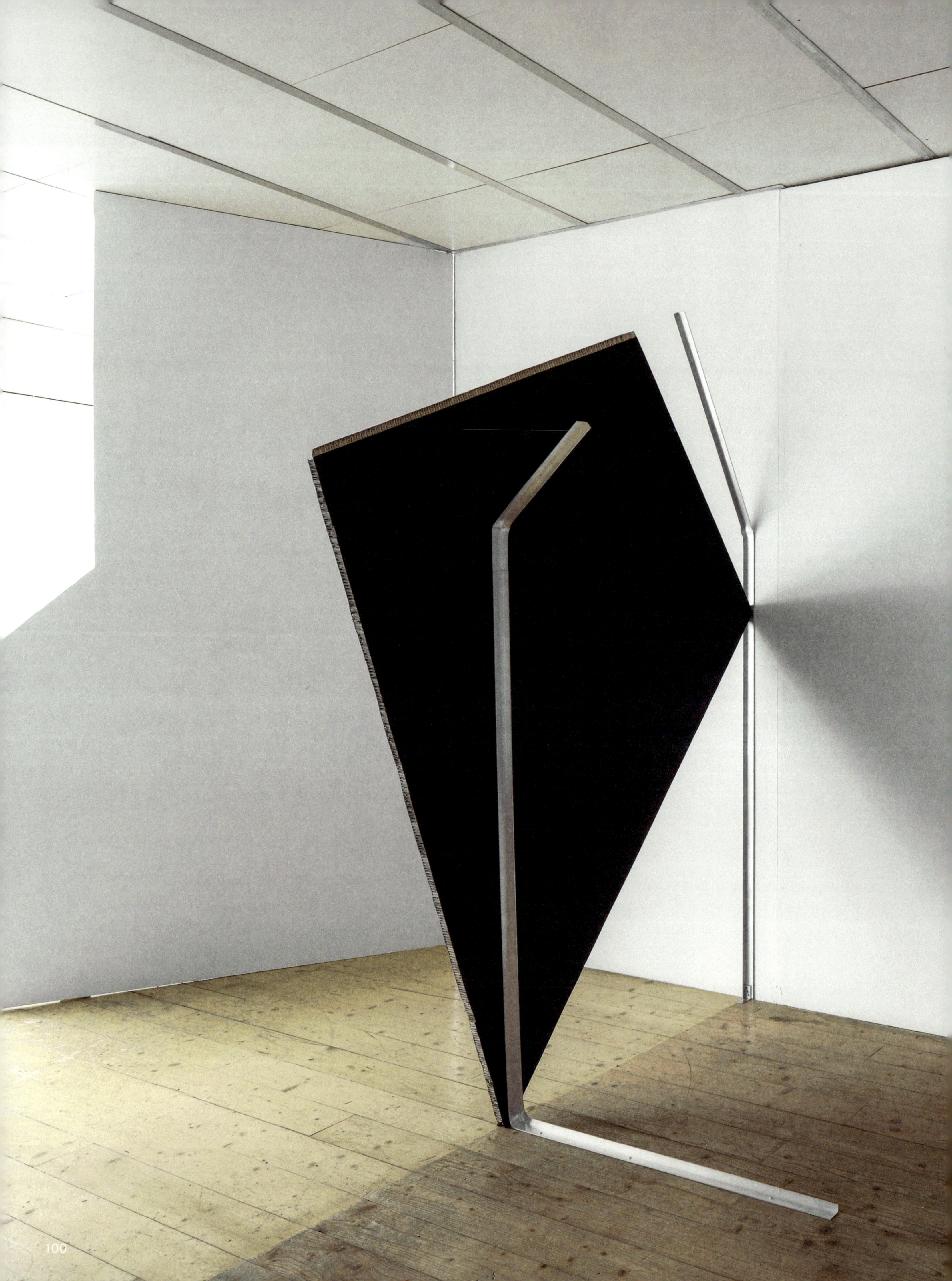

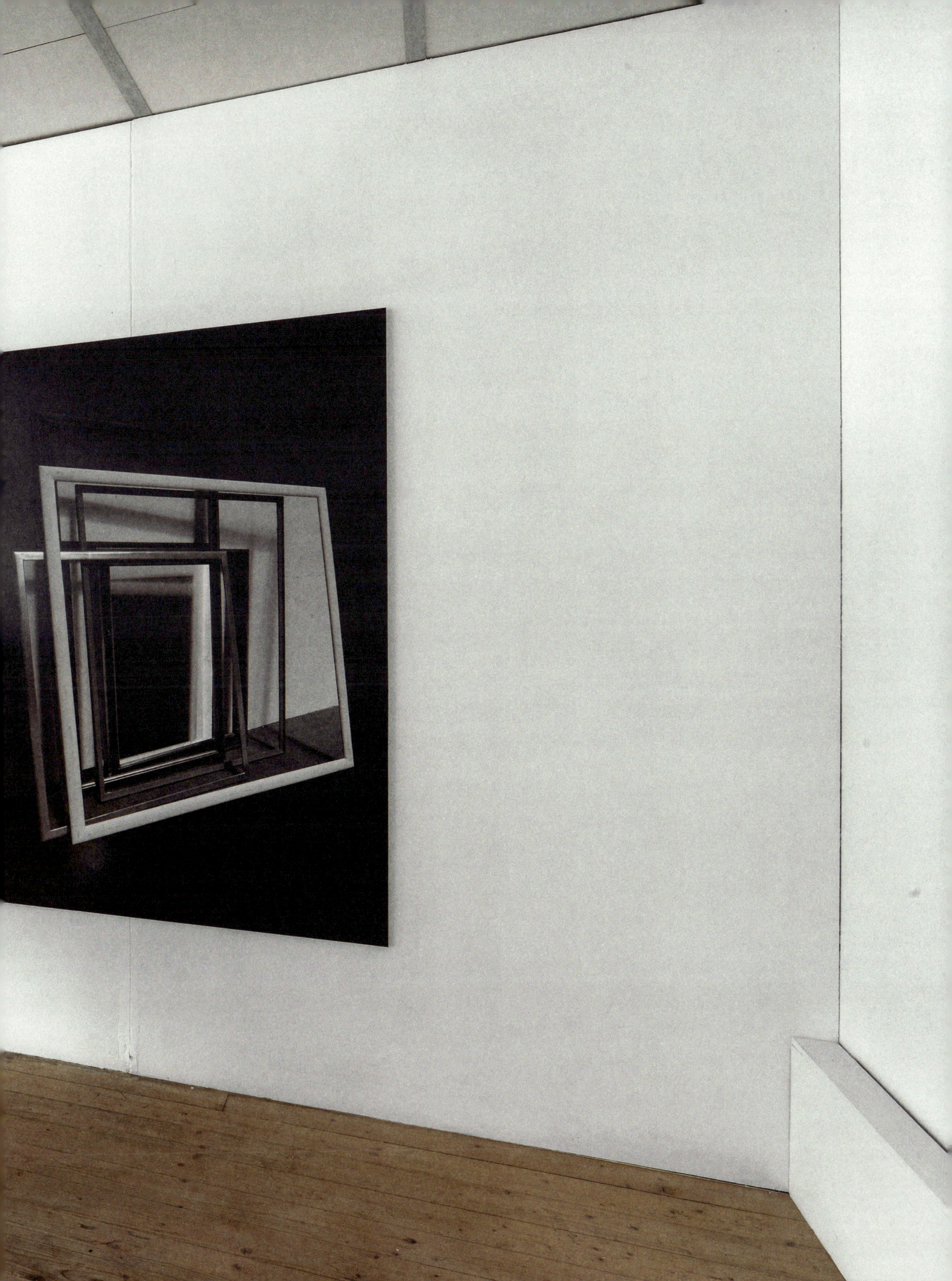

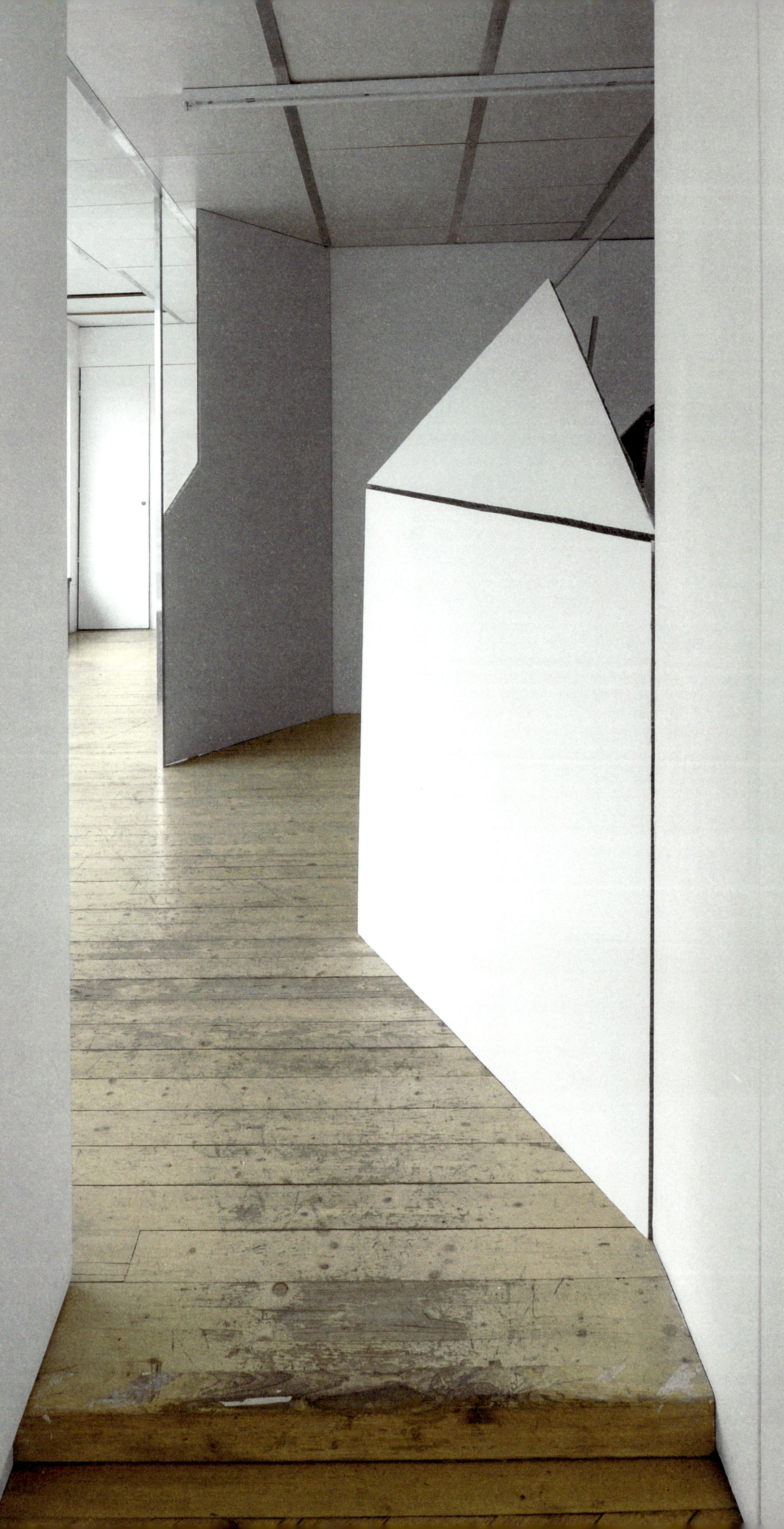

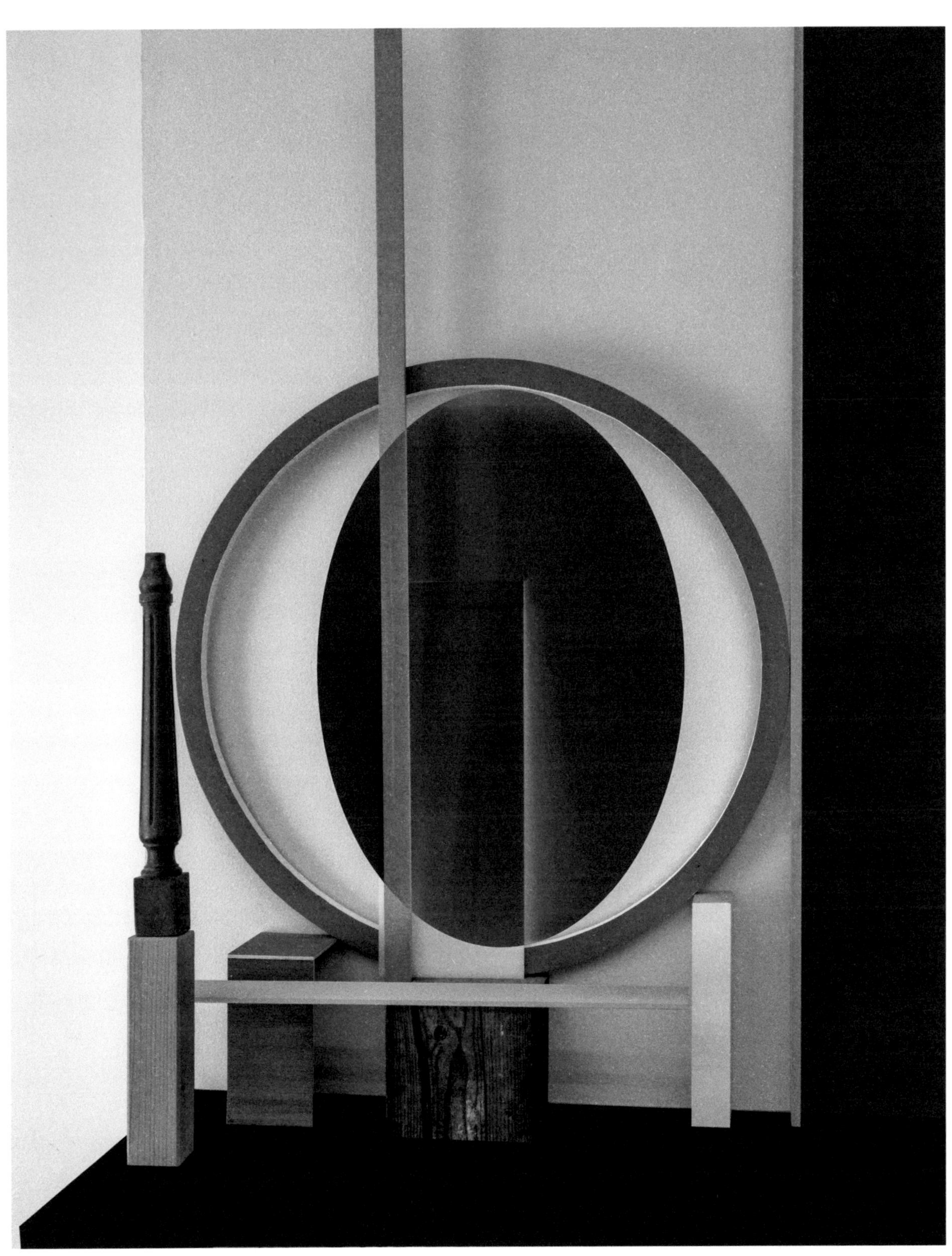

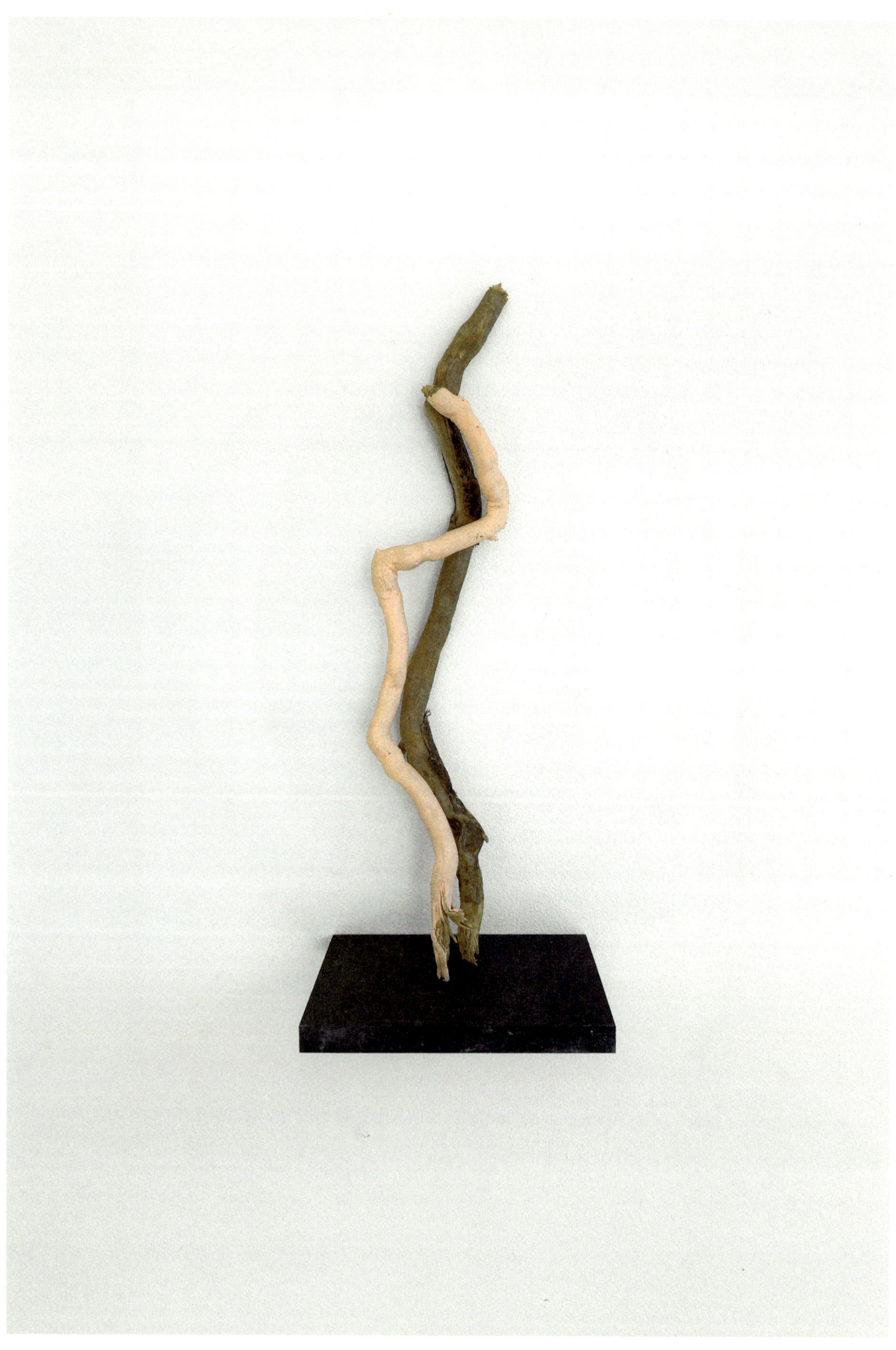

COUPLE

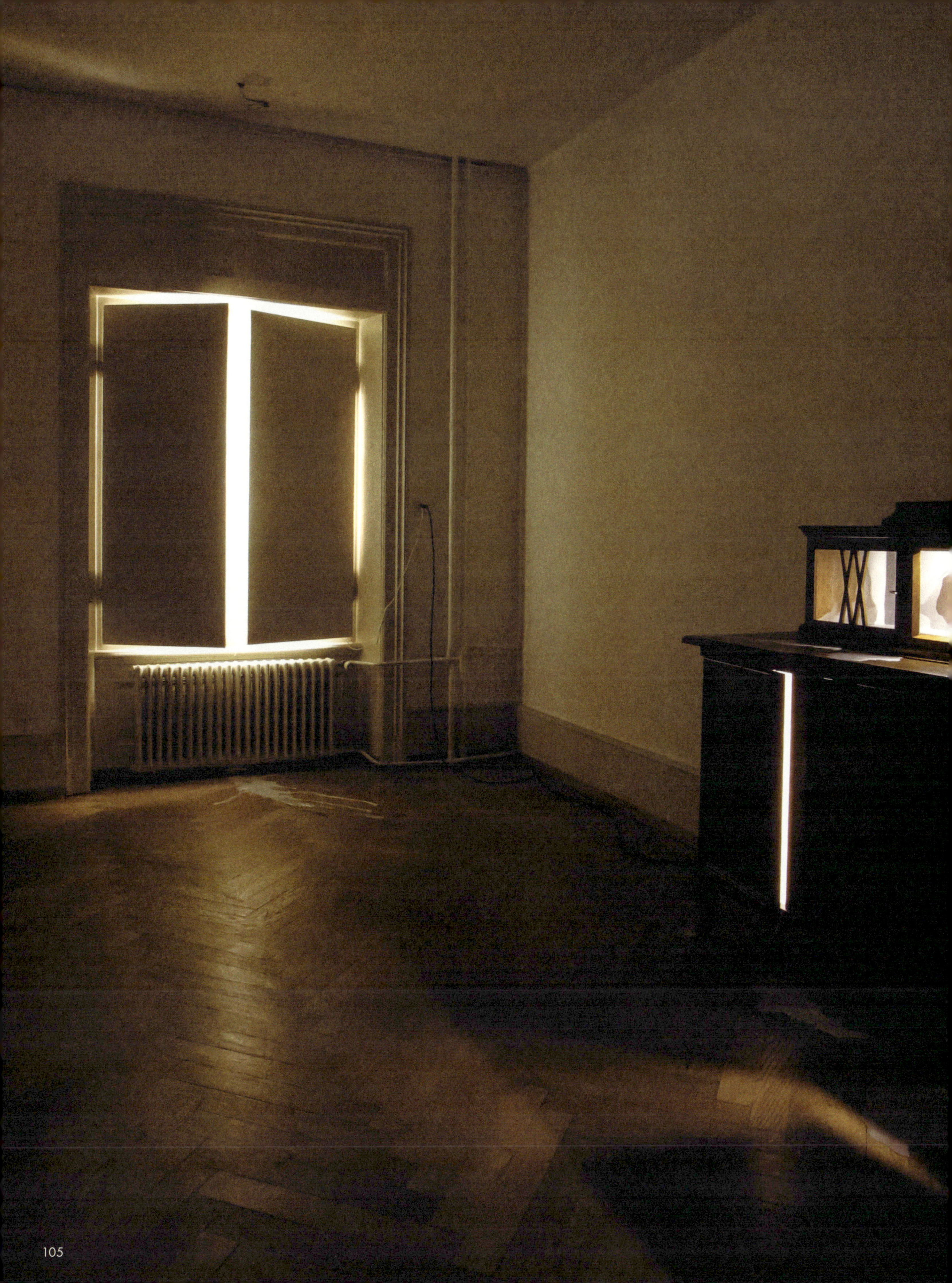

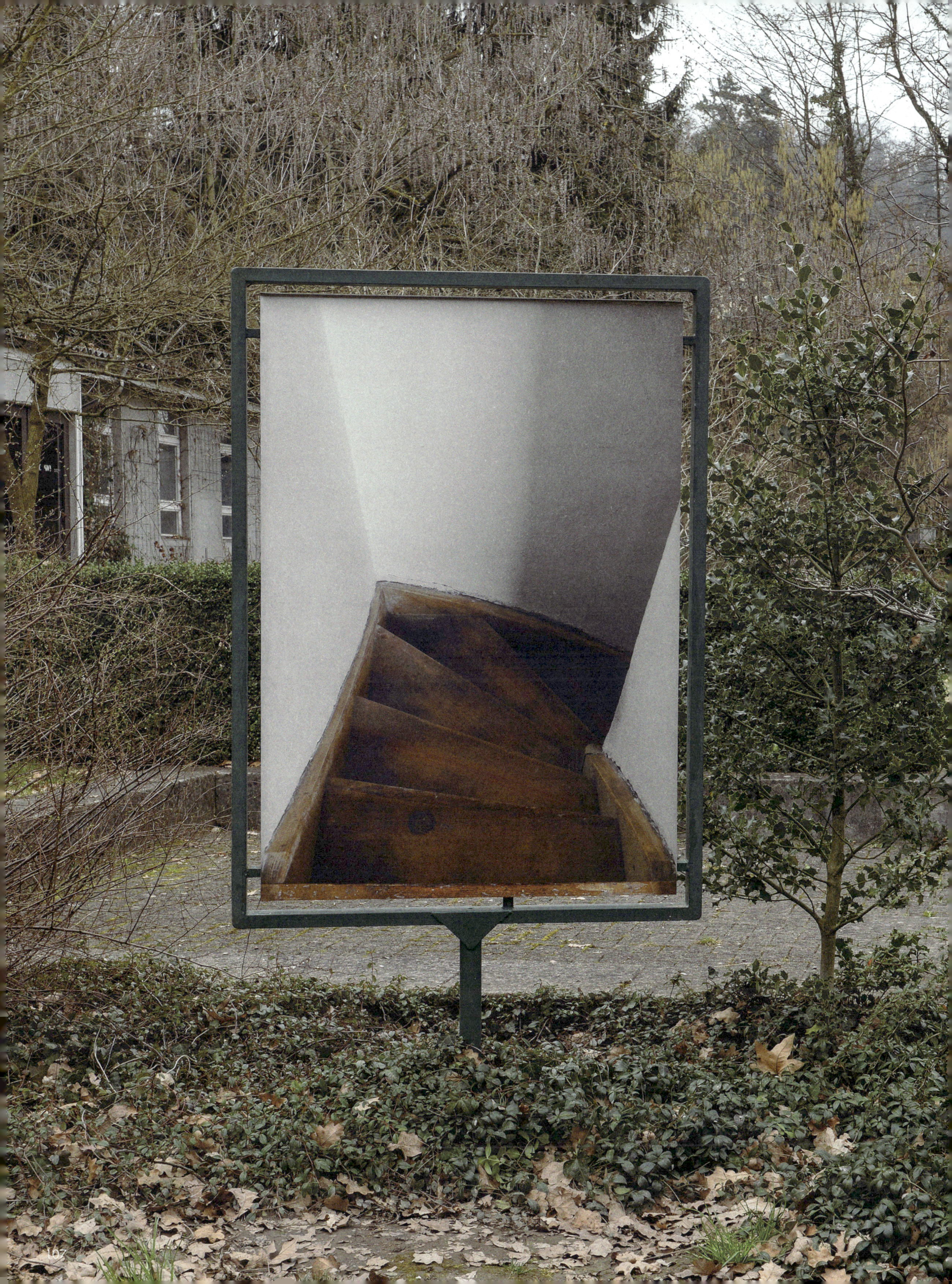

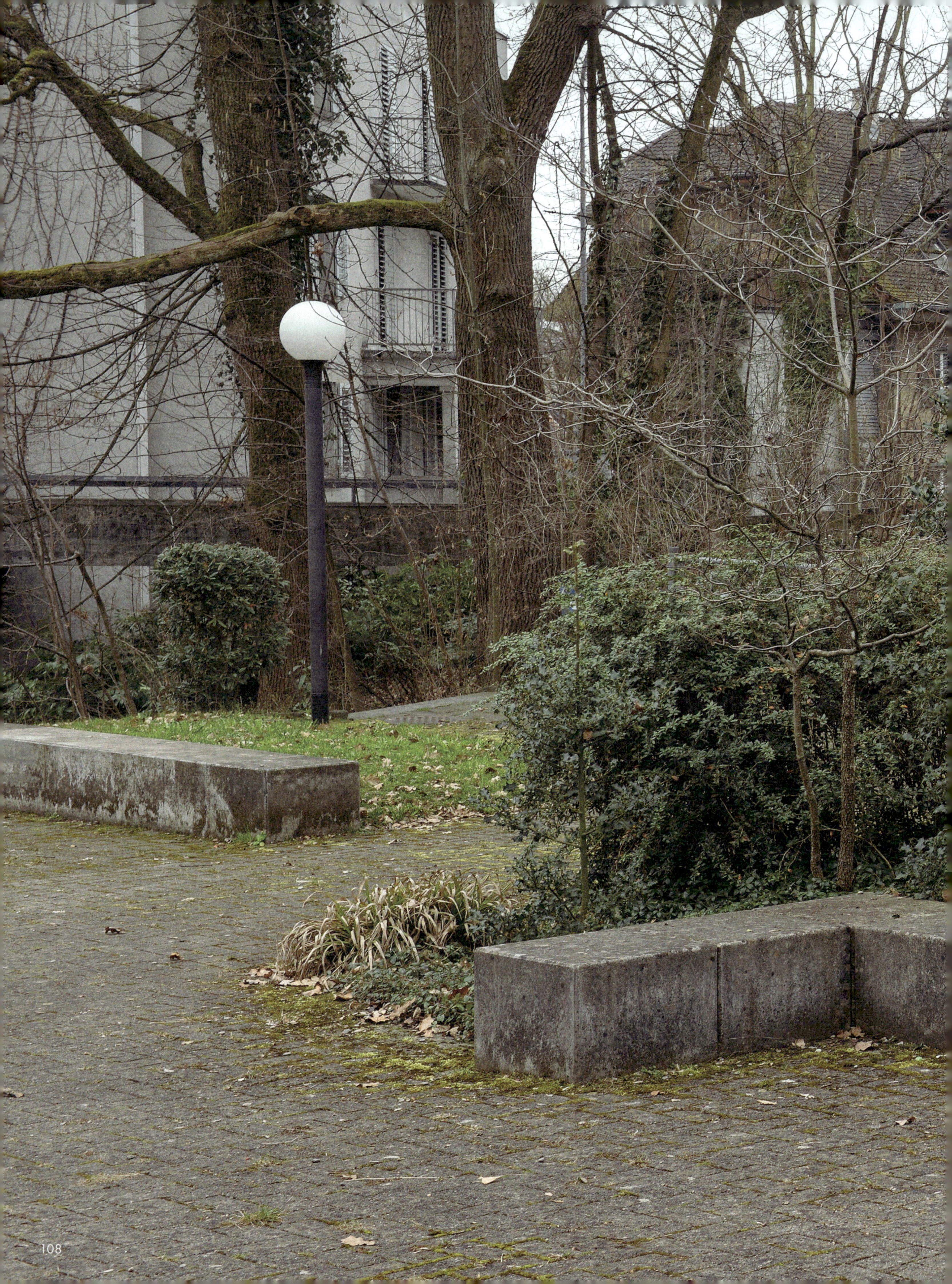

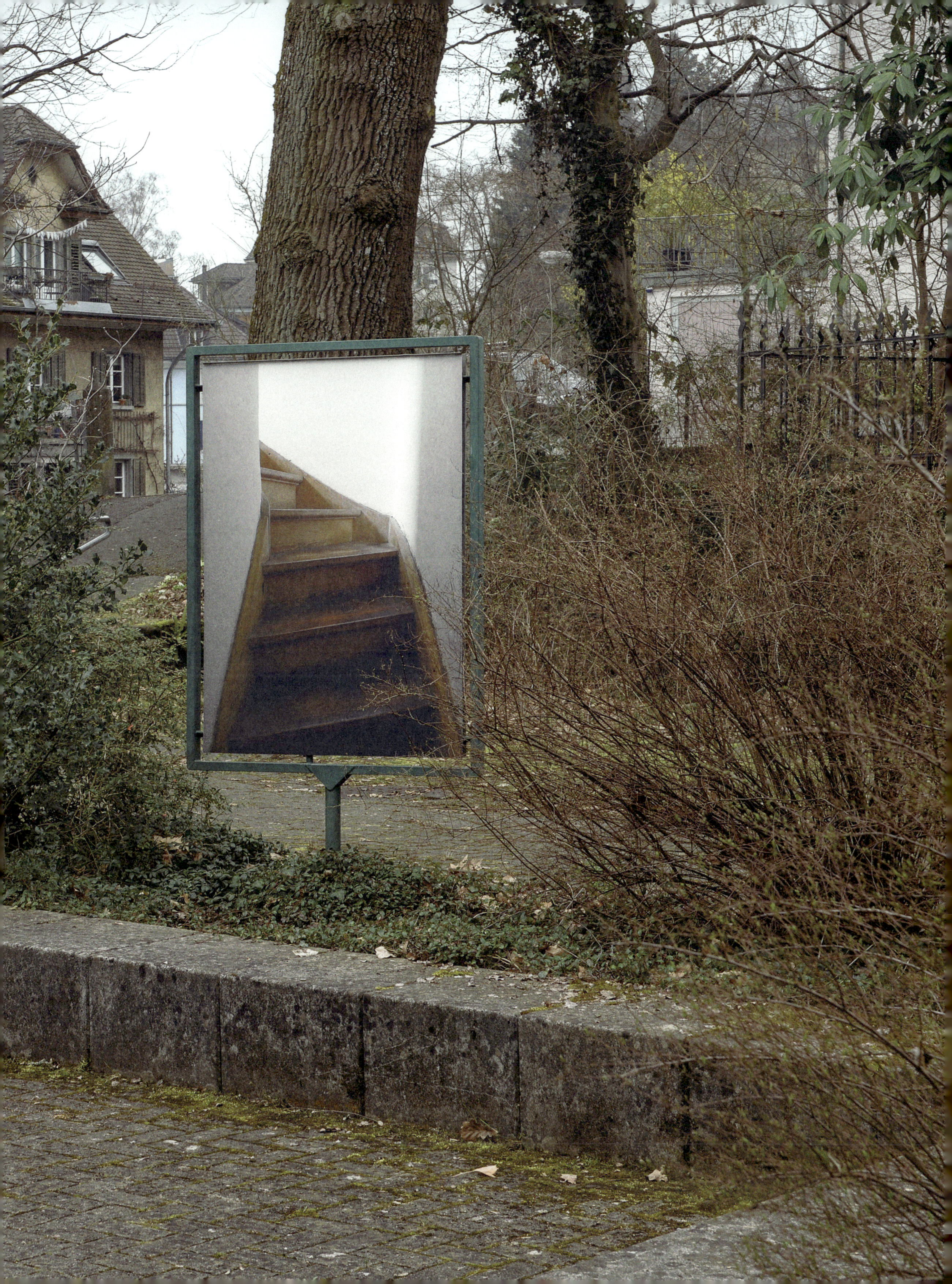

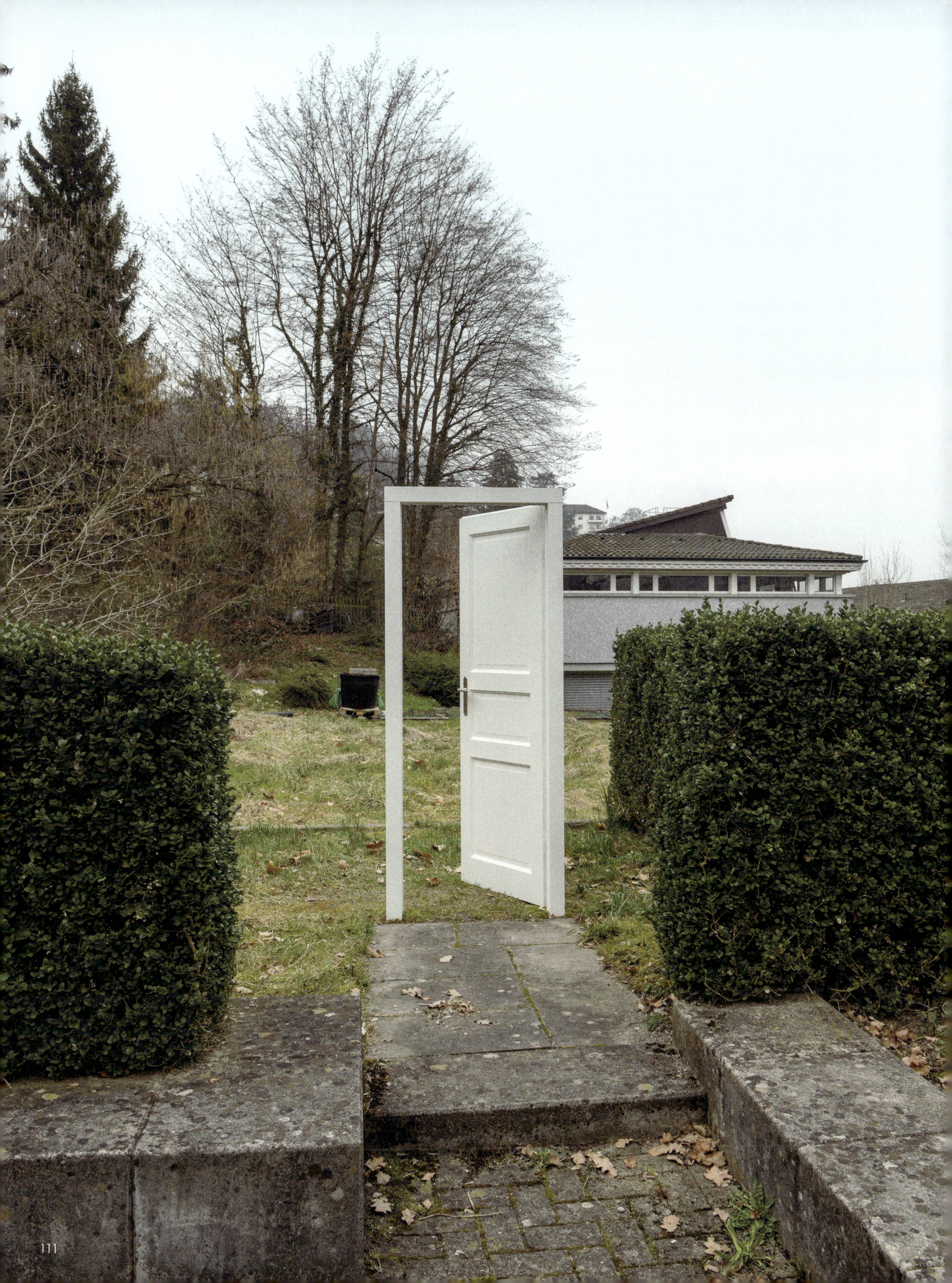

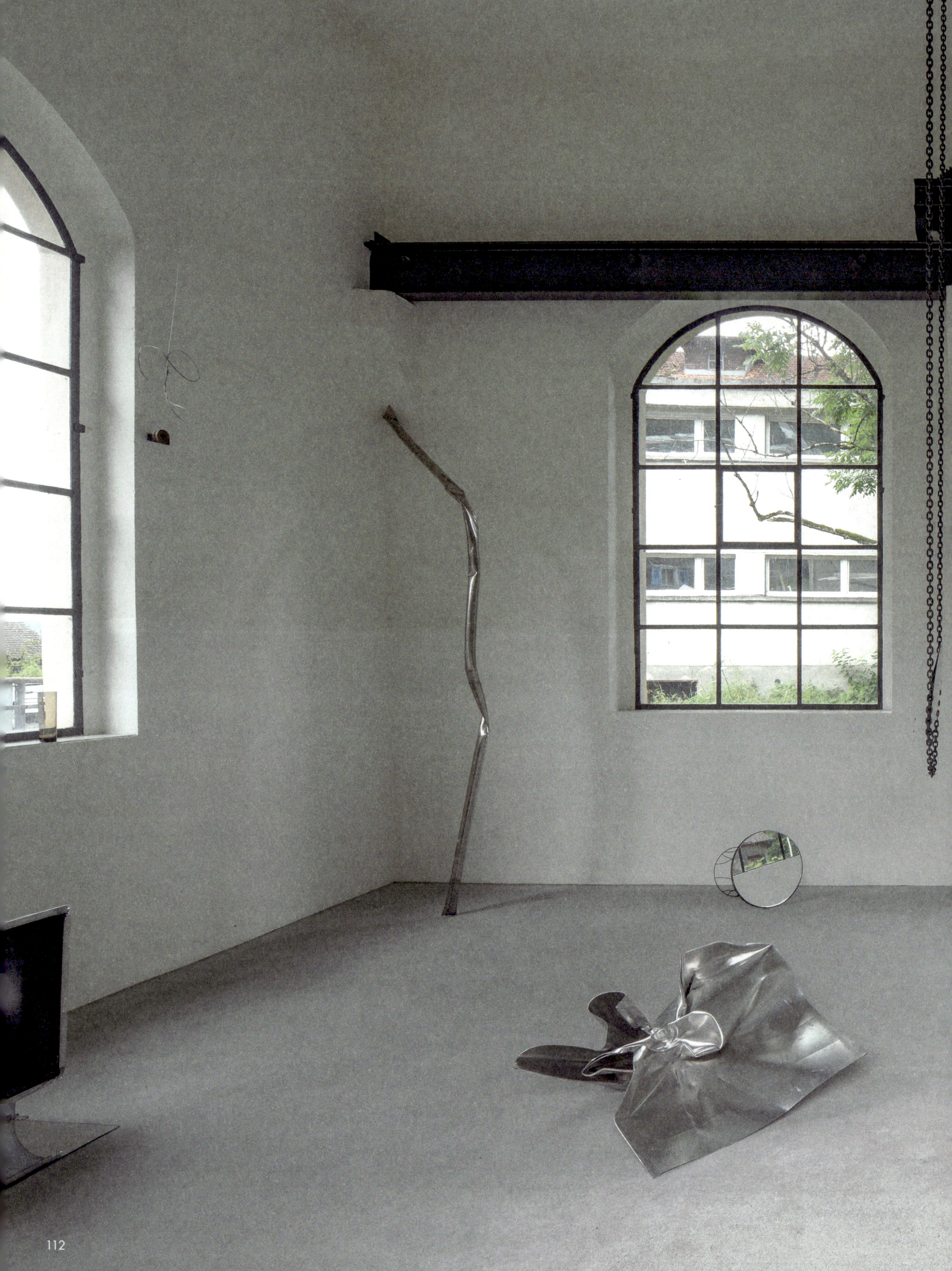

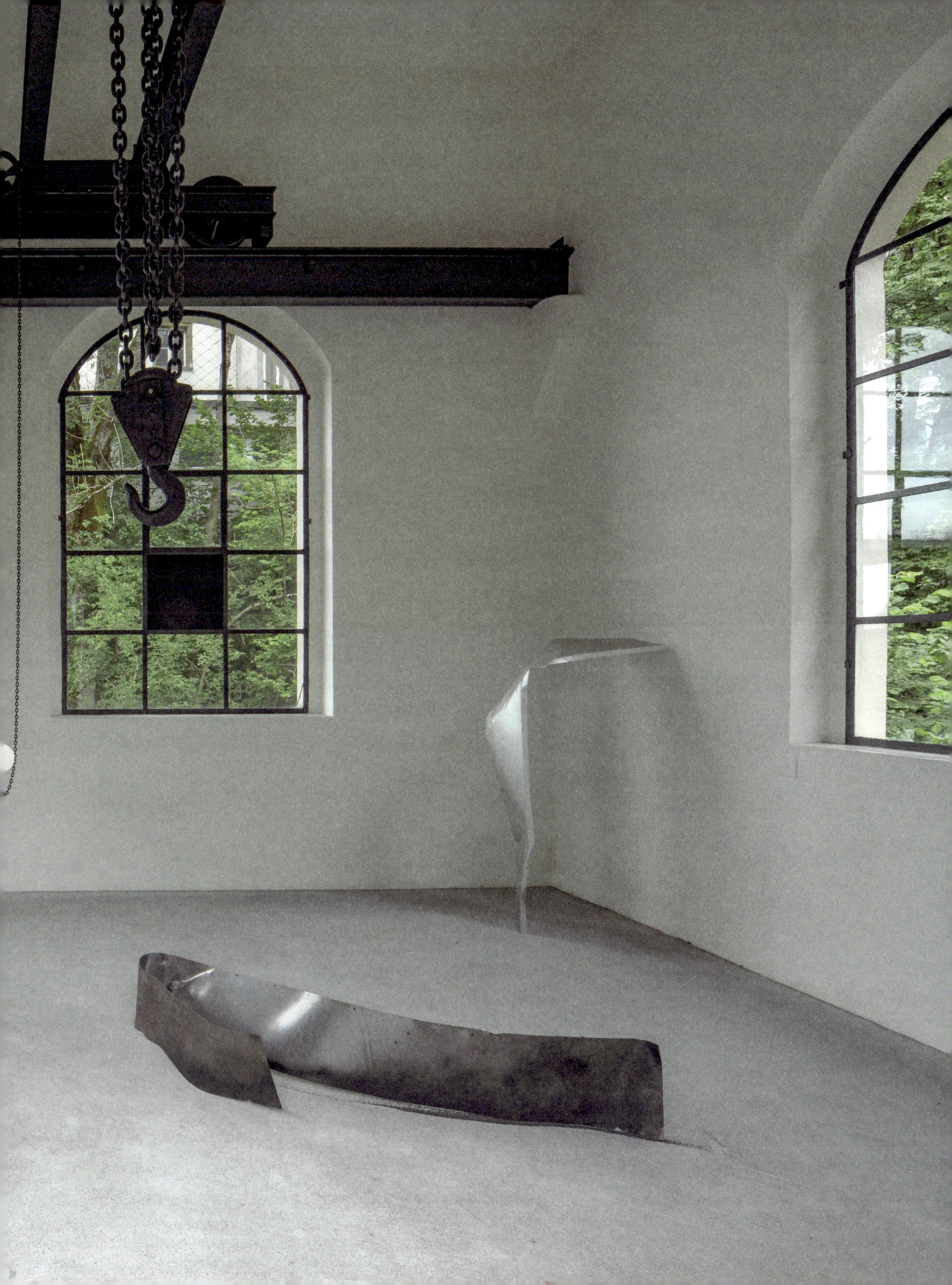

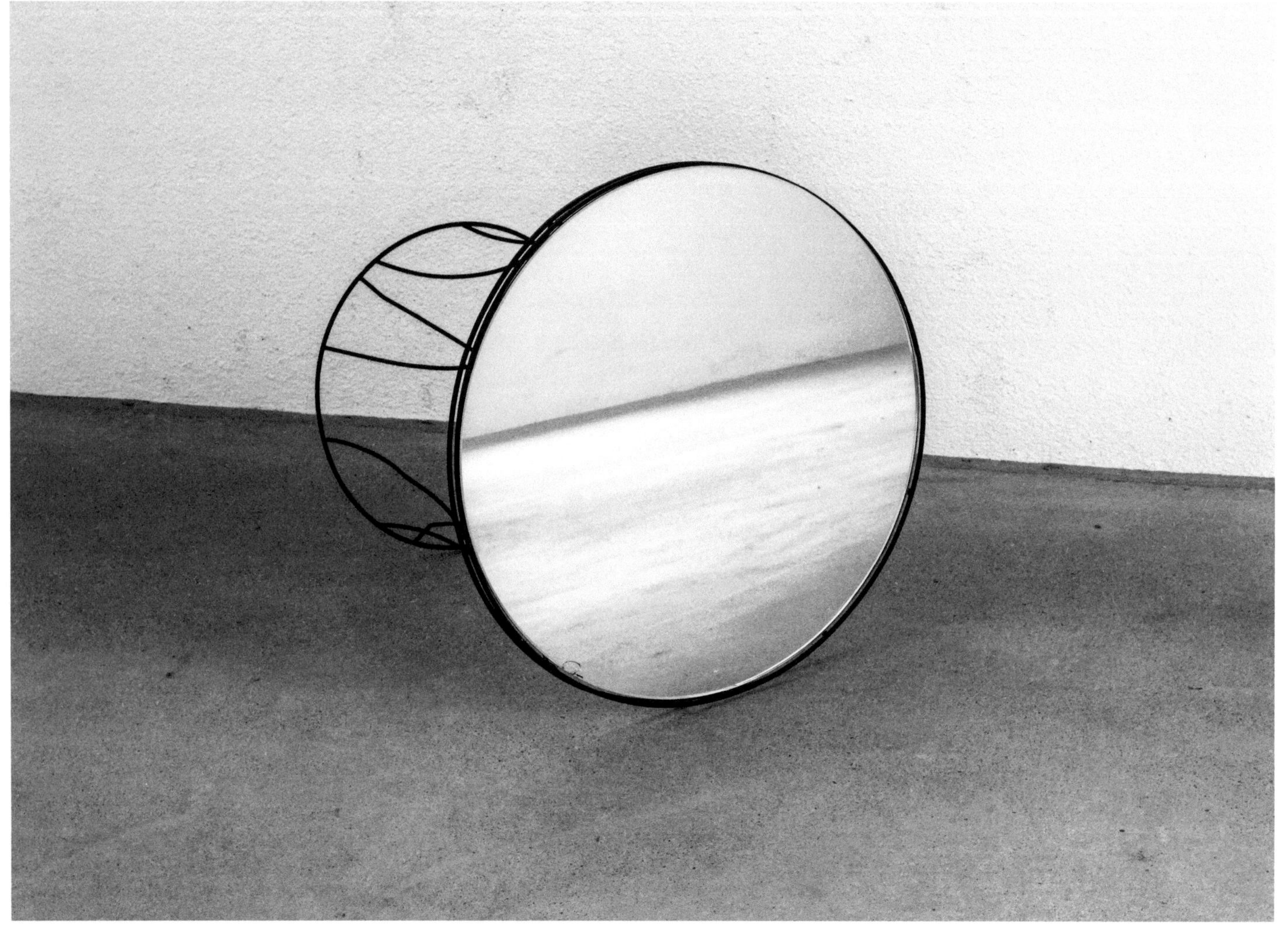

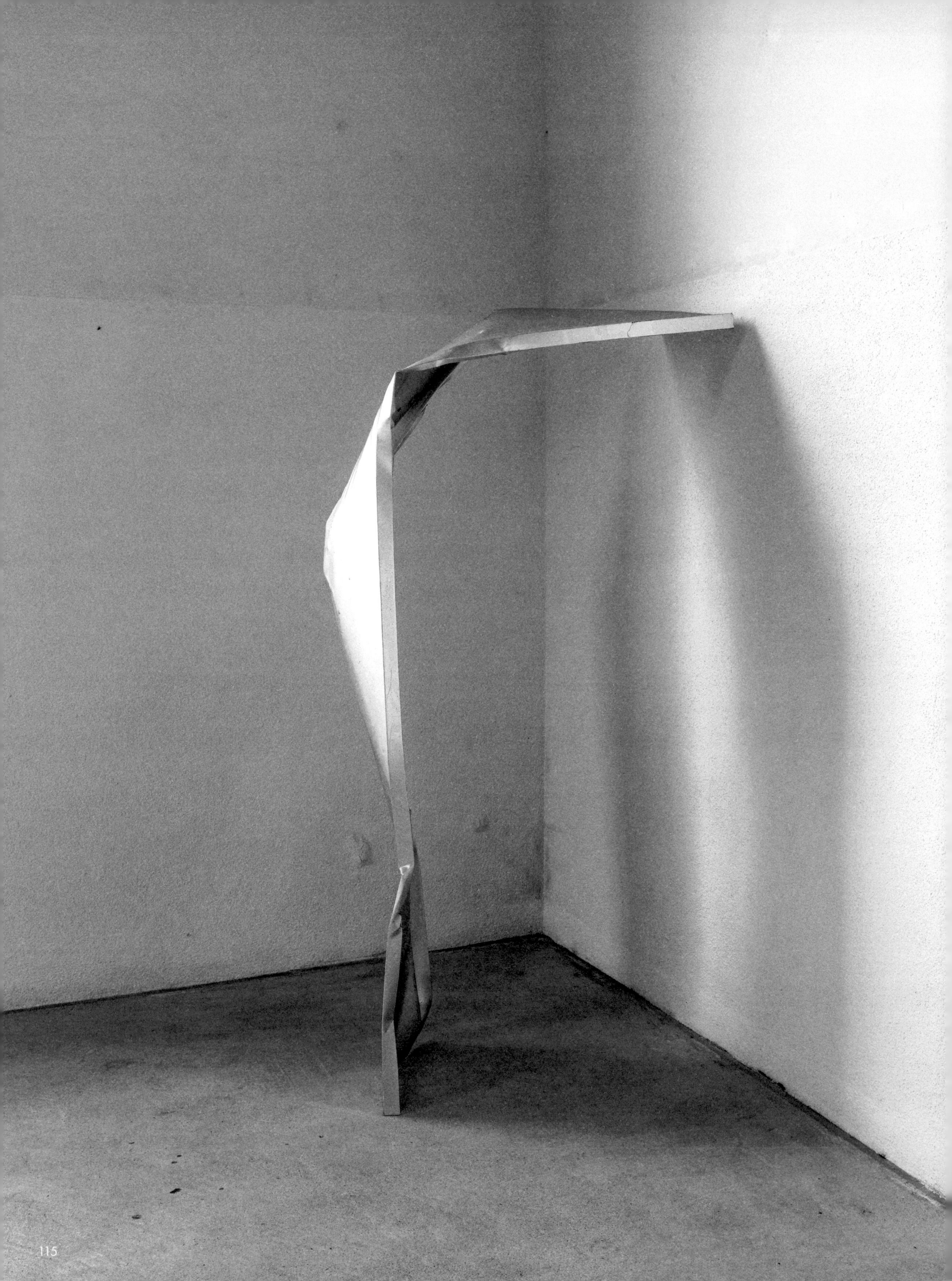

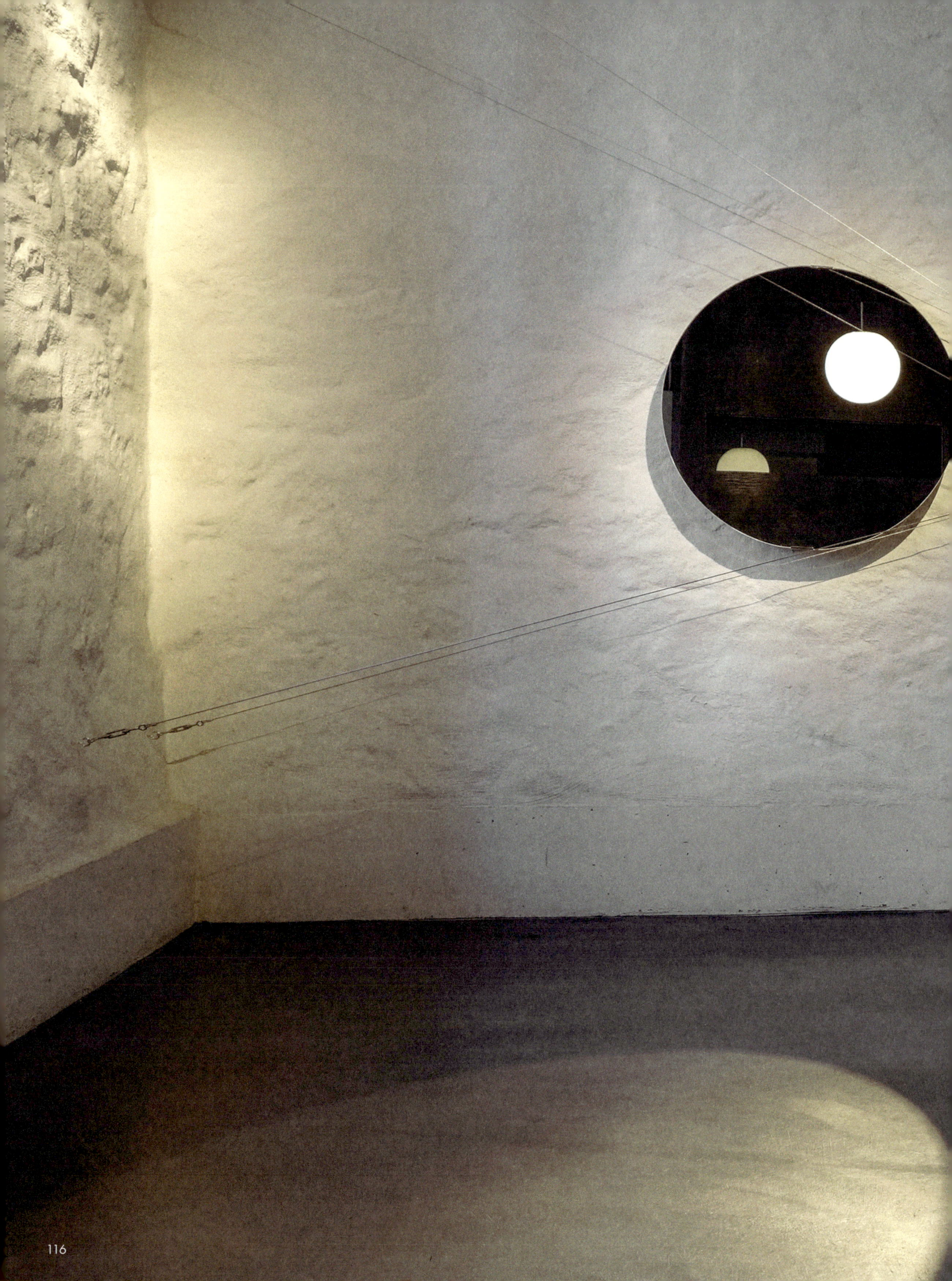

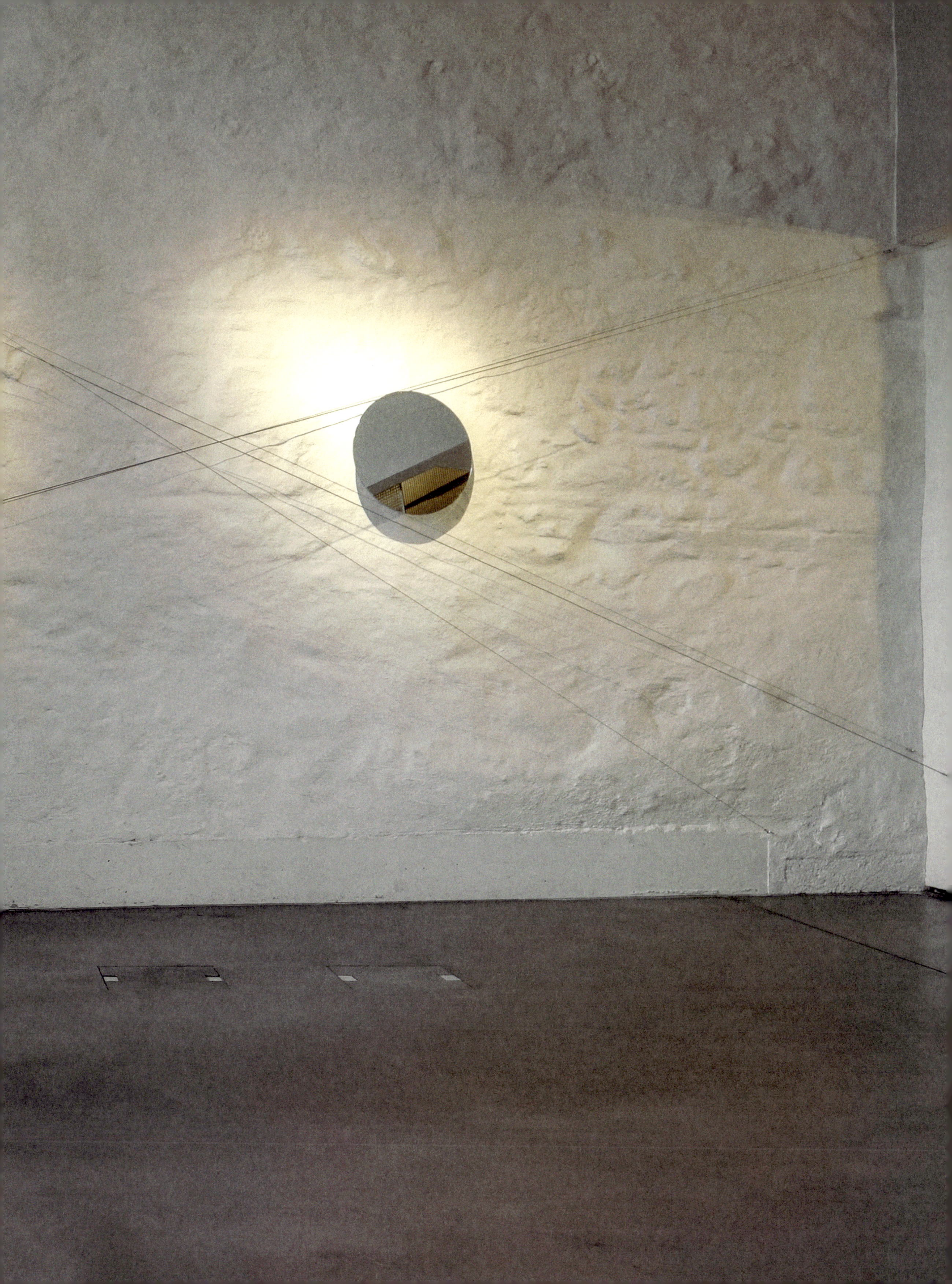

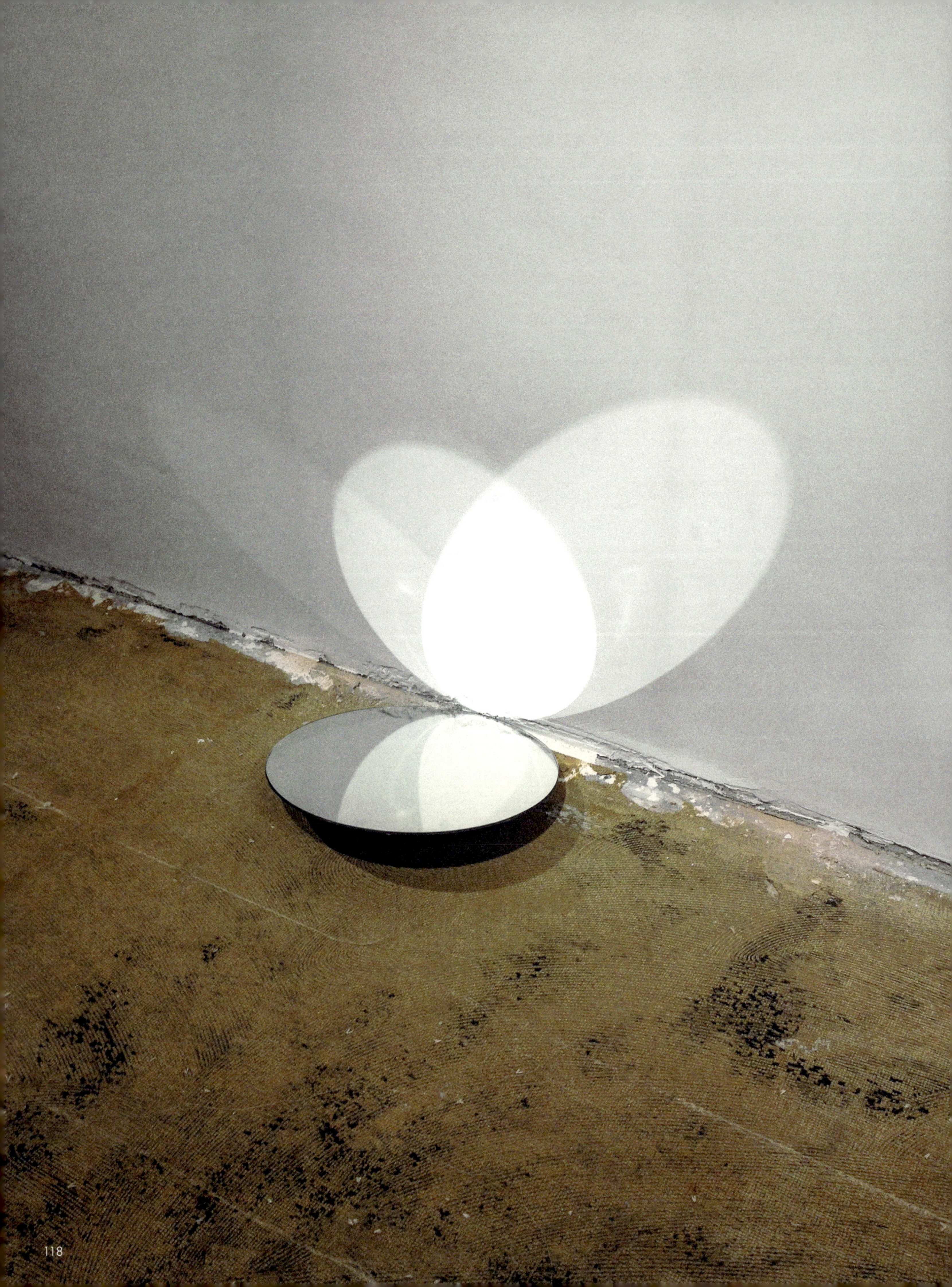

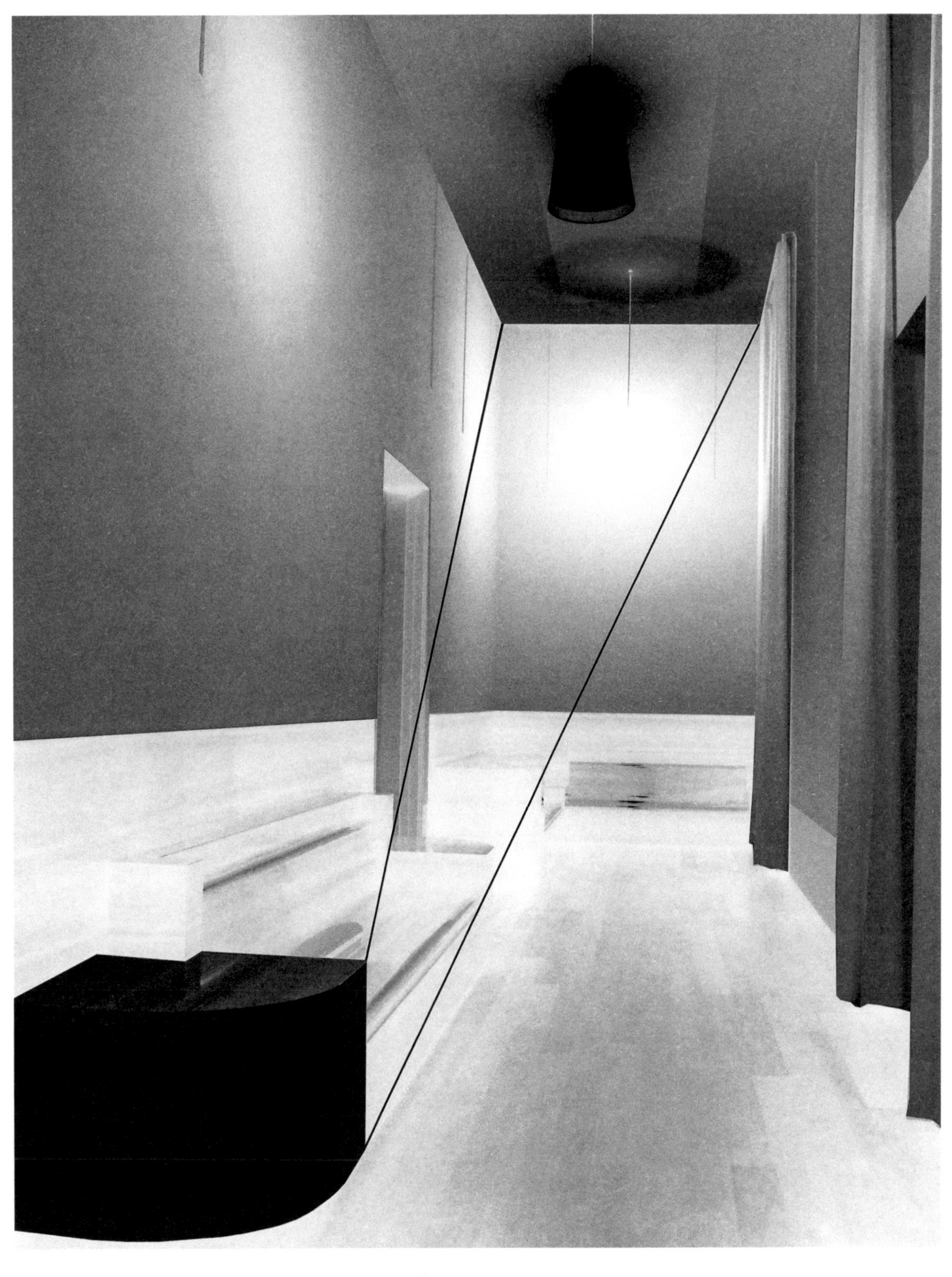

KORRIDOR (GEMÄLDEGALERIE)

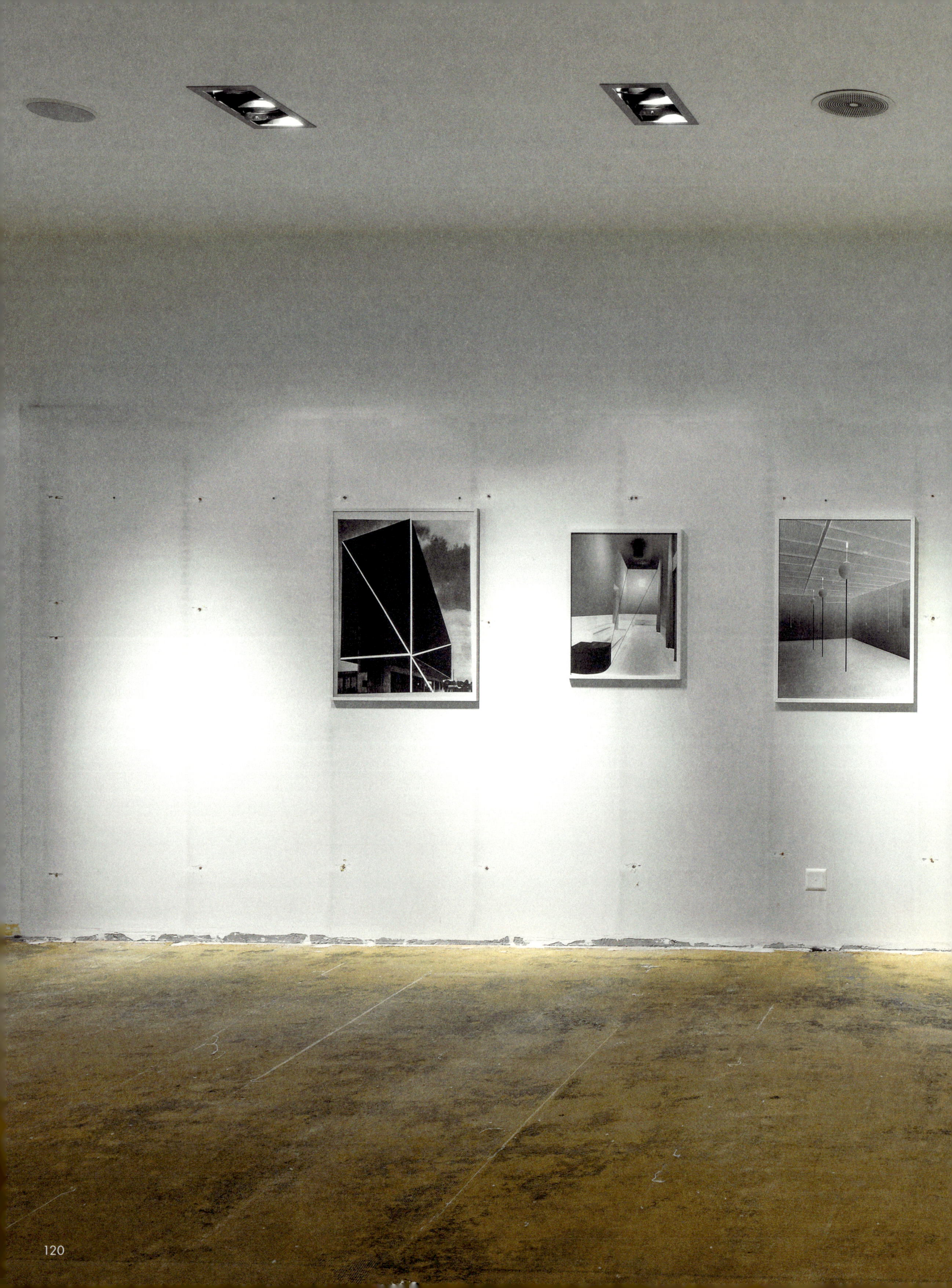

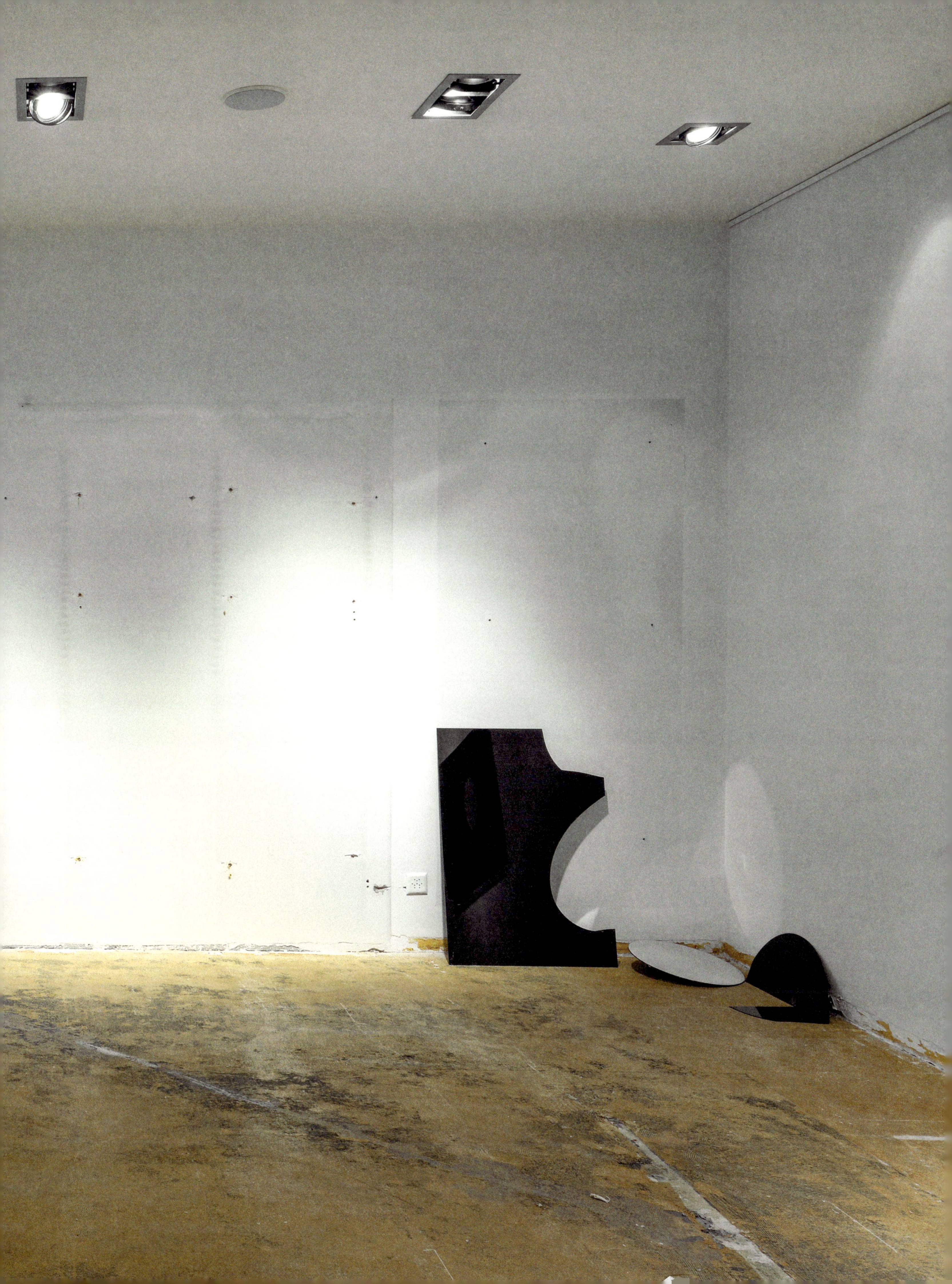

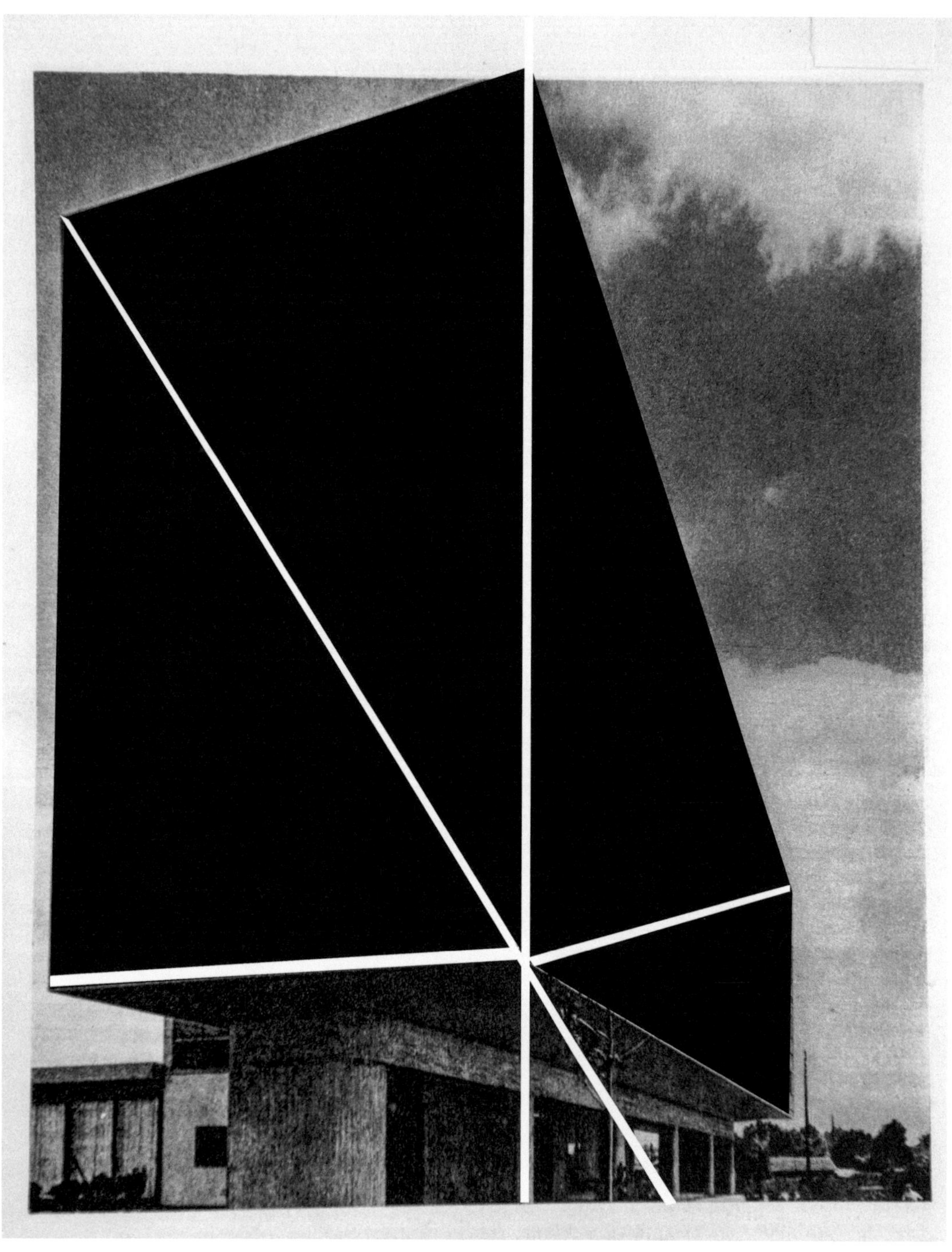

REKONSTRUKTION

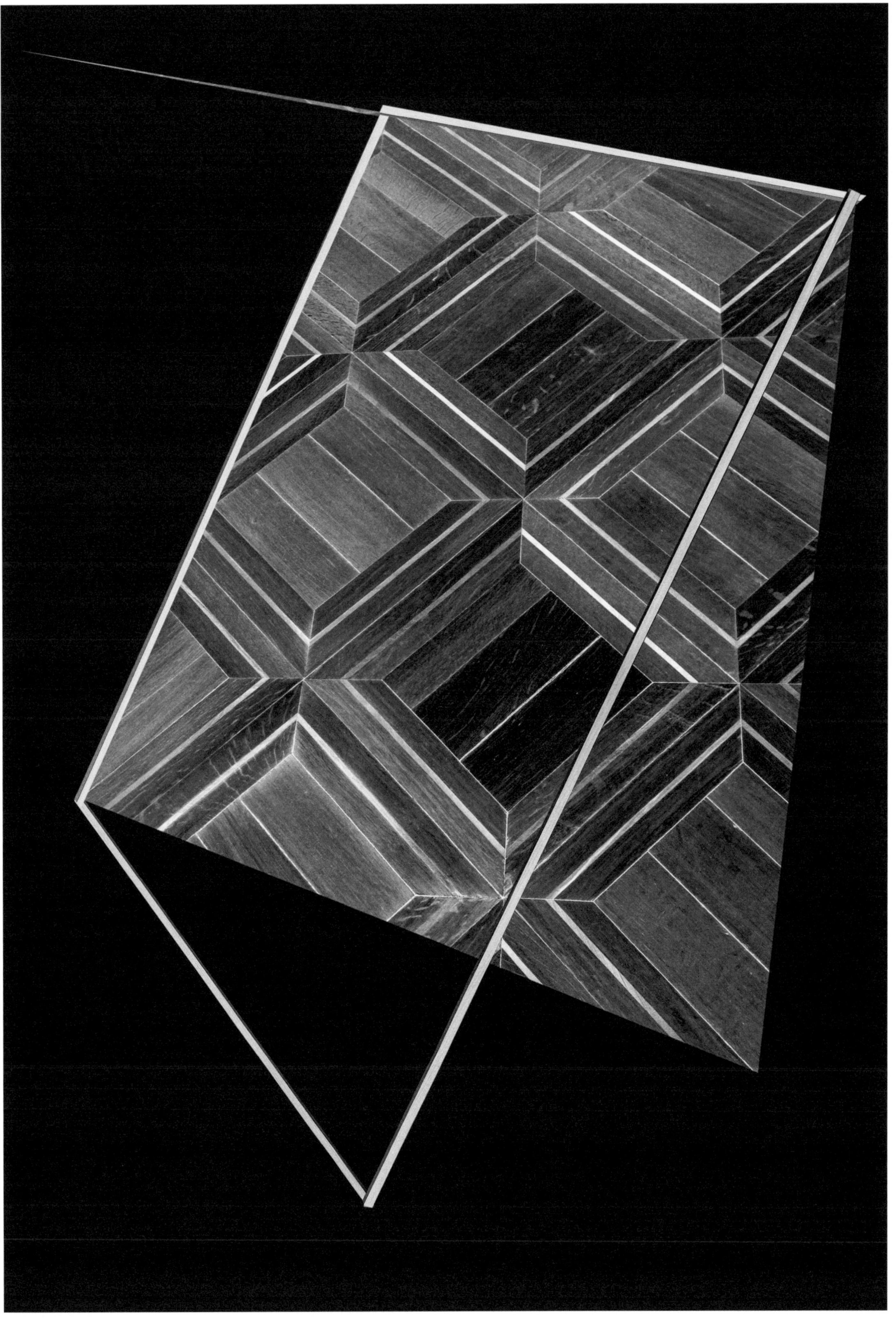

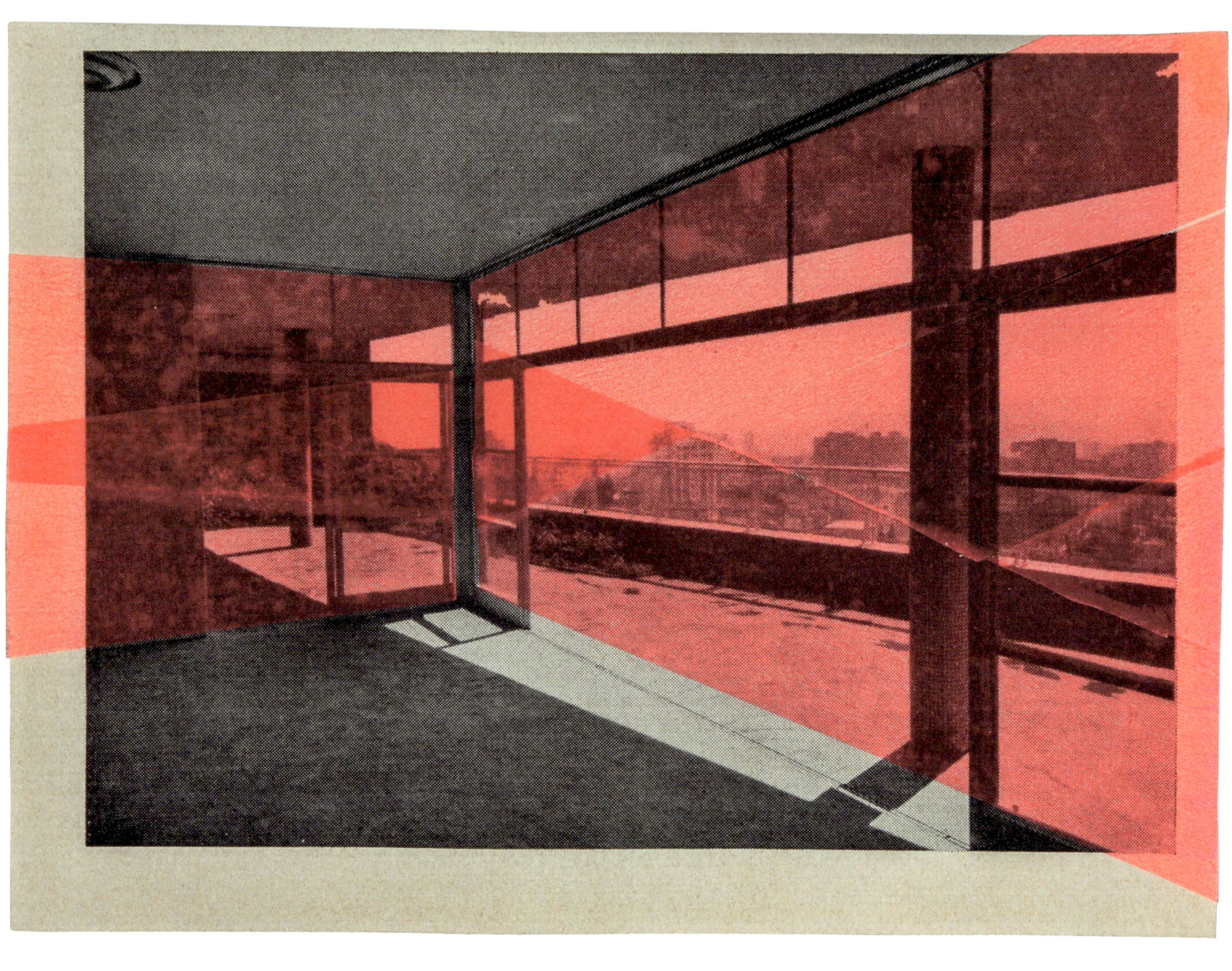

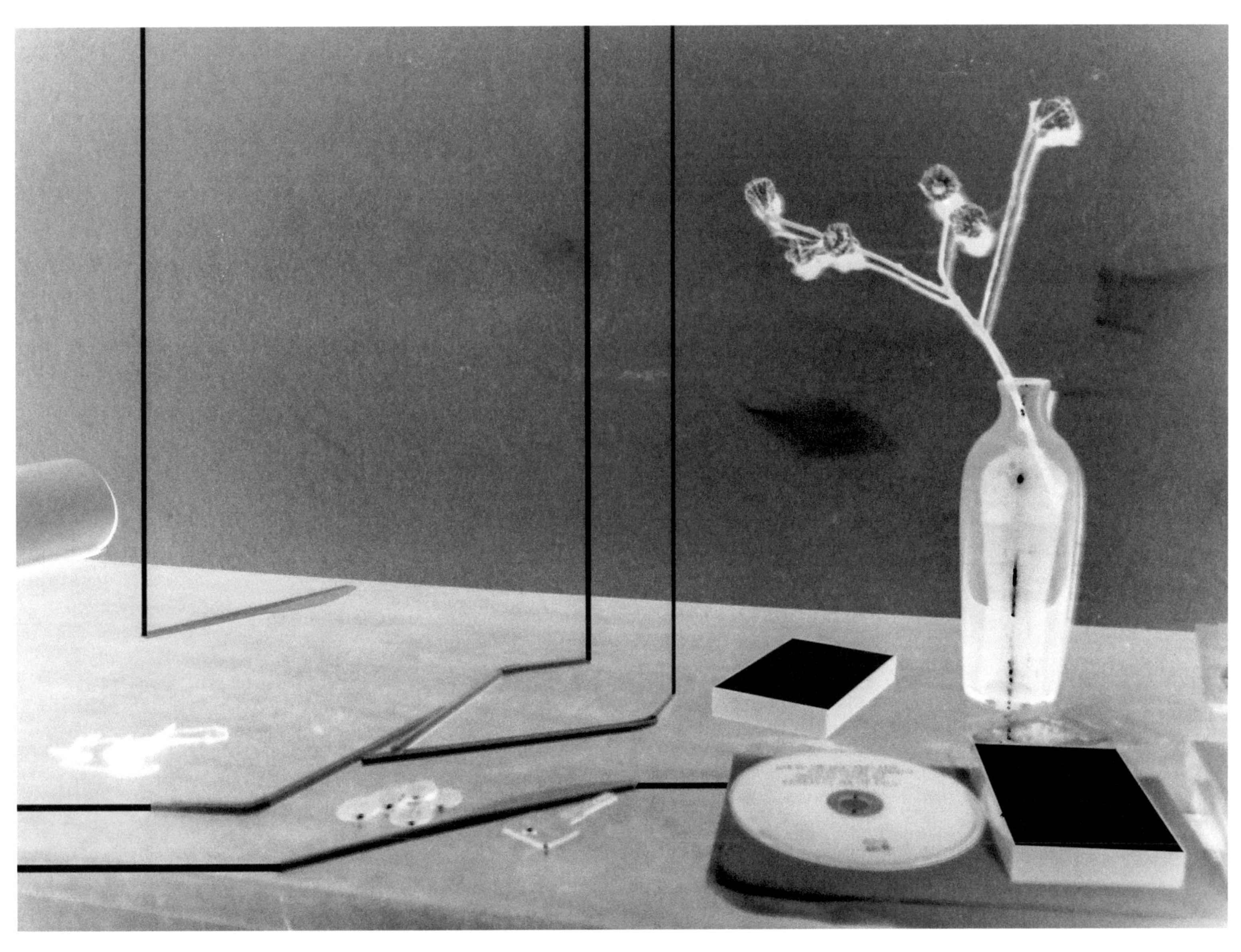

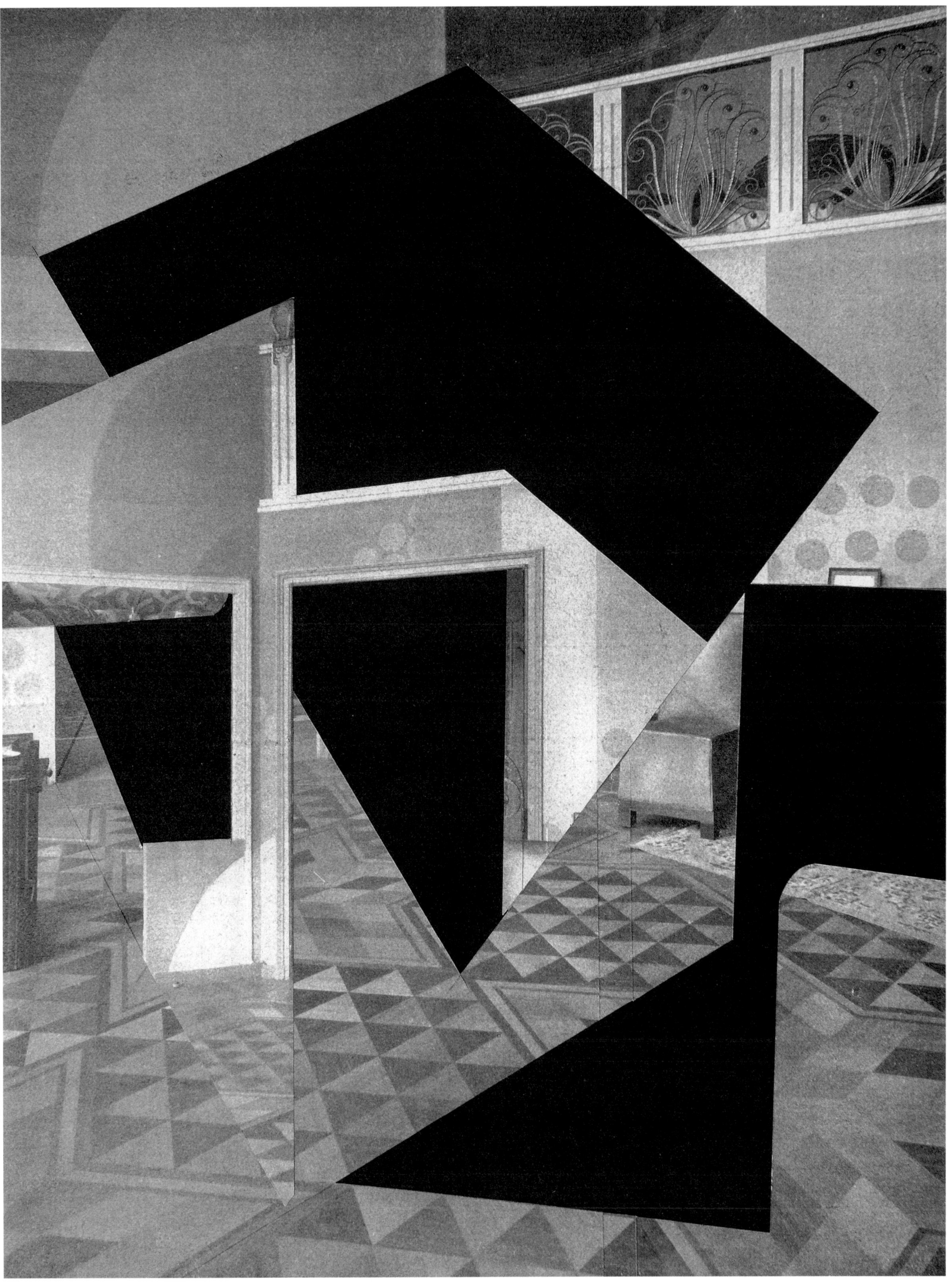

UNTITLED

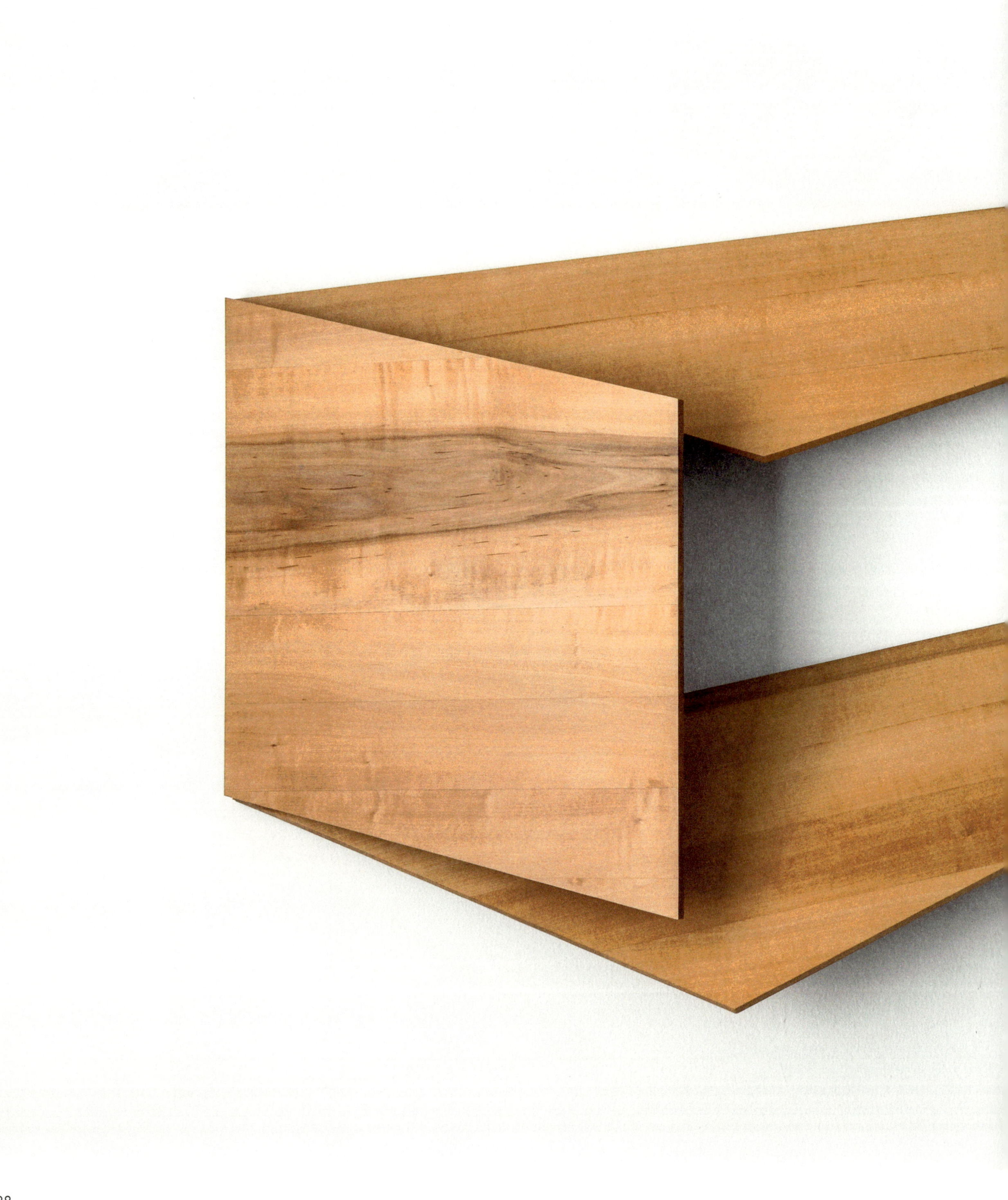

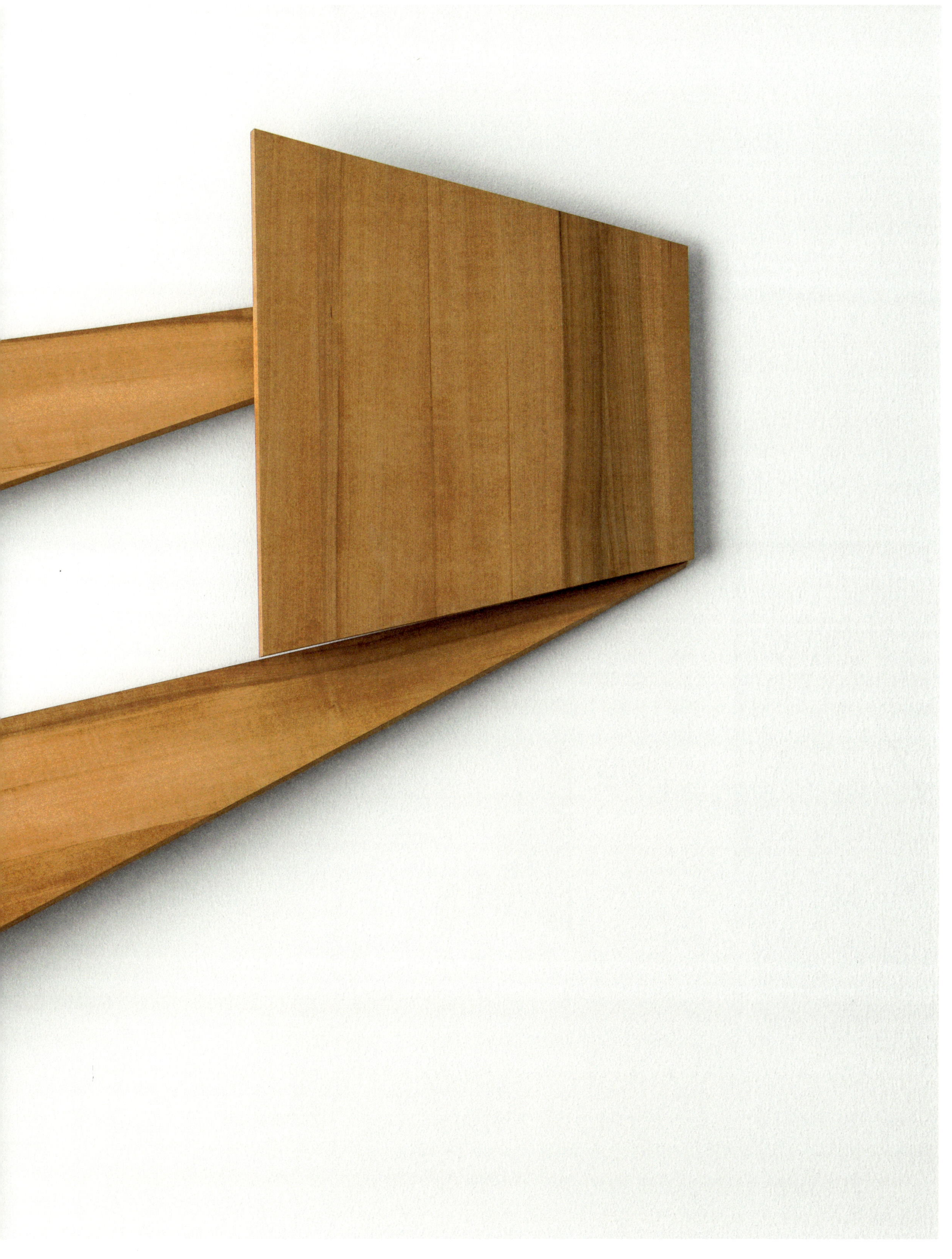

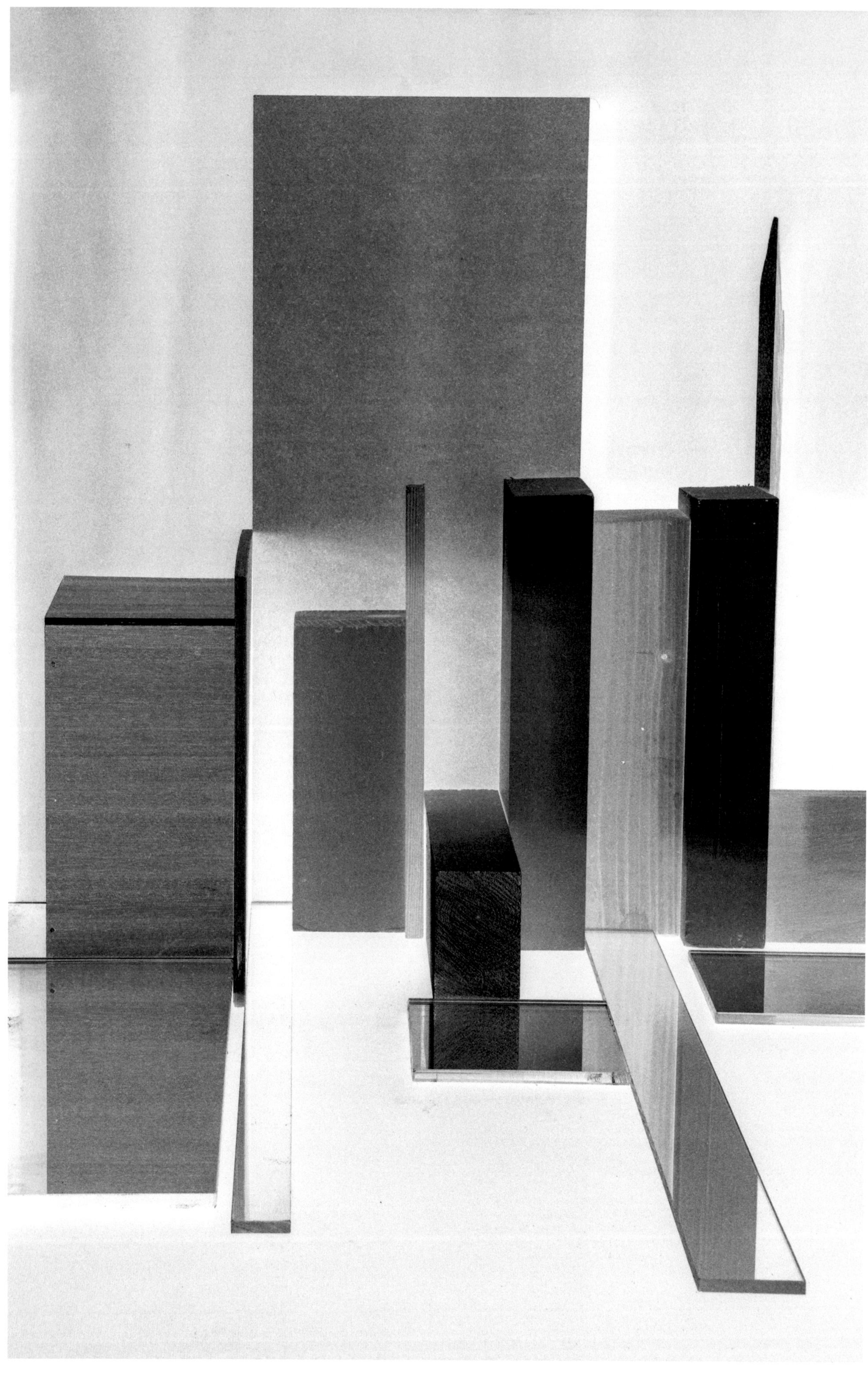

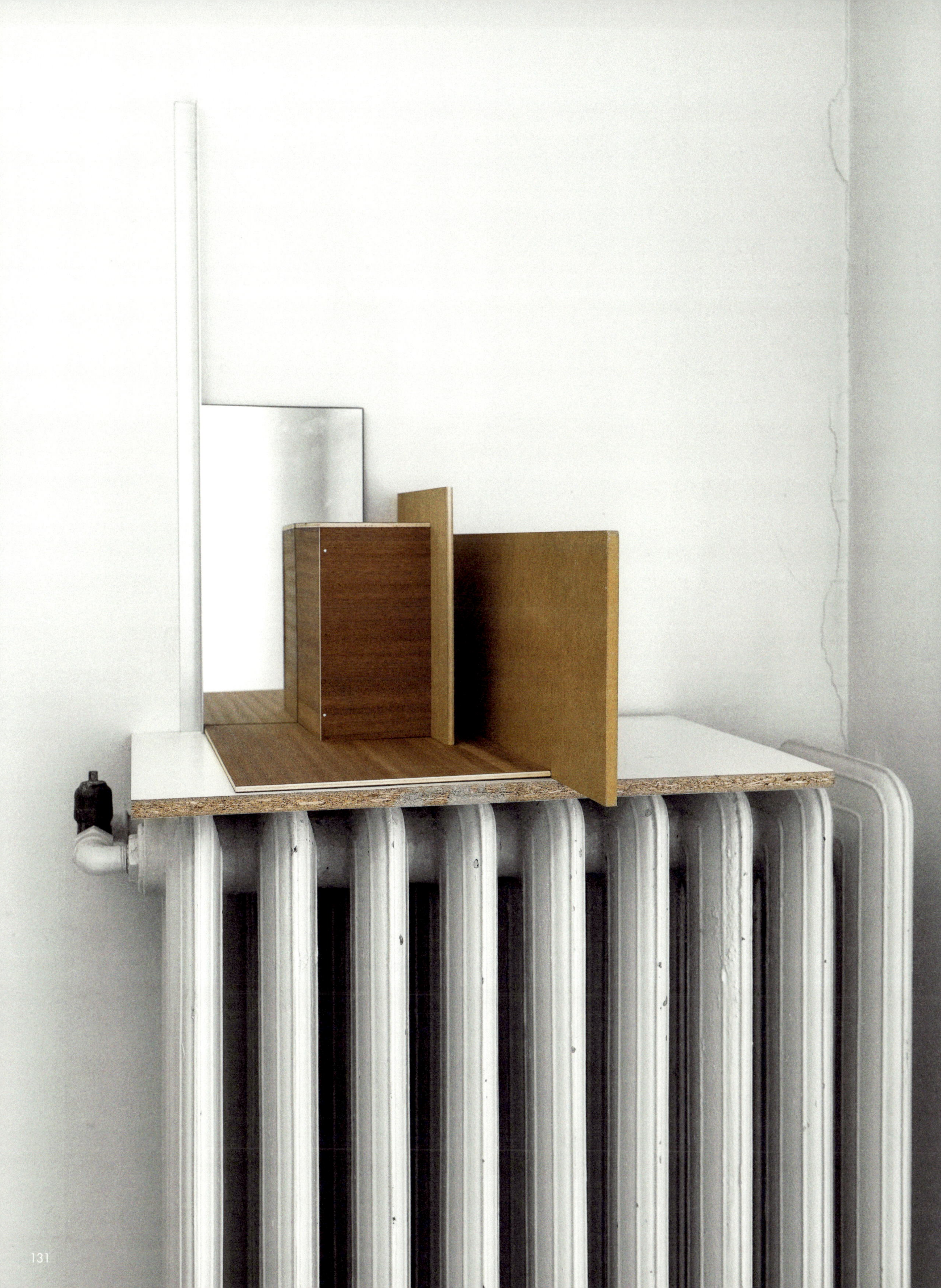

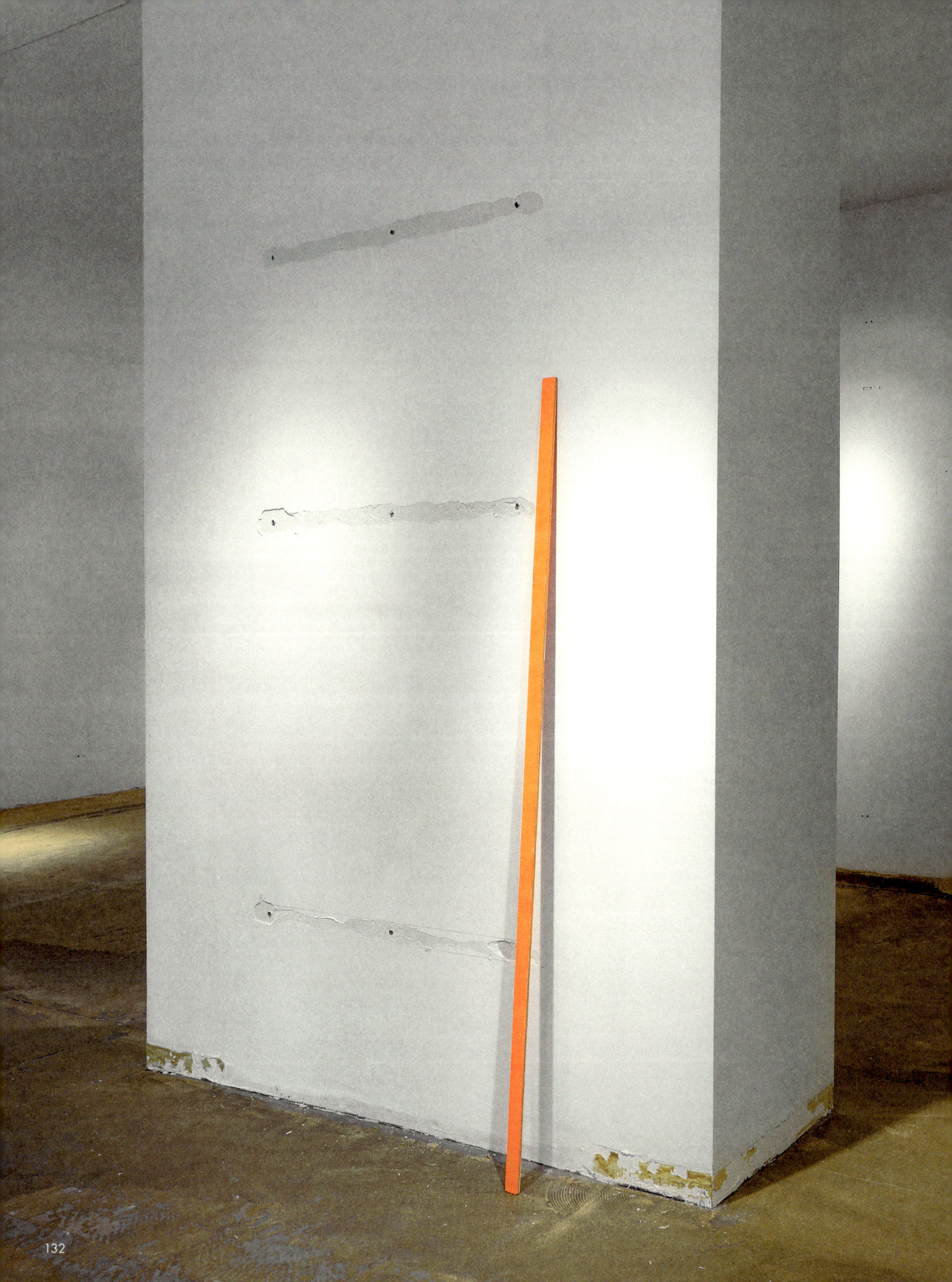

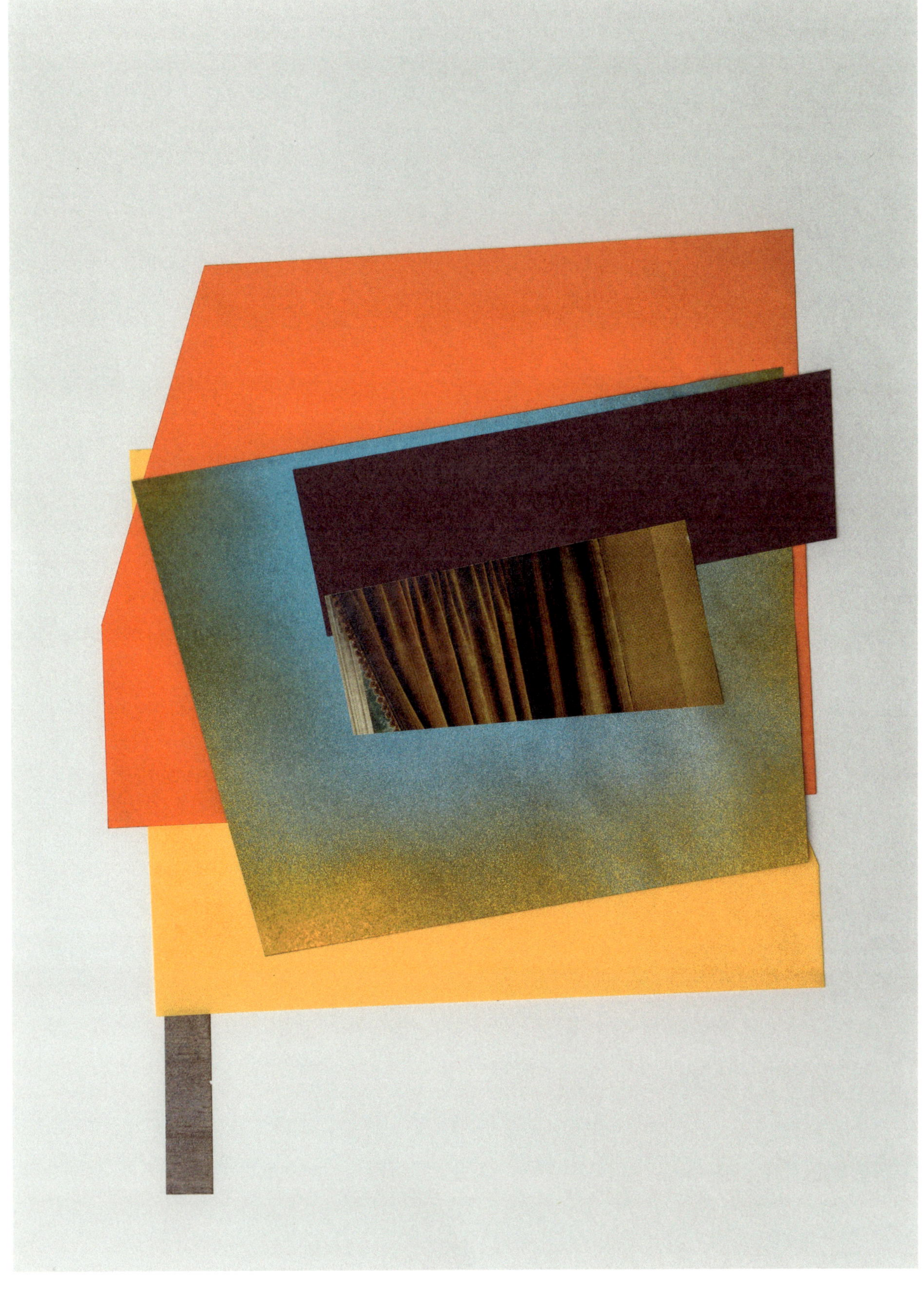

TISCH

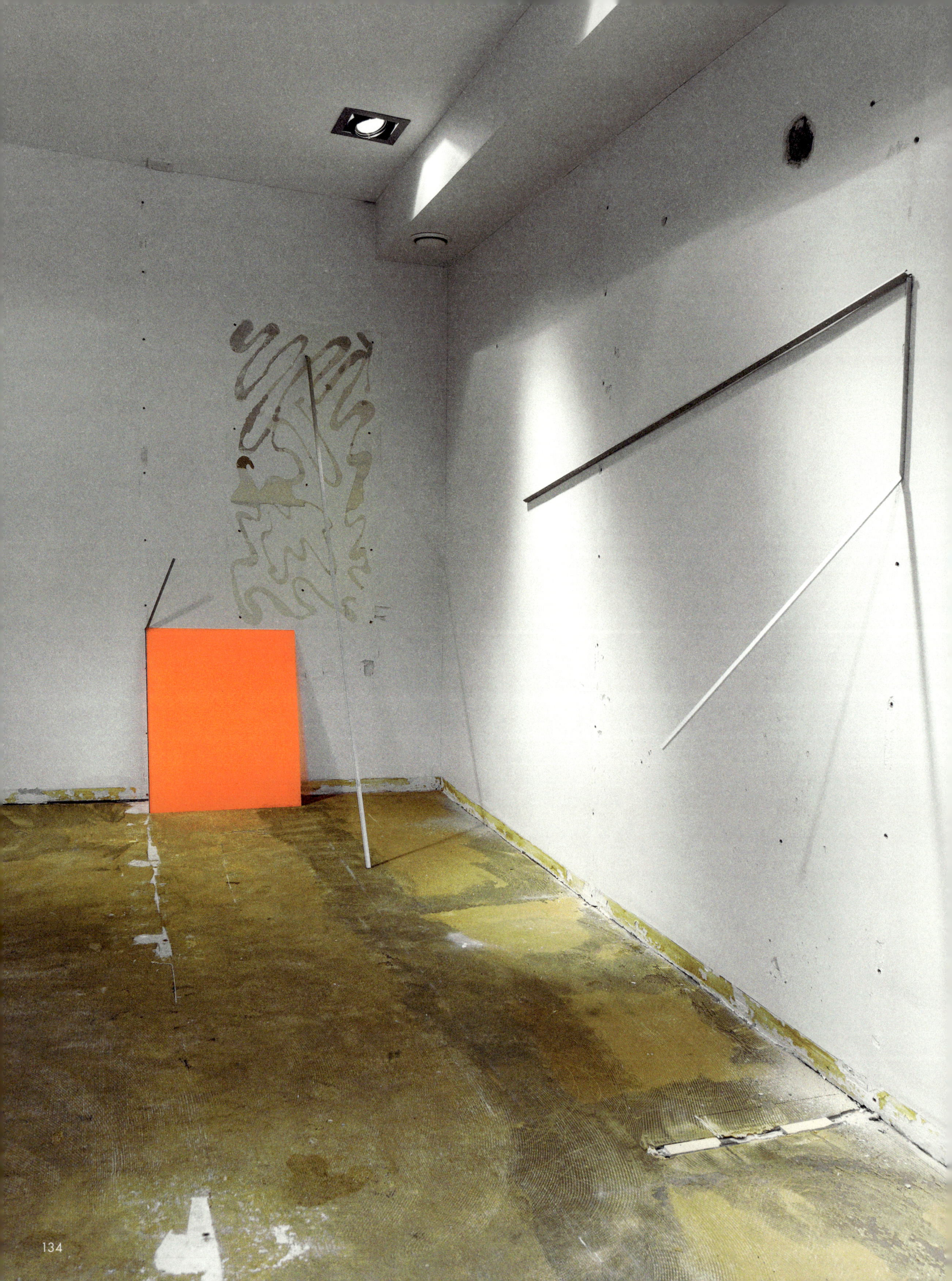

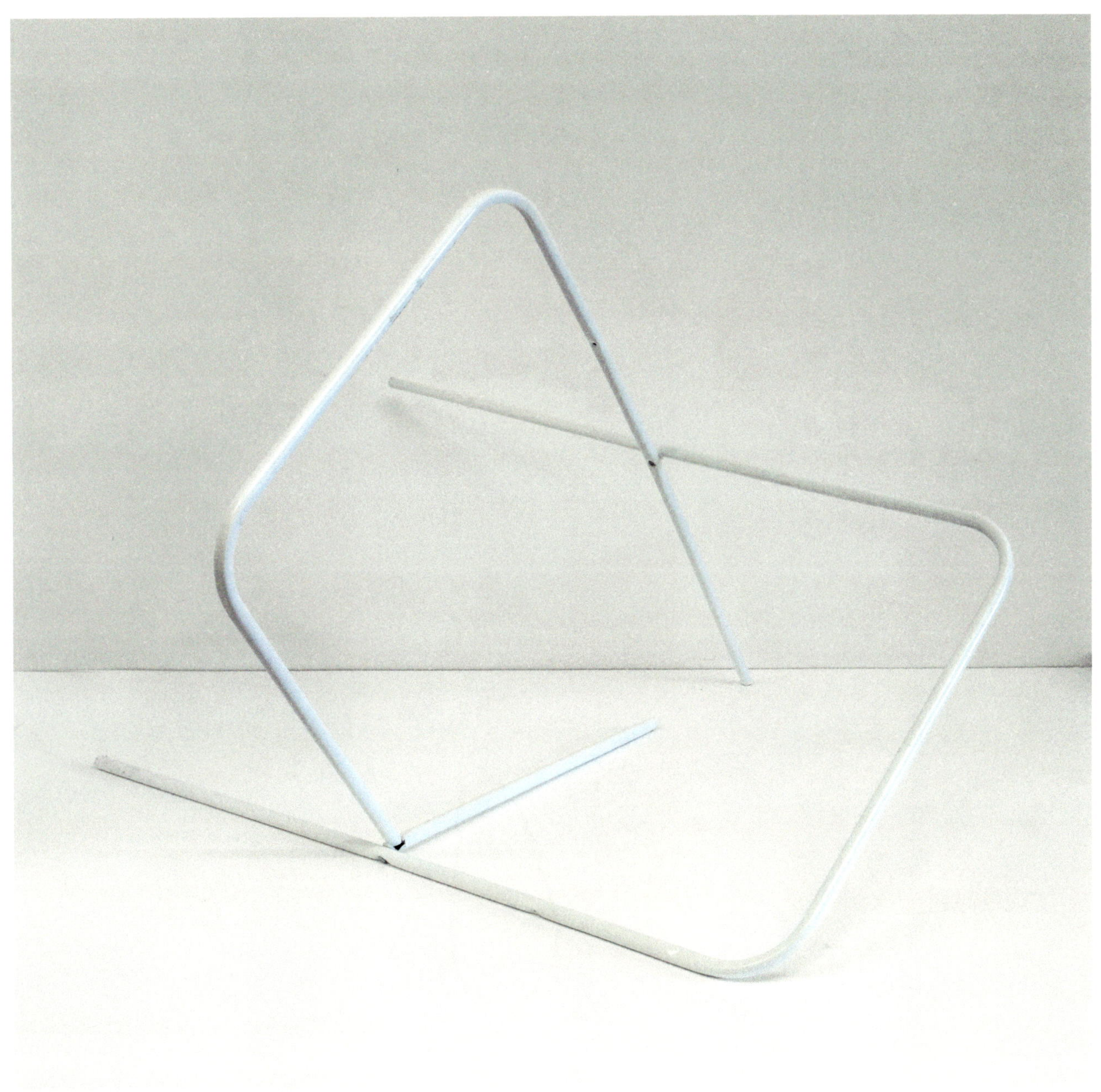

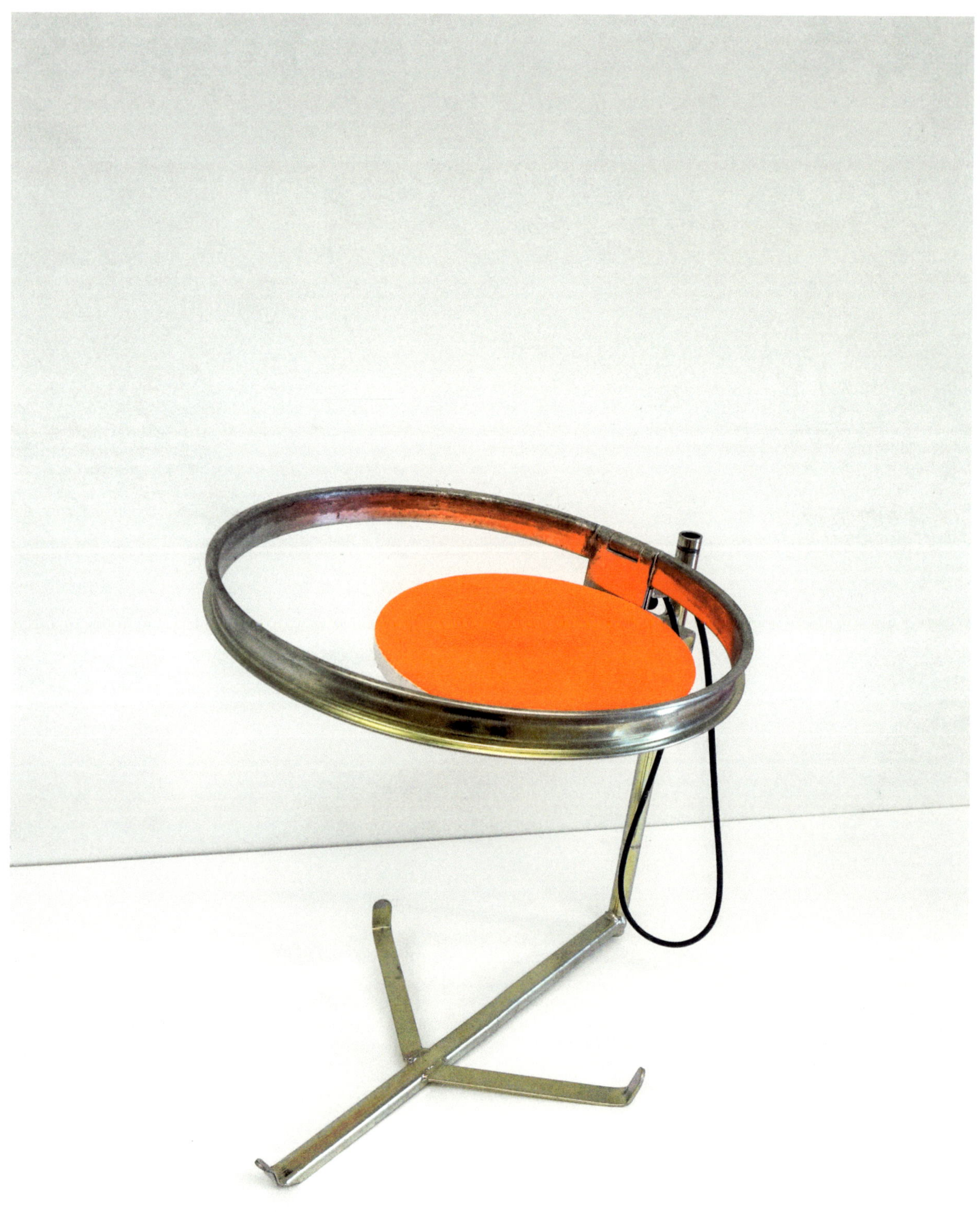

3 CIRCLES

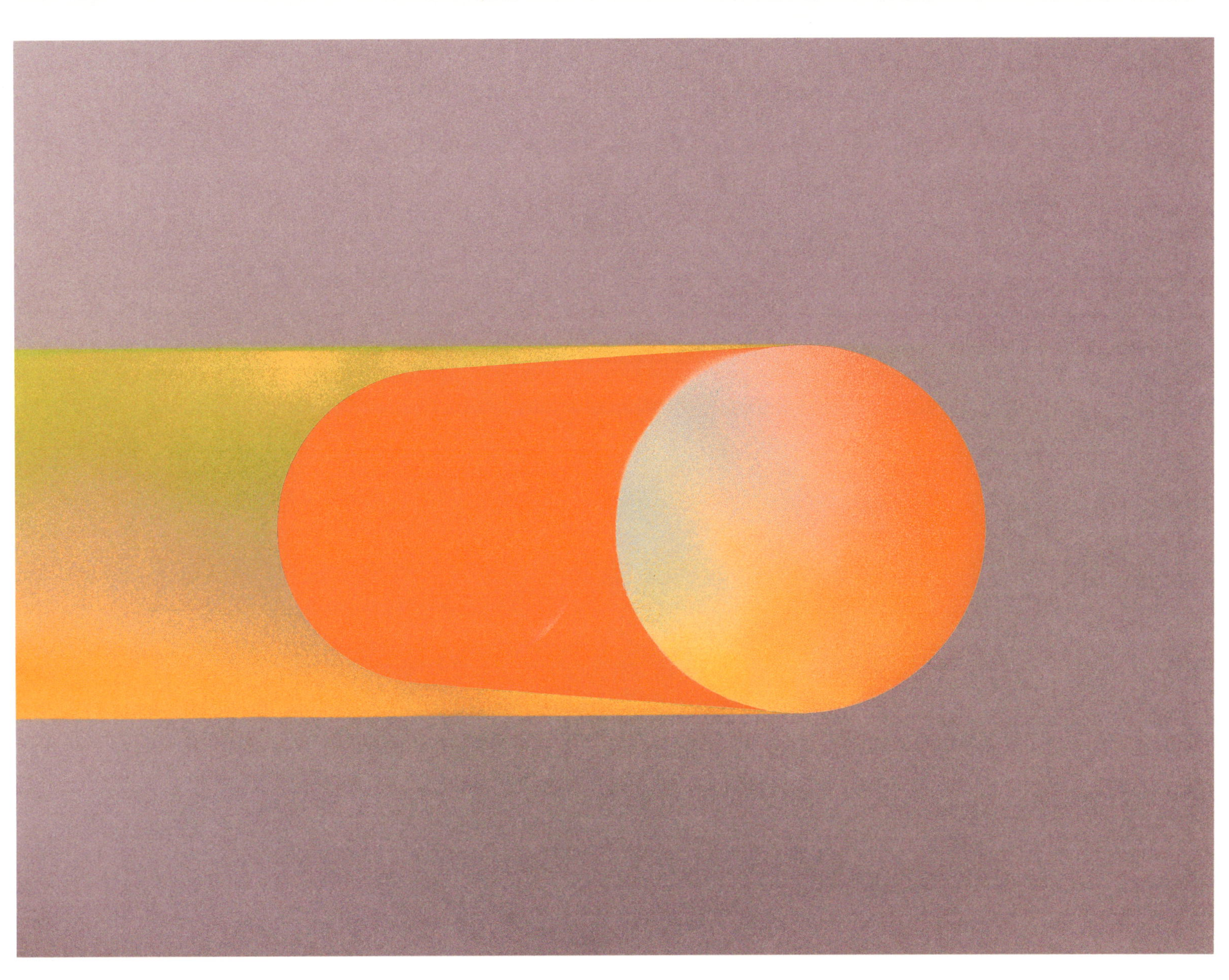

VAKUUM

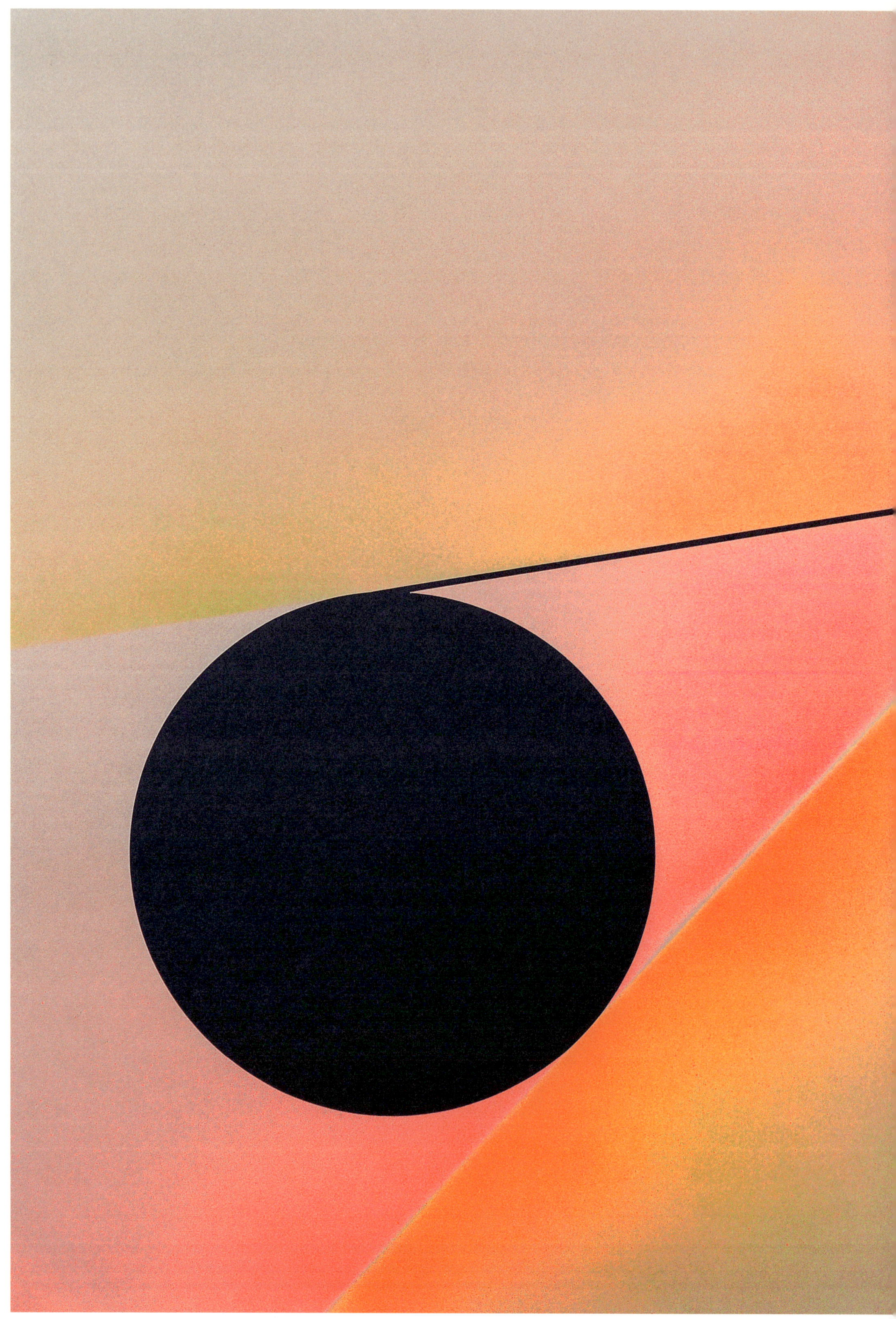

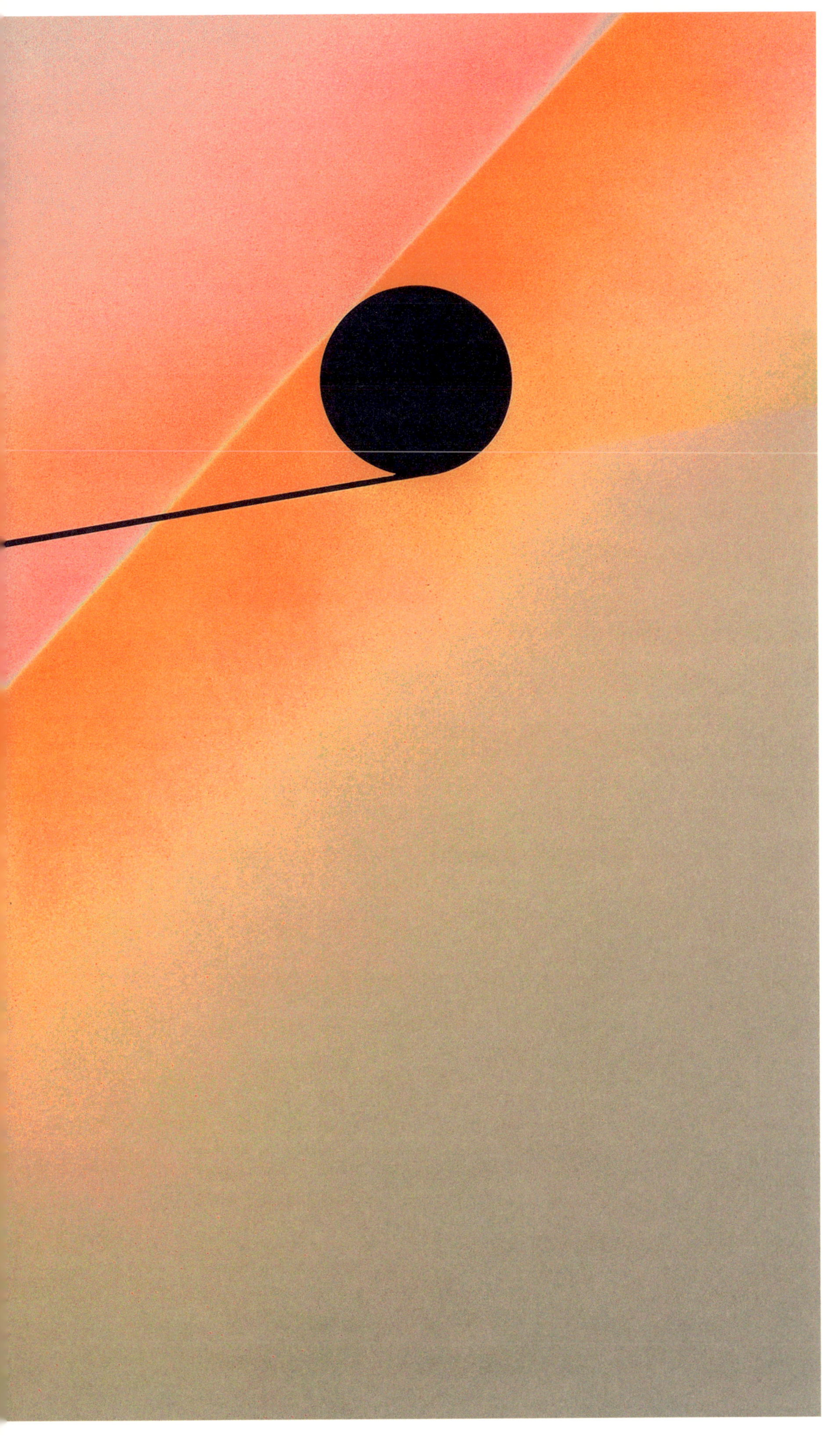

RELATION

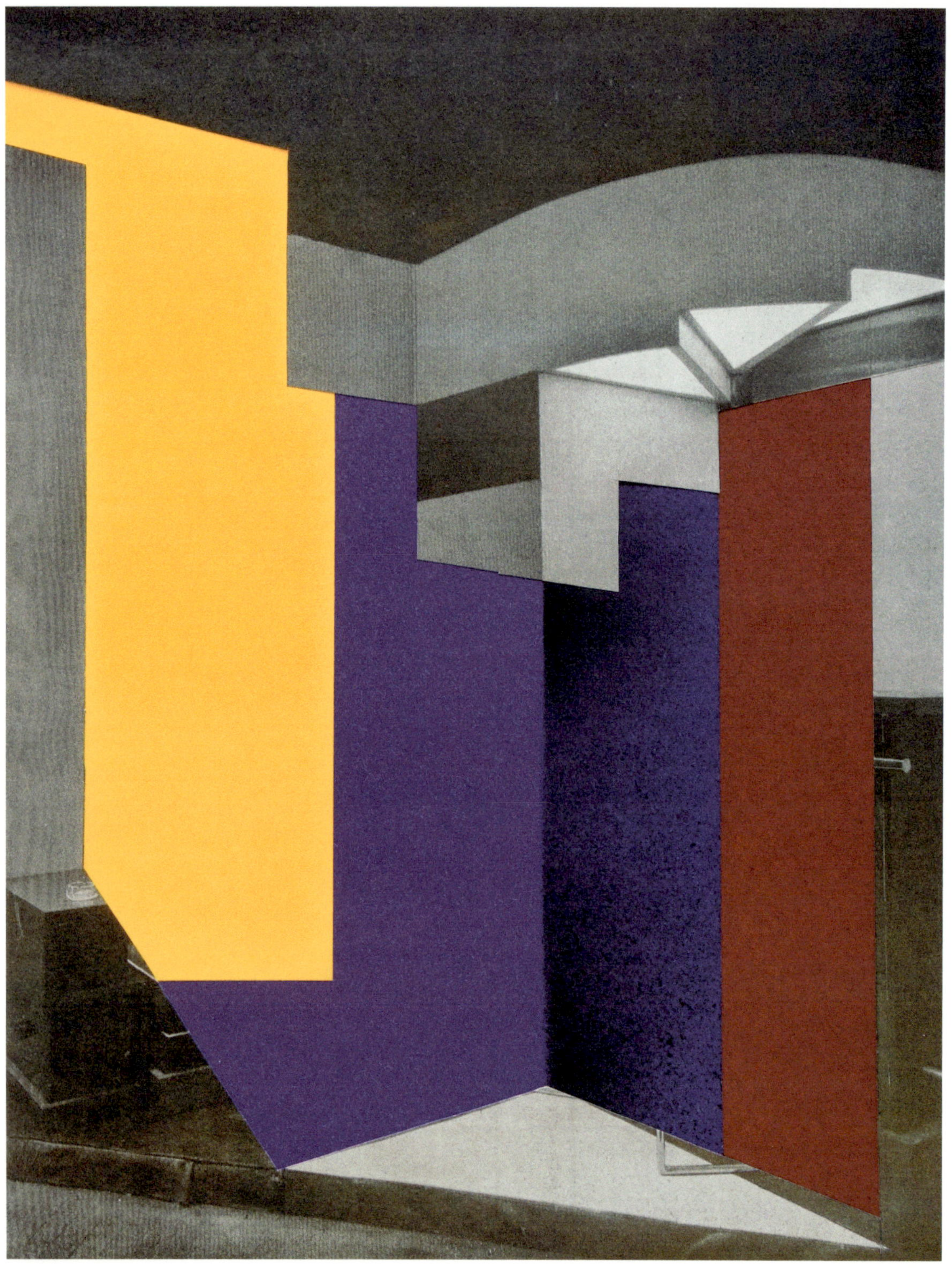

ANGLES

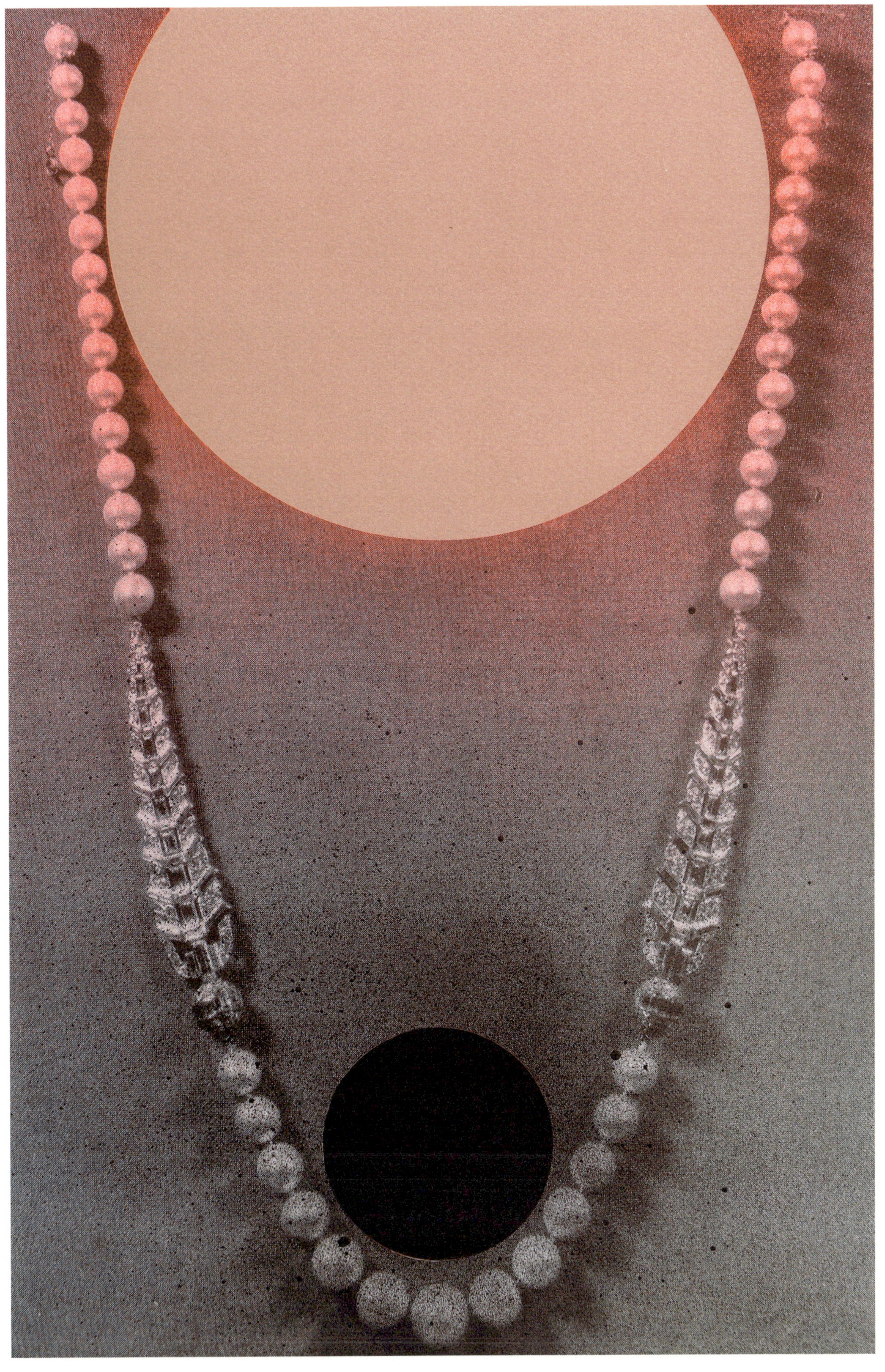

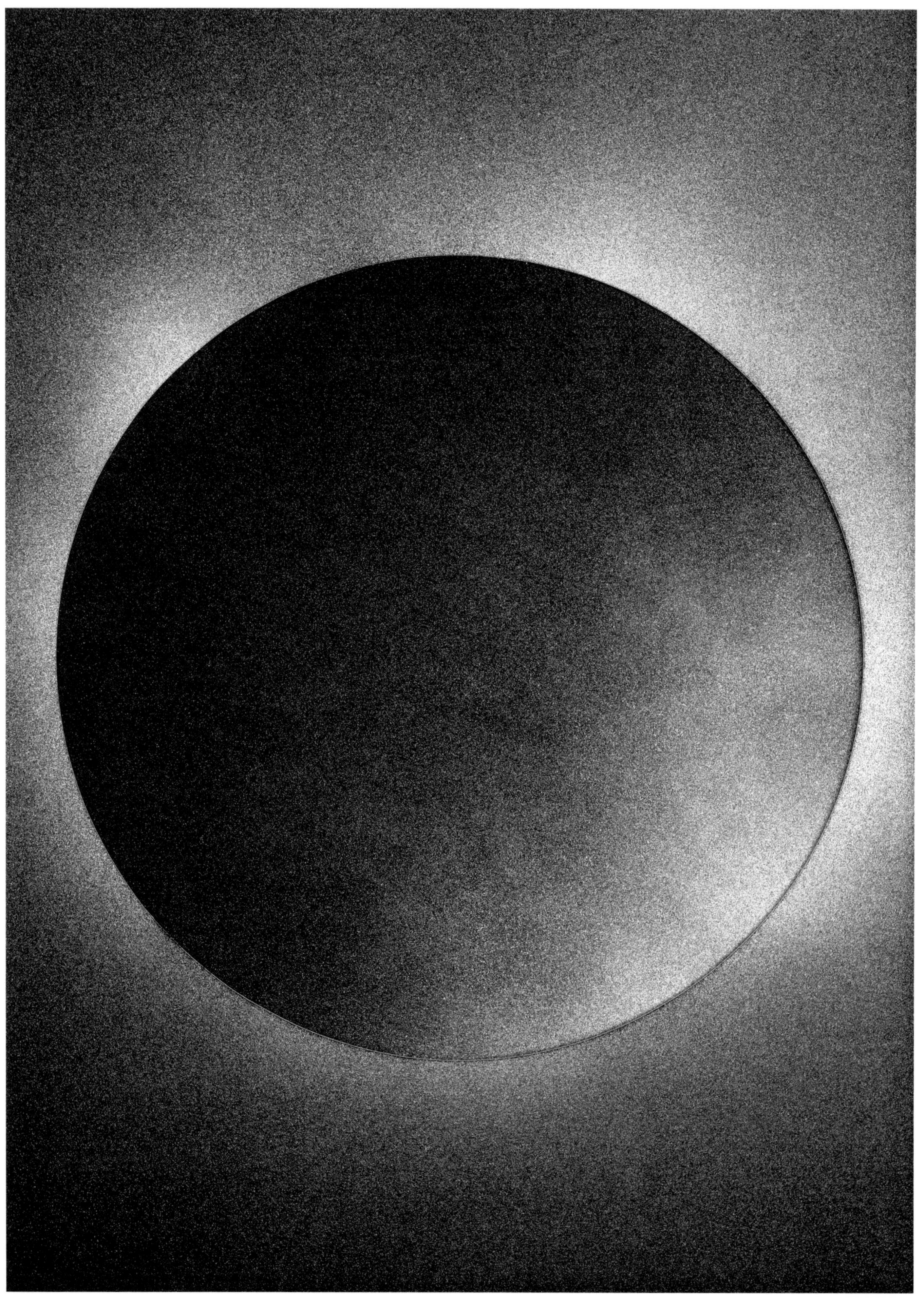

Barbara Davi

TRAIN OF THOUGHT

Mit Texten von   With texts by

Nadine Olonetzky
Eveline Suter

Scheidegger & Spiess   Kunstmuseum Luzern

Nadine
Olonetzky

SCHNITT
WIRD LINIE,
LINIE WIRD STAB
BARBARA DAVIS
POETISCHER
KONSTRUKTIVISMUS

Rätsel sind das Normale. Wir versuchen zwar so zu tun, als sei klar, was oben und unten, was vorne und hinten ist. Wie der Weg, das nächste Etappenziel aussieht. Was Tiefe hat, was Oberfläche ist. Was eine Linie, was ein messerscharfer Schnitt ist. Und wie man eine Kurve von einer Krümmung unterscheidet, was also vor, was hinter dem Horizont steht. Oder was im Licht, was im Schatten liegt. Wir versuchen möglichst aufrechtzuerhalten, dass die Wirklichkeit ein überschaubarer Raum mit einer ruhig fliessenden Zeit ist, und wir uns vorwärtsbewegen, ohne Bruch, ohne Abgrund. Zu einem Treffpunkt zum Beispiel, bei einem Baum vielleicht. Unter der Sonne, die unsere Erde beleuchtet.

Missverständnisse, Verwirrungen sind natürlich an der Tagesordnung. Und wenn wir genau hinschauen, entdecken wir Unverständliches, Unordnung, verwirrende Perspektiven, sogar Fremdkörper. Oder Linien, die eigentlich scharfe Schnitte sind. Barbara Davi gibt uns mit ihren Collagen und Fotoarbeiten Bilder für diese Rätselhaftigkeit. Eine Rätselhaftigkeit, die schön und geheimnisvoll, unheimlich und brutal ist, die aber in allem eingewoben scheint und so vielleicht den eigentlichen Kern der Welt ausmacht. In ihren Arbeiten ist etwas Unerklärliches, Fremdes, das uns aber gleichzeitig vertraut ist.

Die Sonne in BURNING, 2017 (Collage mit Acrylspray auf Farbfotokopie), S. 5 zum Beispiel. Wie ein zu gross geratener, mit synthetischen Farbfolien versehener Scheinwerfer leuchtet sie auf eine Welt – oder genauer – aus einer Welt heraus, in der gleichzeitig eine Sonnenfinsternis zu herrschen scheint: Düster ist sie in ihrem Schwarz-Weiss. Und leicht ist vorstellbar, dass Vögel eben erst verschreckt von dem knorrigen Baum geflattert sind und der apokalyptisch verdunkelte Himmel voller Partikel aus Russ, Staub und Farbe ist – schön und giftig ist die Szenerie.

In DIE FLUTEN DES SAMBESI STÜRZEN 107 METER IN DIE TIEFE, 2008 (Collage mit Acrylspray aus der Serie DURCH AFRIKA), S. 17 dann lässt uns Barbara Davi einen dramatischen Wasserfall entdecken, vor dem tapfere Bäumchen aus einem fast senkrecht abfallenden Hang wachsen. Daneben hängt – wie ein Fremdkörper aus einer anderen Welt – eine verfinsterte Sonne mit kohleschwarz stäubendem Strahlenkranz. Wieder streift uns der Gedanke an eine Sonnenfinsternis, und gleichzeitig sind wir an Landschaften und wissenschaftliche Phänomene erinnert, die wir irgendwann irgendwo in Büchern gesehen haben. Fremde Länder, altes Wissen. Gesammelte Erkenntnisse und Sichtweisen, die, Bildzeichen geworden, auf Papier gespeichert und zwischen Buchdeckel geklemmt, im Dunkel von Regalen und Schränken warten. Vielleicht sind ihre Wahrheiten noch gültig, vielleicht längst veraltet, aber sie harren geduldig im Finsteren aus, bis wir vorbeikommen, blättern. Schauen. Staunen. Rätseln. Zu träumen beginnen.

Von einer Reise zu den Pyramiden im heute nicht mehr so fernen Ägypten vielleicht. Doch auch in Barbara Davis Bild SPHINX, 2008, S. 23, einer Collage aus der Serie DURCH AFRIKA, treffen wir auf eine Szenerie, in der das Postkartensujet eine Perspektivenstörung hat. Ein hellblaues, kopfstehendes Dreieck wirft Vorder-, Hintergrund und Raumtiefe durcheinander, verunmöglicht jede leichte Orientierung, und so verirren sich unsere Augen in der Tiefe dieser verschachtelten Kulisse um die berühmte Grosse Sphinx von Gizeh.

Worauf wir uns sofort etwas weiter ins schwarze Afrika hinein-
träumen und im staubtrockenen Gelände auf den fantastischen
TERMITENWOLKENKRATZER, 2008 → S. 24 stossen, ebenfalls
eine Collage aus der Serie DURCH AFRIKA. Und wie könnte
es anders sein – auch dort bemerken wir plötzlich etwas Seltsames,
nicht in die Landschaft, nicht in die Vorstellung von dieser
Landschaft Passendes: ein hohes Rechteck, das hinausführt in
einen Hintergrund aus zart hellgelbem Nichts. Wie der Mann
im Bild stehen wir dann da, die Hände in den Hosen vergra-
ben, starren auf die Phänomene: auf das Organische und das
Architektonische, auf das Bild und die Bildstörung vor uns. Und
obwohl hier keine ins Unendliche gehende Raumtiefe sugge-
riert wird, werden wir vielleicht von jenem «metaphysischen
Gruseln» gepackt, das Mani Matter besingt, als er beim Friseur
seinen Kopf im verspiegelten Raum wie in einem unendlichen
Korridor verschwinden sieht. Was eine Fläche ist, was tatsäch-
lich Tiefe hat, was Vordergrund ist, was dahinter lauert oder
wartet, was realer Raum oder Raum im Bild ist – manchmal ist
das nicht leicht zu entwirren.

Barbara Davi begann 2012 mit dem Wunsch nach Klärung
zu fotografieren: Sie griff zur Fotokamera, um Werke zu doku-
mentieren oder Zwischenstände von Arbeiten festzuhalten,
ganz so, als ob sie mit Skizzen eine Idee überprüfen würde; sie
handhabte die Kamera wie einen Zeichnungsstift. Fotografieren bedeutete für sie also nachzudenken, etwas zu veran-
schaulichen. Diese Bilder brachten sie bald dazu, Gegenstän-
de – eine Sockelleiste, ein Stück Tapete, Plexiglasplatten, ein
Tischbein – auch im Atelier zu Stillleben zu gruppieren und
für ein eigenständiges Bild zu fotografieren. In Arbeiten wie
OPPOSITE A, 2016 (Digitalprint auf Papier) → S. 55 oder RECHARGE,
2015 (Digitalprint auf Papier) → S. 46 ging es ihr nicht mehr um Klärung
einer im Entstehen begriffenen Installation im Raum, sondern
um eine produktive Verunklärung einer räumlichen Situation
im Bild.
    Um die Umschichtung von Bildelementen zu erreichen,
bearbeitet die Künstlerin digital, was sie als Ensemble fotogra-
fierte. Es sind kleine Veränderungen, die dazu führen, dass
Orientierung und Desorientierung im illusionistischen Bildraum
ineinander verschachtelt werden: Was Licht, was Schatten ist,
wird etwa ins Gegenteil verkehrt; positiv wird negativ und um-
gekehrt. Holzklötze, Holzplatten oder Spiegel, Bleche oder
Latten verlieren oder verändern ihre Materialität, werden zu
Kompositionen in Weiss-, Grau- und Schwarznuancen. Während
die einen Kompositionen etwas Räumlich-Architektonisches
beibehalten – etwa STRATEGY, 2015 (Digitalprint auf Papier) → S. 52 –,
erscheinen andere so flächig, als sei jedes Element aus Papier
SOUL, 2016 → S. 49, und dritte wie REPOSE, 2015 (Digitalprint auf
Papier) → S. 51 oder BODY, 2016 (Digitalprint auf Papier) → S. 48 vereinen
beides in sich. Fläche trifft auf Raum in den unterschiedlichsten
Spielarten. Bis auf Ausnahmen sind für Ausstellungsräume geschaffene Installationen nicht das Ausgangsmaterial für diese
Fotografien, und im Atelier geschaffene Kompositionen für
Fotografien werden nach der Aufnahme wieder abgebaut.
Diese Bilder, es sind ruhige Stillleben, haben die beunruhi-
gende Botschaft, dass die Orientierung im Raum nicht selbst-
verständlich ist.

Bereits seit 2008 arbeitet Barbara Davi zudem an Fotocolla-
gen mit Bildmaterial aus Büchern und Zeitschriften. Bei diesen
Kompositionen handhabt sie nun statt der Kamera das Japan-
messer wie einen Zeichenstift: Schnitt wird Linie, Linie wird
Stab. Die Räumlichkeit in einer fotografierten Landschaft schneidet Barbara Davi wie mit dem Seziermesser auf und beraubt
sie so ihres Illusionismus (in ihren Installationen wirken die
Latten, Stäbe und Stangen wie Zeichnungen im Raum). Diese
Dekonstruktion des Ausgangsmaterials, etwa in den Arbeiten
IN DER NACHT VOM 19. ZUM 20. MÄRZ, 2008 (Collage) → S. 26
und REKONSTRUKTION, 2012 (Digitalprint auf Papier) → S. 122 macht
die Konstruiertheit jedes fotografischen Bilds deutlich. Durch
Schnitte wird das, was wir in der Fotografie beziehungsweise
in der in einem Buch abgedruckten Fotografie wie einen Blick
durch ein Fenster wahrnehmen, zu einem Gegenstand aus
Papier – einem Gegenstand allerdings voller Magie. Durch die
erneute Komposition zum Bild bekommen die Schnitte und
Flächen eine neue Räumlichkeit.
    In Barbara Davis Arbeiten trifft Gegenständliches auf
Abstraktes, Farbe auf Schwarz-weiss, gedruckte Fotografie auf
neonbuntes Farbpapier oder gesprayte Fläche, die Musterung
von Holz, Plexiglas oder Metall auf die grelle Künstlichkeit von
Folien – die Kühle der Konstruktion auf den Charme plötzlicher
Einfälle. Das Messer schneidet Stein, der aber Fotografie ist, das
heisst Druck, also Papier. Dabei geht es der Künstlerin nicht um
Trompe-l'œuil-Effekte, optische Täuschungen, vielmehr schickt
sie uns in rätselhaft verschachtelte, irritierend verschattete oder
merkwürdig beleuchtete Räume, in denen Elemente von Abbild
und Erfindung oder Konstruktion aufeinanderprallen oder ineinander übergehen. Aufschneiden, ausschneiden, hinterlegen,
auflegen: Es sind einfache Interventionen, doch das Resultat ist
eine Preziose, wertvoll, merkwürdig, voller Bezüge und Verbin-
dungen. Was Linie, was Stange, was Spickel, was Segel ist –
es bleibt in der Schwebe. Obwohl der Perspektivenmix in den
Collagen von Hannah Höch (1889–1978), der strenge, aber
farblich berückende Konstruktivismus von László Moholy-Nagy
(1895–1946), die amorphen Formen des Dadaisten Hans Arp
(1886–1966) oder die geometrische Verspieltheit von Sophie
Taeuber-Arp (1889–1943) immer wieder wie ein fernes Echo
anklingen, sind offensichtliche Bezüge dazu wie in PHANTOM,
2017 (Collage mit Acrylspray auf Papier, Farbfotokopie) → S. 80 selten.

Barbara Davis Arbeiten scheinen eher Gefühle, Erfahrungen zu verkörpern, ihren Sinn für die Poesie der Konstruktion auszudrücken: In der Collage <u>RAUM, 2008</u>, S. 18 zum Beispiel verdeckt ein dunkles, ausgeschnittenes Objekt die Sicht in die Tiefe eines prunkvollen Saales und lässt uns daran denken, wie oft wir die Hauptsache nicht sehen, weil etwas Unfassbares, etwas Abstraktes – ein amorpher unbenennbarer Gegenstand – davor steht, den Weg versperrt. Anziehend schön und gleichzeitig unheimlich. Während die Scherenschnitte <u>GRAND CANYON, 2010</u>, S. 63–65 an die scharfe Vermessungstechnik mit Laserprojektoren erinnern und gleichzeitig durch ihre Verträumtheit verzaubern, führt <u>UNTITLED, 2017</u>, S. 127 durch Schnitttechnik und Neukomposition eine Fiktion vor Augen. Ebenso faszinierendes Muster wie gespenstische, fast alptraumhafte Kulisse, stehen wir vor einem Raumgebilde, in dem wir durch Öffnungen in schwarze Abgründe stürzen könnten. Als ob hier Ort und Zeit als zwei verschiedene Gegebenheiten durcheinander geraten wären: kein lineares Fortkommen ist in diesem Raum mehr möglich.

Kommt uns das nicht bekannt vor – eigentlich? Ist die Orientierung als Körper und Geist im sogenannten Hier und Jetzt nicht oft pure Improvisationskunst in einer Landschaft voller Schönheiten und ebenso vieler Unverständlichkeiten? Sind wir nicht froh, Gedankenfäden zu spinnen, nein: Gedankenstränge zu flechten, die uns wie die Seile den Bergsteiger auf Spur halten, zu Neuem führen? Vor Abstürzen bewahren, uns von Etappenziel zu Etappenziel bringen, selbst wenn dazwischen grosse (schwarze, dreieckige) Schluchten klaffen, farbige und flache Wände aufragen oder abrupte Wechsel in Erscheinung, Materialität und Bedeutung einmal aufregende, einmal schreckliche Verwirrung stiften? Ja, Rätsel sind das Normale. Barbara Davis Arbeit zeigt ihre poetische Kraft.

Eveline
Suter

GEDANKENRAUM RAUMGEDANKEN ZU BARBARA DAVIS INSTALLATIVEN ARBEITEN

Es war einmal ein Lattenzaun,
mit Zwischenraum, hindurchzuschaun.

Ein Architekt, der dieses sah,
stand eines Abends plötzlich da –

und nahm den Zwischenraum heraus
und baute draus ein grosses Haus.

Der Zaun indessen stand ganz dumm,
mit Latten ohne was herum,

Ein Anblick grässlich und gemein.
Drum zog ihn der Senat auch ein.

Der Architekt jedoch entfloh
nach Afri- od- Ameriko.

Christian Morgenstern[1]

Morgenstern bringt es mit Witz auf den Punkt: Raum ist existenziell – auch wenn er «leer» ist. Raum ist überall und vielgestaltig, dazwischen, innen und aussen, frei oder verschlossen, Raum ist Architektur, Zimmer, Luft, Atmosphäre – Raum ist dieses schwer fassbare Ding, das uns umgibt. Nur als Synonym für Zimmer oder Innenraum kriegt der Raum eine konkrete Form. Barbara Davi arbeitet in ihren Installationen mit dem Raum, mit dem Dazwischen, dem Innen und Aussen ebenso wie mit dem Raumgefühl und der konkreten Architektur, in der sie ihre Arbeiten realisiert. Die Künstlerin stiehlt den Raum nicht wie im Gedicht, sondern bereichert ihn, umspielt ihn, macht ihn bewusst und so in gewisser Weise sichtbarer – den gebauten Raum genauso wie den Zwischenraum.

Barbara Davi greift beispielsweise Raumstücke heraus oder steckt imaginäre Räume ab. Die Mittel sind immer einfach: Aus industriellen Vierkanthölzern, manche in Leuchtfarben gestrichen, aus Fundstücken oder abgeschälten Ästen skizziert sie unregelmässige Vielecke und Volumen. So entstehen leichte, durchlässige, poetische Raumfragmente UNTITLED (RAUMZEICHNUNGEN), 2010, S. 33–36, UNTITLED, 2011, S. 68–71. Diese Konstruktionen sind mehr dreidimensionale Zeichnung als Körper. Die Künstlerin verweist in einem Interview auf die Nähe ihrer Collagen zur Zeichnung: «Das Ausschneiden hat aber auch einen zeichnerischen Ansatz: Linien entstehen und werden teilweise wieder zugeklebt. Es entstehen Spuren, die ich auf dem Bild hinterlasse.»[2] Ausschneiden, Linien und Spuren sind Begriffe, die sich ebenso auf die zeichnerischen Aspekte von Barbara Davis Installationen anwenden lassen. Das ist nicht erstaunlich, haben sich doch diese dreidimensionalen Arbeiten aus Holz aus den Bildcollagen entwickelt. Die Künstlerin entdeckte bei der Arbeit mit Papier und Schere Aspekte, in denen sie räumliches Potenzial sah.[3]

Barbara Davis Vorgehen ist nicht gewaltsam – weshalb sie bisher auch nicht nach «Afri- od- Ameriko» zu fliehen brauchte. Vielmehr tastet sie den Raum gedanklich ab, tritt mit ihm in einen Austausch, antwortet auf seine Atmosphäre und Eigenheiten. So folgt sie beispielsweise den Spuren im Parkettboden und konturiert im ehemaligen Zürcher Textilgeschäft Perla-Mode eine Vitrine, die es dort so nie gab Ausstellung «Inserted Room», 2009, S. 10–16. Die Intervention ist jedoch so selbstverständlich und plausibel, dass man sich nicht ganz sicher ist, ob darin nicht doch einmal Waren zum Verkauf auslagen. Kleine Irritationen fordern einen zweiten, dritten, vierten Blick. Barbara Davis Arbeiten schärfen die Aufmerksamkeit. Im gleichen Jahr ergänzt sie im o. T. Raum für aktuelle Kunst in Luzern die Holzpfeiler mit je vier weiteren Streben PILLARS, 2009, S. 76. Der Logik der Konstruktion folgend, ist jeder Pfeiler nun dreimal zur Decke und dreimal zum Boden hin verstrebt. Der einfache Eingriff betont das Vorhandene, gleichzeitig irritiert die Überdosis an Streben in der einfachen architektonischen Struktur. Allerdings war die Pseudo-Verstärkung nicht nur perfekt ins Raumgefüge integriert, sondern fast schon visionär: Ein paar Jahre später wurde das Gebäude auf der Luzerner Allmend wegen Einsturzgefahr geschlossen.

1   Der Lattenzaun, in: Christian Morgenstern, Gedichte in einem Band, 2003, Insel Verlag, S. 30.
2   Barbara Davi im Interview mit Natalie Hofer, Ausstellungskatalog 460 m.ü.M. – vermessen, hrsg. von Pavillon Tribschenhorn, Jana Bruggmann und Natalie Hofer, Luzern, 2012, S. 91.
3   Ebd., S. 93.

Etwas weniger sanft ging Barbara Davi mit dem Pavillon Tribschenhorn um <u>Ausstellung «460 m.ü.M. – vermessen», 2012</u>, S. 40–44. Die Installation <u>UNTITLED, 2012</u> wirkt, als hätte die Künstlerin ein Stück Ausstellungsraum herausgelöst und ihn aus dem Fenster geschoben, wo er auf halbem Weg stecken blieb. Entstanden ist ein ausgefranster Kasten aus Wandtäfer, der den Blick durchs Fenster kanalisiert und wie ein Fernrohr auf einen Wohnblock des berühmten Architekten Alvar Aalto ausrichtet. Der abgegrenzte Ausblick hat etwas Fotografisches: Jeder Wimpernschlag ergibt ein flüchtiges Polaroid. Der Blick wird nicht nur durch die Installation <u>UNTITLED</u> von innen nach aussen gesogen, der Aussenraum strömt als Luftzug auch durch die Öffnung in den Ausstellungsraum hinein. Oft nutzt Barbara Davi wie hier Kontraste, um Merkmale herauszuheben: Der schlichte, anspruchslose ehemalige Schulpavillon trifft auf modernistische Architektur, Holz auf Beton, Natur auf Siedlung, Innen auf Aussen. Das Wechselspiel von Konstruktion und Dekonstruktion – der Gucklochkasten <u>UNTITLED</u> hat etwas Provisorisches – ist ebenfalls ein wesentlicher Aspekt von Barbara Davis Arbeit. Wie hier entsteht oft der Eindruck des Innehaltens im Auf- oder Abbau (siehe auch <u>«Kabinett», 2016</u>, S. 98–102). Dies ebenso wie ihre teilweise prekäre Leichtigkeit macht die Installationen lebendig, wohnt ihnen doch ein Bewegungsmoment inne.

Barbara Davi hat ein feines Gespür für Räume, ihre Dimensionen, ihren Charakter, ihre Atmosphäre. Dabei nimmt sie die Gestaltung ebenso in den Blick wie die Zwischenräume, das Ganze wie die Details, die man gerne aufgrund ihrer Alltäglichkeit und Selbstverständlichkeit unbeachtet lässt. So verbindet die Künstlerin Aufputz-Kabelkanäle mit Vierkanthölzern zu einer Raumzeichnung <u>KREISLAUF, 2012</u>, S. 40. Oder sie reagiert mit einer gelochten Faserplatte auf die Löcher einer Steckdose, mit Zwischenwänden aus Aluschienen und Fertigplatten auf die Deckenverkleidung der Galerie <u>«Kabinett», 2016</u>, S. 98–102 und mit einer schwarzen Fläche auf die Sitzbank im Museum <u>UNTITLED, 2011</u>, S. 68–71 – abgesehen davon, dass ein schwarzes Rechteck einen ganzen Strauss kunsthistorischer Referenzen mit sich bringt.

Wie Barbara Davi den Raum mit einfachen, präzisen Eingriffen verwandelt, so haucht sie auch gefundenen Gegenständen mit wenigen Handgriffen neues Leben ein. Oft verwendet die Künstlerin architektonisch-räumliche Elemente beziehungsweise häusliche Objekte wie Tisch, Stuhl, Bett, Türe oder Teile eines Mülleimers – lauter Dinge, die uns im Alltag umgeben. Eine Bettstatt wird zersägt zu Kommas oder einem Yin-Yang-Zeichen <u>UNTITLED, 2016</u>, S. 83, Stuhlbeine ergänzt die Künstlerin zu fragilen Stützen <u>LINES, 2015</u>, S. 79 und zwei Ästlein fügt sie zu einem aneinander geschmiegten Paar <u>COUPLE, 2016</u>, S. 104. Abstrakte Materialkombinationen wirken teilweise wie architektonische Modelle, wobei der Titel <u>RECHARGE, 2015</u>, S. 130 auch darauf verweist, dass die Fundstücke im veränderten Zusammenhang mit neuer Energie angereichert werden, dass etwas Abgelegtes eine frische Bedeutung erhält. Barbara Davi recycelt nicht nur Möbel, Holzplatten, Plexiglas, Äste oder andere Materialien, sie arrangiert ihre Sammlung auch immer wieder neu und testet Kombinationen in Ausstellungen und im Atelier <u>KONFIGURATION, 2015</u>, S. 86. Zudem bildet der Fundus die Basis für ihre fotografischen Arbeiten, wodurch auch ein Verweissystem zwischen den verschiedenen Medien entsteht.

Zu Beginn ihrer künstlerischen Laufbahn fügt Barbra Davi die Fundstücke zu kleinteiligen Installationen, die teilweise an eine Wunderkammer erinnern <u>SIEBEN EPISODEN, 2006</u>, S. 81. Die Muscheln, Perlen, getrockneten Blätter, Samenkapseln oder historischen Fotografien verleihen den Arrangements einen traumartigen, märchenhaften Charakter. An die Stelle der Kleinteiligkeit sind unterdessen klarere, abstraktere Formen getreten. Die verwendeten Objekte sind nackter, oft auch industrieller in ihrer Anmutung: ein Klappstuhl ohne Stoff, verbogene Aluminiumprofile oder Lochschienen. Die erzählerische Komponente ist weniger wichtig, im Fokus steht die Befragung des Raums und seiner Wahrnehmung. Geblieben ist das intuitive Vorgehen, bei dem das Material Inspirationsquelle und Auslöser ist. Das verstärkt konstruktive Vorgehen zeigt sich nicht nur bei der Wahl von industriellen Systemen und Baumaterialien, die Künstlerin entwirft auch Objekte, ohne von gefundenem Materialien auszugehen. Beispielsweise das Wandobjekt <u>IMPACT, 2015</u>, S. 128, das zu einer Werkgruppe gehört, die Barbara Davi für den Vorraum eines gediegenen Sitzungszimmers zusammengestellt und angefertigt hat. <u>IMPACT</u> gleicht einer eingeklappten – oder dem Titel gemäss zusammengestauchten – Schachtel, umfasst also latent einen Raum, den man gedanklich öffnen kann. In Bezug auf den Umgang mit Raum ebenso wie auf die materielle und formale Anlehnung an seine Umgebung mit edlen Holztüren verhält sich das Wandobjekt wie die raumgreifenden Installationen: Es antwortet auf den Ort und verändert den Blick auf ihn.

Licht ist neben Raum ein weiteres immaterielles Element, das Barbara Davi in ihren Werken einsetzt. Sie bezieht die Fenster der Ausstellungsräume in ihre Installationen ein, verwendet Spiegel als Reflektoren <u>MIRROR, MIRROR, 2015</u>, S. 116, <u>UNTITLED, 2016</u>, S. 118, <u>UNTITLED, 2015</u>, S. 138 oder nutzt den Schatten, um die Raumzeichnung zu erweitern <u>LEANING, 2016</u>, S. 134. Zudem imitiert Barbara Davi spielerisch Lichteffekte. So wirft ein Tisch einen unechten Schatten <u>CIRCUMSTANCE, 2014</u>, S. 56–61 und das gelbliche Lichtfeld auf der Wand ist kein Sonnenschein, der durchs Fenster fällt, sondern gemalt <u>KONSTRUKT, 2011</u>, S. 73. Auch die Neonfarben, die Barbara Davi gezielt in ihre mehrheitlich unbunten Werke einfügt, sind in gewisser Weise Lichtelemente. Sie leuchten nicht nur aufgrund ihrer Knalligkeit aus dem Weiss, Grau, Schwarz und Braun hervor, sondern lassen auch ihre Umgebung farbig widerscheinen <u>UNTITLED (RAUMZEICHNUNGEN), 2010</u>, S. 33–36. Und die fotografischen Arbeiten sind ja sowieso Lichtzeichnungen.

Die Titel von Barbara Davis Einzelausstellungen «Kabinett», «showRoom», «fumoire», «outdoors», «460 m.ü.M. – vermessen», «Geo-pictura», «Inserted Room», «Pillars and Panels», «Fluidum» wiederspiegeln ihr Interesse an räumlichen Fragestellungen. Sie verfolgt dieses im Wechselspiel der Medien Installation, Objekt, Collage und Fotografie, die sich gegenseitig befruchten. Barbara Davis Installationen sind ein «friendly Take-over» der Präsentationsräume, weshalb ihr Anblick nicht wie in Morgensterns Gedicht «grässlich und gemein» ist, sondern anregend und bereichernd. Ihre sensiblen, präzisen Eingriffe treten in einen subtilen Dialog mit dem Raum, sie stellen Fragen und verweisen auf Eigenschaften. Die Künstlerin arbeitet mit dem, was uns im Alltag begegnet. So berühren ihre Arbeiten unmittelbar, auch wenn ihnen teilweise rätselhafte Momente innewohnen. Die Irritationen springen nicht ins Auge, aber sie gewinnen, je länger wir die Werke anschauen und darüber nachdenken, desto mehr Intensität.

Barbara Davi schafft poetische Raumgefüge, verändert Perspektiven und zeigt uns das neu, was uns umgibt. Dabei nutzt sie die Grundelemente skulpturaler Arbeit – Raum, Leerraum und Licht –, egal in welchem Medium sie arbeitet. Ob realer oder imaginierter Raum, skizzierter oder gebauter Raum, Barbara Davi macht ihn durchlässig, lässt uns hindurchschauen, gedanklich hindurchgehen und dem Gedankengang um die Ecken folgen.

Nadine
Olonetzky

CUT BECOMES LINE, LINE BECOMES BAR

BARBARA DAVI'S POETIC CONSTRUCTIVISM

Riddles are the norm. We try to pretend as though all is clear; what is top and bottom, front and back. What the path looks like, the next milestone; what has depth, what's flat; what's a line, a razor sharp cut. How one differentiates a curve from a bend, what is before the horizon, and what beyond; what is in the light, or shadows. We try to maintain, as greatly as we can, that reality is an assessable space with a calmly flowing time, and that we move forward without pause, without abyss: To a meeting point, for example, near a tree, perhaps. Under the sun that illuminates our earth.

Misunderstandings, confusions are, of course, on the daily agenda. And when we look carefully, we discover incomprehensible things: disorder, confusing perspectives, even alien bodies—lines that are, in fact, sharp cuts. With her collages and photo works Barbara Davi offers images for this mysteriousness; a mysteriousness that is beautiful and arcane, uncanny and brutal, yet seems to be so woven into everything that perhaps it actually comprises the true core of the world. Her works comprise something inexplicable, foreign, which is, at the same time, familiar to us.

In <u>BURNING, 2017</u>, p. 5, for instance, it is the sun. Shining onto the world like a spotlight that has grown too large, furnished with synthetic, colored foils—or more precisely—shining out from a world where, simultaneously, a solar eclipse appears to dominate: cheerless in its black-and-white. It is easy enough to imagine that frightened birds just fluttered from the gnarled tree, and the apocalyptically darkened sky is full of grime, dust, and paint particles—a beautiful, toxic scene.

In <u>DIE FLUTEN DES SAMBESI STÜRZEN 107 METER IN DIE TIEFE, 2008</u> (collage with spray from the series <u>DURCH AFRIKA</u>), p. 17, Barbara Davi then lets us discover a dramatic waterfall, in front of which stalwart trees grow from a nearly vertical slope; an eclipsed sun with coal-black dusted aureole hangs next to it, like an alien body from another world. For a moment our thoughts touch upon a solar eclipse again, and at the same time we are reminded of landscapes and scientific phenomena that we've seen some time, somewhere in books. Foreign countries, old knowledge: Collected realizations and perspectives that have become graphic symbols, saved on paper and trapped between the covers of a book wait in the dark of shelves and closets. Perhaps their truths are still valid; perhaps they have long been outdated, but they wait patiently in the dark until we pass by, leaf through, look, wonder, puzzle, begin dreaming.

Maybe it is about a journey to the pyramids in what is today a no-longer so distant Egypt. But also in Barbara Davi's image <u>SPHINX, 2008</u>, p. 23, a collage from the <u>DURCH AFRIKA</u> series, we come upon a scene in which the perspective of the postcard subject is distorted. A light-blue triangle upside down jumbles foreground, background, and spatial depth, disables any easy orientation, causing our eyes to become lost in the depths of this convoluted backdrop for the famous The Great Sphinx of Giza.

Whereupon we immediately dream further into Africa; and in a landscape that is dry as a bone, we come across fantastical termite high rises in TERMITENWOLKENKRATZER, 2008, p. 24, which is also a collage from the DURCH AFRIKA series. And how could it be any different? There, too, we suddenly notice something strange; not in the landscape, not consistent with our idea of landscape: an upright rectangle that brings us out into a delicate, pale yellow void in the background. Like the man in the picture, we stand there, hands buried deep in pockets, staring at the phenomena: at the organic and the architectural, at the image and the image distortion in front of us. And although no eternal spatial depth is suggested here, we might be seized by the "metaphysical creeps" that Mani Matter sings of when, while at the hairdressers, he sees his head disappear in a mirrored room, as though down an endless corridor. What is surface, what is true depth, what is foreground, what lurks behind or waits, what is real space or space in the image—sometimes is not so easy to unravel.

Barbara Davi began to take photos in 2012 with the desire to clarify: she reached for the camera to document works or capture their interim states, as though she wanted to verify an idea by means of sketches handling the camera like a drawing pencil. For her, taking photos meant contemplating, illustrating something. These images soon led her to also group together objects—a floorboard, a bit of wallpaper, Plexiglas panels, a table leg—into still lifes in her studio and photograph them for a separate image. In works such as OPPOSITE A, 2016 (digital print on paper), p. 55 and RECHARGE, 2015 (digital print on paper), p. 46 she was no longer concerned with clarification of the process of a spatial installation in the process of emerging, but instead, a productive blurring of a three-dimensional situation in the image.

In order to achieve a shift in the pictorial elements, the artist digitally edits what she had photographed as an ensemble. Small changes lead orientation and disorientation to become interlaced in the illusionistic image space: what is light and what is shadow become reversed; positive becomes negative and vice versa. Logs, wood panels, or mirror, sheet metal and battens lose or change their materiality, become compositions in white, gray, and black nuances. While some compositions retain something of a spatial architecture—for example, STRATEGY, 2015 (digital print on paper), p. 52—others appear so two-dimensional that every element seems to be made of paper SOUL, 2016, p. 49, and yet others, such as REPOSE, 2015 (digital print on paper), p. 51 or BODY, 2016 (digital print on paper), p. 48, unite both within them. Surface meets space in the most diverse varieties. Other than a few exceptions, installations created for exhibition spaces are not the starting material for these photographs, and compositions created in the studio for photographs are dissembled again after the shooting. These images, calm still lifes, have the unsettling message that orientation in space is not self-evident.

Beginning already in 2008, Davi also worked on photo collages with pictorial material from books and magazines. For these compositions, rather than a camera, she now wielded a Japanese knife as drawing pen: cut becomes line, line becomes bar. Barbara Davi cuts out the three-dimensionality in a photographed landscape as though with a dissecting knife, thus robbing it of its illusionism (in her installations, the battens, bars, and poles look like drawings in space). This deconstruction of the starting material, for instance, in the works IN DER NACHT VOM 19. ZUM 20. MÄRZ, 2008 (collage), p. 26 and REKONSTRUKTION, 2012 (digital print on paper), p. 122, clarifies the constructed nature of all photographic images. Actually, we perceive what is shown in a photograph or a photo printed in a book, as though a view through a window. Deliberate incisions make us aware that these images suggesting three-dimensions are objects made of paper—however, without forfeiting their magic—and through the composition as an image, incisions and surfaces gain new three-dimensionality.

In Barbara Davi's works, representative meets abstract, color meets black-and-white, printed photographs meet neon colored paper; and sprayed surfaces on the patterns of wood, Plexiglas, and metal meet the artificiality of transparencies—the coolness of construction meets the charm of sudden ideas. Knife cuts stone, which is, however, a photograph, a print on paper. The artist is not after trompe-l'œuil effects or optical illusions; instead, she sends us into mysterious, intricate, and strangely lit spaces where elements of copy and invention and construction collide or blend into one another. Slicing, cutting out, depositing, and applying: they are simple interventions, but the result is precious, valuable, odd, full of references and connections. What's a line, a bar, a marking, a sail—that remains up in the air. Although the perspective mix in Hannah Höch (1889–1978)'s collages, László Moholy-Nagy (1895–1946)'s strict but colorfully enchanting constructivism, the Dadaist Hans Arp (1886–1966)'s amorphous forms, and Sophie Taeuber-Arp (1889–1943)'s geometric playfulness continually resound like a distance echo, clear references, such as in PHANTOM, 2017 (Collage, acrylic spray on paper, color photocopy), p. 80, are rare.

Instead, Davi's works seem to embody feelings and experiences, to express her sense of the poetry of construction: in the collage RAUM, 2008, →p. 18, for example, a dark, cut-out object blocks the view into the depths of a splendid hall, which lets us contemplate how often we do not see the c l o u, the main issue because something incomprehensible, abstract—an amorphous, unnamable object—stands before it blocking the way. Appealingly beautiful and, at the same time, uncanny. Whereas the paper cut work GRAND CANYON, 2010, →pp. 63–65, 67 are reminiscent of precision laser cutting techniques, and at the same time, possess an enchanting dreaminess; UNTITLED, 2017, →p. 127 unfolds a fiction before our eyes through cutting technique and new composition. Patterns that are just as fascinating as they are eerie, and nearly nightmarish backdrops confront us with a spatial structure where we could fall through the gaps into black abysses. As though time and place had become jumbled as two different facts: linear progression is no longer possible in this space.

Actually—Doesn't this seem familiar? Isn't orientation as body and mind in the so-called here and now often pure improvisation within a landscape that is full of just as many beautiful as incomprehensible things? Aren't we glad to spin threads of thought, or better yet, to weave strands of thought that like a mountain climber's ropes keep us on track, leading us to something new? Protect us from falling, bring us from milestone to milestone, even when large (black, triangular) chasms gape in between, colorful and flat walls loom or abruptly change in appearance, materiality, and meaning, leading to confusion that is at times exciting, at times horrifying? Yes, riddles are the norm. Barbara Davi's works show their poetic power.

Eveline
Suter

SPACE OF THOUGHT
SPATIAL THOUGHTS
ON BARBARA DAVI'S INSTALLATION WORKS

One time there was a picket fence
with space to gaze from hence to thence.

An architect who saw this sight
approached it suddenly one night,

removed the spaces from the fence,
and built of them a residence.

The picket fence stood there dumbfounded
with pickets wholly unsurrounded,

a view so loathsome and obscene,
the Senate had to intervene.

The architect, however, flew
to Afri- or Americoo.

Christian Morgenstern[1]

Morgenstern hits the nail on the head, and does so with humor: space is existential—even when it is "empty." Space is everywhere and manifold, in between, inside and out, open and closed, space is architecture, room, air, atmosphere—space is the difficult to grasp entity surrounding us. Only as a synonym for a room or interior does space turn into concrete form. Barbara Davi works with space in her installations, with the interstices, the inside and outside, as well as with a spatial sense and the concrete architecture in which she realizes her works. The artist doesn't steal space like in the poem, but instead, enriches it, plays around it, makes it conscious and thus visible in a particular way—the built space as well as the "space to gaze from hence to thence."

Barbara Davi hones in on pieces of space, for instance, or stakes out imaginary spaces. The means are always simple: She sketches out irregular polygons and volumes using industrial squared timber, some painted in luminous colors, found pieces, or stripped branches. This gives rise to light, permeable, poetic spatial fragments UNTITLED (RAUMZEICHNUNGEN), 2010, pp. 33–36, UNTITLED, 2011, pp. 68–71. Rather than bodies, these constructions are three-dimensional drawings. In an interview, the artist mentions the proximity of her collages to drawing: "The cutting out does, also, have a graphic approach: Lines emerge and are, in part, sealed again. Traces accrue, which I leave behind on the image."[2] When speaking of the graphic aspects of Barbara Davi's installations, these same terms—cutting out, lines, and traces—can be used. This is not surprising, since these three-dimensional works made of wood evolved from the picture collages. In the work with paper and scissors, the artist discovered aspects in which she saw three-dimensional potential.[3]

Barbara Davi's approach is not violent—which is why she hasn't had to flee to "Afri- or Americoo." Instead, she feels out the space conceptually, enters into an exchange with it, responds to its atmospheres and particularities. In this way, for example, she follows traces in the parquet floor of the former Zurich clothing shop Perla-Mode and contours a display case that was never there exhibition "Inserted Room," 2009, pp. 10–16. But the intervention is so natural and plausible that it is not entirely clear whether or not goods had once been placed in it for sale. Little disturbances exact a second glance, a third, a fourth. Barbara Davi's works focus our attention. In the same year she added a stay to each of the four wooden pillars in UNTITLED at the Raum für aktuelle Kunst in Lucerne PILLARS, 2009, p. 76. Following the logic of the structure, every pillar is now braced three times toward the ceiling and three times toward the floor. The simple intervention emphasizes what is present, and also the excess of stays in the simple architectural structure. The pseudo-reinforcement was, however, not only perfectly integrated in the spatial structure, but was also nearly visionary. A few years later the building in Lucerne's Allmend area was closed due to danger of collapse.

1   Der Lattenzaun, in Christian Morgenstern, Gedichte in einem Band, 2003, Insel Verlag, p. 30. English translation by Max Knight http://www.alb-neckar-schwarzwald.de/morgenstern/morgenstern_poems.html (visited June 30, 2017).
2   Barbara Davi in an interview with Natalie Hofer, exhibition catalogue 460 m.ü.M. – vermessen, eds. Pavillon Tribschenhorn, Jana Bruggmann, and Natalie Hofer, Lucerne, 2012, p. 91.
3   Ibid., p. 93.

Barbara Davi was a bit less gentle with the Tribschenhorn pavilion <u>exhibition "460 m.ü.M. – vermessen," 2012</u>⭢ pp. 40–44. The installation <u>UNTITLED, 2012</u> looks as though the artist had detached a piece of the exhibition space and pushed it out the window, where it got stuck halfway. What arose is a frayed box made of wall panels that channels the view through the window and directs it like a telescope to an apartment building designed by the famous architect Alvar Aalto. The marked-off view has something photographic about it: Every blink of the eye yields a fleeting Polaroid. The Untitled installation not only draws the view from inside to outside; outside space also flows as an airstream through the opening into the exhibition space. Davi often uses contrasts as she does here to emphasize features: The simple, modest former school pavilion meets modernist architecture; wood meets concrete, nature meets settlement, inside meets outside. The interplay of construction and deconstruction is likewise a key aspect in Davi's work—the peephole box <u>UNTITLED</u> has something provisional about it. A sense of pausing in assembly or disassembly often arises as it does here (also in <u>"Kabinett," 2016</u>⭢ pp. 98–102). Along with a precarious lightness that is sometimes present in the installations, this brings them to life; after all, a moment of movement is inherent in them.

Barbara Davi has a fine sense for spaces, their dimensions, their character, and their atmospheres. In this, she views the design just as much as the interstitial spaces, the whole and also details that are so common or obvious one tends to not even notice them. In this way, the artist combines surface-mounted conduits with squared timber to a spatial drawing <u>KREISLAUF, 2012</u>⭢ p. 40. Or she reacts to the holes in an electrical outlet with perforated fiberboard, to the gallery's ceiling paneling with partitions made of aluminum rails and prefabricated slabs <u>"Kabinett," 2016</u>⭢ pp. 98–102, and to the bench in the museum with a black surface <u>UNTITLED, 2011</u>⭢ pp. 68–71—leaving aside the fact that a black rectangle brings an entire bouquet of art-historical references along with it.

Davi breathes new life into found objects with just a few moves in the same way that she transforms space with simple, precise interventions. The artist often uses architectural-spatial elements, or household objects such as tables, chairs, beds, doors, or parts of a trashcan—simple things that surround us in our everyday lives. A bed is sawn into commas or a yin-yang symbol <u>UNTITLED, 2016</u>⭢ p. 83; the artist completes chair legs, creating a fragile support <u>LINES, 2015</u>⭢ p. 79; and she joins two branches to a snuggling couple <u>COUPLE, 2016</u>⭢ p. 104. Abstract combinations of materials seem, in part, like architectural models whereby the title <u>RECHARGE, 2015</u>⭢ p. 130 also points out that in changed circumstances, the found pieces can be reinforced with new energy; that something discarded can be given a new meaning. Barbara Davi not only recycles furniture, wood panels, acrylic glass, branches, and other material; she also continually rearranges her collection and tests out combinations in exhibitions and in the studio <u>KONFIGURATION, 2015</u>⭢ p. 86. In addition, this inventory forms the basis of her photographic works, which likewise creates a reference system between the various media.

At the start of her artistic career, Barbra Davi joined the found pieces to detailed installations, which are, in part, reminiscent of curiosity cabinets <u>SIEBEN EPISODEN, 2006</u>⭢ p. 81. The shells, pearls, dried leaves, seed capsules, and historical photographs make the arrangements seem dreamy, like a fairytale. Clearer, more abstract forms now appear rather than the attention to detail. The objects used are bare, often seemingly industrial: a folding chair without fabric, bent aluminum profiles, or perforated rails. The narrative component is less important; focus is on the questioning of space and its perception. What remains is an intuitive approach in which the material is a source of inspiration and catalyst. The reinforced structural approach is shown not only in the selection of industrial systems and building materials, the artist also designs objects without starting from found materials. The wall object <u>IMPACT, 2015</u>⭢ p. 128, for example, belongs to a work group that Barbara Davi compiled and produced for the foyer of a tasteful conference room. <u>IMPACT</u> resembles a folded—or like its title, crushed—box, which encompasses a latent space that one can theoretically open up. In terms of its way of dealing with space, as well as the material and formal dependence on its environment with noble wooden doors, the wall object behaves like the extensive installations: It responds to the site and changes the gaze upon it.

In addition to space, light is a further immaterial element that Davi employs in her works. She includes the window of the exhibition spaces in her installations, uses mirrors as reflectors <u>MIRROR, MIRROR, 2015</u>⭢ p. 116; <u>UNTITLED, 2016</u>⭢ p. 118; <u>UNTITLED, 2015</u>⭢ p. 138 or uses a shadow to expand a three-dimensional drawing <u>LEANING, 2016</u>⭢ p. 134. In addition, Barbara Davi playfully imitates light effects. In this way, a table casts a faux shadow <u>CIRCUMSTANCE, 2014</u>⭢ pp. 56–61 and the yellowish light field on the wall is painted rather than sunshine coming through the window <u>KONSTRUKT, 2011</u>⭢ p. 73. Also the neon colors that Davi inserts in her mainly non-colorful works are a type of light element. They not only brashly radiate from the white, gray, black, and brown, but also let their surroundings colorfully reverberate <u>UNTITLED (RAUMZEICHNUNGEN), 2010</u>⭢ pp. 33–36. And the photographs are, anyway, light drawings.

The title of Barbara Davi's solo exhibitions "Kabinett," "show-Room," "fumoire," "outdoors," "460 m.ü.M. – vermessen," "Geo-pictura,""Inserted Room," "Pillars and Panels," and "Fluidum" reflect her interest in spatial issues. She pursues this in the inter-play of mutually enriching media—installation, object, collage, and photography. Davi's installations are a "friendly take-over" of the presentation spaces, which is why their view is not "loathsome and obscene" as in Morgenstern's poem, but stimu-lating and rewarding. The sensitive, precise interventions enter into a subtle dialogue with the space; they ask questions and point out characteristics. The artist works with what we encoun-ter in everyday life. Thus, her works touch us directly, even when they embrace, in part, enigmatic moments. Although not striking, the disturbances become more intense the longer we look at the works and think about them.

Barbara Davi creates spatial structures, changes per-spectives, and shows us anew what surrounds us. In doing so, regardless of the medium in which she works she uses the basic elements of sculptural work—space, empty space, and light. Whether real or imagined space, sketched or built space, Barbara Davi makes it permeable, allows us to look through it, pass through it intellectually, and follow our thoughts around the corner.

Biografie / Biography

Barbara Davi, 1971 in Luzern ge-
boren, studierte von 1989 bis
1994 an der Zürcher Hochschule
der Künste (ZHdK) und von 1988
bis 1989 sowie 2005 bis 2006 an
der Hochschule Luzern – Design
& Kunst (HSLU). Nach Atelierauf-
enthalten in Paris, Berlin und
Chicago lebt und arbeitet sie in
Luzern. /
Barbara Davi, born in Lucerne in
1971, studied at the Zurich University of the Arts (ZHdK) from 1989
to 1994 and at The Lucerne School
of Art and Design at the Lucerne
University of Applied Arts and
Sciences (HSLU) from 1988 to 1989
and 2005 to 2006. Following
studio residencies in Paris, Berlin,
and Chicago, she now lives and
works in Lucerne.

www.barbaradavi.ch

Impressum / Imprint

Dieses Buch erscheint anlässlich
der Ausstellung /
This book is published on the
occasion of the exhibition:
    Barbara Davi
    "Train of Thought"
    Kunstmuseum Luzern
    21.10. – 3.12.2017

Konzept / Concept:
    Barbara Davi,
    Megi Zumstein,
    Claudio Barandun
Lektorat Deutsch /
Copy editing german:
    Christian Schmidt,
    Nadine Olonetzky
Übersetzung / Translation:
    Lisa Rosenblatt
Korrektorat Deutsch:
    Beate Bücheleres-Rieppel
Proofreading English:
    Charlotte Eckler
Gestaltung / Design:
    Hi – Megi Zumstein &
    Claudio Barandun
Lithografien, Druck und Bindung /
Lithographs, printing, and binding:
    DZA Druckerei zu
    Altenburg GmbH, Thüringen

© 2017
    Verlag Scheidegger &
    Spiess AG, Zürich
© für die Texte / for the texts:
    die Autorinnen /
    the authors
© für die Bilder / for the images:
    Barbara Davi

Bildrechte / Image Credits:
    S./p. 14: Silvio Waser
    S./pp. 40 – 44: Atelier Blank
    & Chiovelli
    S./p. 60: Times Museum

Verlag Scheidegger & Spiess AG
Niederdorfstrasse 54
8001 Zürich – Schweiz
www.scheidegger-spiess.ch

ISBN 978-3-85881-560-6

Alle Rechte vorbehalten;
kein Teil dieses Werkes darf in
irgendeiner Form ohne vorherige
schriftliche Genehmigung des
Verlags reproduziert oder unter
Verwendung elektronischer Systeme
verarbeitet, vervielfältigt oder
verbreitet werden. /
All rights reserved; no part of this
publication may be reproduced,
stored in a retrieval system or trans-
mitted in any form or by any
means, electronic, mechanical,
photocopying, recording or other-
wise, without the prior written
consent of the publisher.

Der Verlag Scheidegger & Spiess
wird vom Bundesamt für Kultur
mit einem Strukturbeitrag für die
Jahre 2016–2020 unterstützt. /
Scheidegger & Spiess is being
supported by the Federal Office
of Culture with a general subsidy
for the years 2016–2020.

Die Publikation dieses Buchs
wurde unterstützt durch /
The publication of this book was
supported by

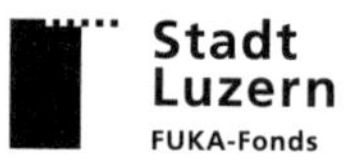

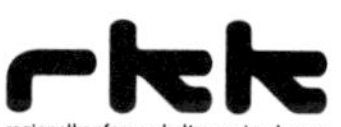

Casimir Eigensatz Stiftung

**Stadt
Luzern**
FUKA-Fonds

rkk
regionalkonferenz kultur region luzern

**Kunstmuseum
Luzern**

Ein spezieller Dank geht an /
Special thanks go to
Megi Zumstein und Claudio
Barandun, Nadine Olonetzky,
Eveline Suter, Fanni Fetzer,
Team Kunstmuseum Luzern, Silvia
Davi, Nils Nova, Lux und Ava.